"Emerging Conversations in Coaching and Coaching Psychology *is an unusual book amongst various edited volumes. It opens conversations on a whole range of debates: those that are already well attended, those that are so controversial that very few want to participate in and those that are fairly new but a welcome addition to both academic and practitioner domains of knowledge. What unites these contributions is the rigour of the approach and intention to raise the quality of debates to the level they deserve. An important read for serious stakeholders of the coaching profession.*"

– Professor Tatiana Bachkirova, Director of the International
Centre for Coaching and Mentoring Studies, Oxford
Brookes University, UK

"*Coaching is reaching a point of maturity as a craft, a field of research and an industry.* Emerging Conversations in Coaching and Coaching Psychology *is an excellent navigational aid in plotting the path ahead. With a breadth of expertise and insight across a range of increasingly relevant chapter topics, this recommended text repeatedly encourages us to challenge and re-examine coaching orthodoxies and will doubtless serve to enrich our individual and collective practice.*"

– Dr David Tee, PhD, Wales Coaching Centre,
University of South Wales, UK

"*Great conversations leave me energised and inspired, tingling with new ideas and possibilities for enriching my experience of being alive and sharing those possibilities with others. This book reads like an opportunity to dip into a range of great conversations supported and informed by a growing body of evidence and experience that can expand and enrich our coaching philosophy and practice and enable us to demonstrate the valuable contribution that psychologically informed coaching can make in an uncertain world.*"

– Alison Clarke, Chair Practice Board, British Psychological Society

Emerging Conversations in Coaching and Coaching Psychology

This rich collection offers new perspectives on the future of coaching and coaching psychology, with insight from a broad range of contributors reflecting a wide variety of viewpoints. It captures the ongoing evolution of coaching practice, inviting contribution to conversations as they unfold.

Mary Watts and Ian Florance skillfully bring together authors from backgrounds in law, finance, education, psychology and human resources to examine the nature of change and assess current and future developments. *Emerging Conversations in Coaching and Coaching Psychology* considers influences from within coaching itself, discussing topics including ethics, diversity, supervision and reflective learning, and from other disciplines, assessing the offerings of psychometric assessment, trauma studies and neuroscience. It also considers the impact of social changes as seen in business, education and leadership, and concludes with a look at the future of coaching.

This book will be of great interest to coaches and trainee coaches interested in changes and developments in the field, who aren't afraid to ask questions and who are open to reflecting on their own assumptions and approaches to practice.

Mary Watts, PhD, is Emeritus Professor of Psychology at City, University of London, UK.

Ian Florance is Founder and Managing Director of OnlyConnect Ltd. and Executive Director of the European Test Publishers Group.

Emerging Conversations in Coaching and Coaching Psychology

Edited by Mary Watts
and Ian Florance

Routledge
Taylor & Francis Group

LONDON AND NEW YORK

First published 2021
by Routledge
2 Park Square, Milton Park, Abingdon, Oxon OX14 4RN

and by Routledge
52 Vanderbilt Avenue, New York, NY 10017

Routledge is an imprint of the Taylor & Francis Group, an informa business

British Library Cataloguing-in-Publication Data
A catalogue record for this book is available from the British Library

Library of Congress Cataloging-in-Publication Data
Names: Watts, Mary H., editor. | Florance, Ian, 1953– editor.
Title: Emerging conversations in coaching and coaching psychology / edited by Mary Watts, PhD and Ian Florance.
Description: Abingdon, Oxon ; New York, NY : Routledge, 2021. | Includes bibliographical references and index.
Identifiers: LCCN 2020045120 (print) | LCCN 2020045121 (ebook) | ISBN 9781138078765 (paperback) | ISBN 9781138078758 (hardback) | ISBN 9781315114514 (ebook)
Subjects: LCSH: Personal coaching. | Counseling psychology.
Classification: LCC BF637.P36 E54 2021 (print) | LCC BF637.P36 (ebook) | DDC 158.3—dc23
LC record available at https://lccn.loc.gov/2020045120
LC ebook record available at https://lccn.loc.gov/2020045121

ISBN: 978-1-138-07875-8 (hbk)
ISBN: 978-1-138-07876-5 (pbk)
ISBN: 978-1-315-11451-4 (ebk)

Typeset in Times New Roman
by Apex CoVantage, LLC

MIX
Paper from
responsible sources
FSC
www.fsc.org   FSC™ C013985

Printed in the United Kingdom
by Henry Ling Limited

Contents

Acknowledgements

It would be impossible to name the many people who have contributed significantly to this book but, named or unnamed, we give you huge and heartfelt thanks.

Our first thanks go to our chapter authors who have put many hours of thought and writing into their chapters and challenged themselves to confront many difficult questions and issues – which has led frequently to deep yet constructive critical thinking about their own, very personal ways of understanding and practicing coaching.

We, including chapter authors, would like to thank the many clients, students and colleagues who over many years have helped to shape who we are now and how each of us has come to be engaged in our personal areas of 'Emerging Conversations'.

We also thank the many people who have read drafts of chapters and given enormously helpful and constructive feedback, those who have been interviewed, and all those whose work has in some way guided and influenced our thinking as we have prepared this book. Whilst we take full responsibility for all that is written here, we acknowledge that it is built upon the foundations of all that has gone before – and we hope that it will provide an interesting and unique kind of foundation for works that follow. It is our hope that the emerging conversations highlighted in this book will continue to develop and new ones emerge.

We thank also the Routledge team, for their constant support – nudging when necessary, endlessly patient, and above all believing is us and our shared vision. Every step of the way they have modelled for us the key ingredients of a trusting and effective coaching relationship. In particular, thank you Susannah Frearson for your leadership of our large combined team, every member of which has had a significant part in bringing this book to print.

Finally, and perhaps foremost, we thank our families and friends for their patience in respect of the many hours that we have shut ourselves away to work on this project, and for the many times we have been distracted thinking about it, even when not overtly 'shut away'. We could not have completed this book without your love, support and encouragement.

Ian would particularly like to thank the man who taught him most of what he knows about coaching – the late Juan Coto: a great coach, a superb teacher, and a kind man.

Mary would particularly like to thank the late Professor Peter Jarvis who always believed in me and who profoundly influenced the 'lenses' through which I understand learning and change. Your person and way of being in this world, along with your prolific writing, have influenced me, and many others, more than you will ever know.

We dedicate this book to Juan Coto and Peter Jarvis.

Huge thanks from Mary and Ian

Contributors

Mark Adams CPsychol MISCP (Accred) is a chartered psychologist, HCPC-registered practitioner psychologist and accredited member of the International Society for Coaching Psychology. He has 21 years' experience of working in education as a teacher, educational psychologist, and coaching psychologist. Mark is Director of Aspen Psychology Services, Bristol, providing consultation, coaching and training services to education settings and practitioners, while also supporting others to develop proficiency in coaching skills. Mark has now accumulated over 800 hours of direct coaching time with individuals and teams, and is the author of *Coaching Psychology in Schools*, published by Routledge in November 2015.

Carol Braddick has worked as a leadership coach through her company Graham Braddick Partnership for over 15 years. In her coaching and consulting practice, she works with global leaders and teams in large, medium-sized and entrepreneurial organisations. Cautiously optimistic about the potential to use technology in coaching, she views emerging technologies as one of the ways to advance the practice of coaching. She follows the growing market of stand-alone digital coaching tools as well as hybrid tech-enabled solutions that complement work with human coaches. She actively supports the coaching community on its learning curve to become savvy adopters of technology and experts at blending new and current approaches in service of their clients' challenges.

Carol is a founding fellow of the Institute of Coaching at Harvard Maclean and a member of the Disruptive Tech Working Group of the Future of Coaching Collaboration. Before establishing her coaching and consulting practice, Carol worked as Senior Consultant and Team Leader in the Talent Development practices of two leading consulting firms, Hewitt and Towers Perrin (now AON Hewitt and Willis Towers Watson, respectively). Originally from New York, she now works from the UK and Tucson, Arizona.

Sarah Corrie is a registered coaching psychologist and consultant clinical psychologist. Sarah has extensive experience in both the public and private sector, delivering coaching and psychological interventions as well as working as a freelance supervisor and trainer. She is a founding member and former chair of the British Psychological Society's Special Group in Coaching Psychology and has a particular interest in how coaching might contribute to some of the most challenging issues of our time, including mental health. Sarah has authored over 80 journal articles and nine books, including *The Art of Inspired Living: Coach Yourself with Positive Psychology,* and *Supervision in the Psychological Professions: Building your own Personalised Model* (co-authored with David A. Lane and Mary Watts). Amongst her other roles, Sarah is a faculty member of the Professional Development Foundation and a visiting professor at Middlesex University. In 2016, she was the recipient of the British Psychological Society's Achievement Award for Distinguished Contributions to Coaching Psychology.

Claudia Filsinger is an associate at the International Centre for Coaching and Mentoring Studies at Oxford Brookes University, where she was previously lecturing in coaching, business and management. She researched and has published on gender diversity coaching and gained extensive expertise in coaching women at all career stages as an associate of The Executive Coaching Consultancy. As a founder of Moving Maps Ltd she contributes to innovation in the coaching field through emerging coaching and supervision practices based on systemic and experiential approaches. Her corporate background is in sales with leading IT and publishing companies. Originally from Germany and now living in Oxford, she has spent most of her career working internationally, therefore virtual coaching is another area of her special expertise.

Ian Florance is Founder and Managing Director of OnlyConnect Ltd. He is also Executive Director of the European Test Publishers Group, an organisation of European psychometric test publishers which he helped to found 30 years ago. Ian worked in educational, trade and academic publishing before spending over 20 years at NFER-NELSON, the UK psychometric test publisher, as well as ASE its business consultancy arm.

Ian trained as a coach with the London-based Meyler Campbell Limited and has delivered leadership coaching as well as strategic consultancy in the UK, Italy, Denmark, France and Romania among other countries. He undertakes monthly interviews for the *Psychologist*, the British Psychological Society's journal. In addition to authoring, editing and ghost-writing a number of coaching-related books, Ian has a parallel career as a poet, novelist and librettist.

Dr. Andreas Kleinschmidt supports senior leaders as executive coach and as coach for public speaking. He is co-founder of a seed fund and moderates high level media and investor events, including with CEOs and heads of states. Previously, he acted as an international spokesperson for Siemens. For his work as journalist he received a CNN journalist award.

Professor David A. Lane is Director and co-founder of the Professional Development Foundation, which has pioneered work-based professional development

for 40 years. As well as contributing to research and the professional development of coaching, Professor Lane has coached in a wide range of organisations
including major consultancies, multinationals, and public sector and government bodies. He was Chair of the British Psychological Society Register of
Psychologists Specialising in Psychotherapy and convened the European Federation of Psychologists Associations group on Psychotherapy. He has served
on committees of the APECS, BPS, CIPD, WABC and EMCC, as well as being
a founder member of the Global Coaching Community.

Dr. Jak Lee has worked in education for over 30 years. She was a teacher and
school senior leader and has now been an educational psychologist (EP) for
20 years. Since 2002, she has also worked as a coaching psychologist and
for eight years led a team of teachers and psychologists coaching educational
practitioners to support their performance, development and well-being. As
part of her EdD, she conducted research into the benefits of coaching in secondary schools. Jak is now Assistant Programme Director of the professional
Doctorate in Educational Psychology at the University of Bristol and works as
an associate senior psychologist with Aspen Psychology Services supporting
children/young people, parents and educational practitioners in Bristol and the
surrounding areas. She also has experience of education in the UK 'from the
other side' as a mother of two.

Andrew A. Parsons has been leading and supporting teams for over 25 years
in both multinational and small- to medium-sized enterprises. He has a PhD
(physiological sciences), a masters degree in psychology and is an accredited
mental health first aider. He supports people in transition in personal and professional lives. His work has been recognised by the Parliamentary Review as
best practice practitioner for establishing a coaching support service for cancer
patients and their families. He is a fellow of the Institute of Coaching as well as
a member of the UK European Mentoring and Coaching Council and several
psychological associations.

Hamira Riaz is a chartered psychologist and associate fellow of the British
Psychological Society. With two doctorates and a specialism in neuropsychology, she designed and managed clinical services for dementia, epilepsy and
Parkinson's surgery, head injury, Gulf War syndrome, NEAD (non-epileptic
attack disorder) and other medically unexplained symptoms, first in the NHS
and later the MoD. She transitioned to the corporate world in 2004 on joining
YSC (a global strategy consultancy), where for almost a decade she advised
senior leaders in multinational companies on talent strategy and benchmark-
ing, executive assessment, coaching and leadership development. She now
splits her time between her role as VP Strategic Leadership at Volvo Group, a
small clinical private practice and not-for-profit activity.

Hamira is a longstanding member of the British Psychological Society
Media Panel. She is a regular commentator on subjects ranging from existential

societal death anxiety to women in leadership, most recently as ambassador for the 'We are Undefeatable' campaign supporting people living with chronic health conditions and resident psychologist on Channel 5's documentary, 'Lawrence of Arabia: Britain's Great Adventurer'.

Louise Sheppard is an experienced executive coach, team coach and coaching supervisor. She has worked with more than 50 organisations globally. Louise's background is in business and leadership development. She started her career with Unilever Plc. and then worked as a management consultant. She is a partner at Praesta Partners LLP and an accredited executive coach and coaching supervisor with APECS. Louise has a doctorate in coaching and mentoring awarded by Oxford Brookes University and an MA in professional coaching from Middlesex University. She enjoys researching, writing and speaking at conferences on coaching and coaching supervision-related topics.

Noreen Tehrani is a past chair of the Crisis, Disaster and Trauma Section of the British Psychological Society and has specialised in working with trauma for many years. She was directly involved in dealing with the Shoreham air crash, the Westminster and London Bridge terrorist attacks and the Grenfell Tower disaster. She has also supported first responders and victims of a wide range of traumatic incidents including child abuse, murders, rapes, fatal accidents and road crashes. Currently she is working with the College of Policing to help reduce the incidence of primary and secondary trauma in police officers and staff. Noreen has written many articles, papers and book chapters including two books on trauma: *Workplace Trauma – concepts, assessment and intervention* and *Managing Trauma in the Workplace.*

Dr. Tim Walker holds a doctorate in Counselling Psychology and is also an accredited Coaching Psychologist. Before retraining, he spent over 20 years in management and consulting roles working with major brands, including Arcadia Group/Debenhams, The BBC, HMV Media Group, Lloyds TSB, Tesco and Universal Music Group, alongside a ten-year tenure as a lecturer in Marketing and Strategy for the Creative Industries at Warwick Business School and University.

Tim has worked as a senior psychologist within the UK's National Health Service, developing a clinical interest and expertise in complex mental health issues. He has also lectured extensively on postgraduate and doctoral psychology programmes at City, University of London. His own doctoral research was focused on burnout and resilience, and he retains a strong interest and specialism in this area. Tim draws on this broad experience in his private practice to offer clinical, coaching and consultancy services to individuals and organisations.

Mary Watts is Emeritus Professor of Psychology at City, University of London, where she formerly held the roles of Pro-Vice-Chancellor for Learning and Teaching and Dean of the School of Health Sciences. She is currently

Director of the Meyler Campbell Mastered programme (business and executive coaching). Registered as a health and counselling psychologist with the Health and Care Professions Council (HCPC), she is also Chartered with the British Psychological Society (BPS), is registered with them as a coach and psychotherapist and is a fellow of Advance HE. She was a founder member of the BPS working group, which set the standards for health psychology training, former chair of the Division of Counselling Psychology, the Special Group in Coaching Psychology and the Psychotherapy Implementation Group (which set the standards and established the register for BPS psychotherapists). Mary has an independent coaching, supervision and consulting practice. In 2014, she received the British Psychological Society Achievement Award for Distinguished Contributions to Coaching Psychology.

Dr. Sasha Webster is an executive and leadership coach working with individuals who want to develop themselves as modern leaders. In her work, Dr. Sasha shows how the ability to lead is within us all and is triggered the moment we, as individuals, reject the disempowering belief of current culture, that is preoccupied with what is wrong with us (and how it must be fixed), and instead to focus on, and celebrate, all that is right with us. Dr. Sasha specialises in helping others access this part of themselves in order that they can be in alignment with who they are and who they want to become. Modern leadership must be about acknowledging that to be credible as a leader is to be congruent as a person.

Chapter 1

Introduction

Why are conversations emerging in coaching?

Ian Florance and Mary Watts

The approach this book takes

As its title suggests, this book looks at current issues in coaching; conversations that have emerged fairly recently or which are continuing, having reached no obvious consensus. It is not a post-hoc report of achieved goals, rather an initial planning meeting for a journey. In the spirit of coaching, *Emerging Conversations* is an invitation to join conversations as they unfold: conversations which are designed to excite and challenge, causing us to question our presuppositions and assumptions and our comfort in 'knowing'; conversations that stimulate our curiosity, and help us to explore and discover new ways of thinking, doing, and being.

The editors were clear that the book couldn't be comprehensive. Change in all aspects of life – in coaching as much as anywhere – seems to be accelerating, and certain issues moved on while the book was being written: to give one instance, Carol Braddick was very clear when drafting her chapter on technology that new solutions would appear in between the book's submission and its publication. The conclusion suggests some areas we have not dealt with. However, to give a very current example, planning for this book started before we had heard of the COVID-19 pandemic; we are doing final preparation as much of Europe goes into a further lockdown pre-Christmas 2020. Mary added the Afterword to reflect this situation during the writing process, but there will be much more to say. Carol Braddick, for instance, has raised how critical technology will be to how coaching responds to the issue, but we await genuine research and survey findings. The key activity in thinking about emerging conversations is to 'watch this space!'

By their nature, some topics discussed here have attracted less research effort and practical learning than one might expect to see in this type of book. In several cases the underpinning evidence is contradictory. Sarah Corrie's chapter on research in this book argues why this should be an issue of concern, but a lack of conclusive evidence is the nature of emerging conversations. We therefore asked authors to use references to research and theory where they could, but to be comfortable using the first-person voice and expressing personal views where appropriate. This is therefore a colloquy of voices expressing informed opinion, including occasional warnings against too much certainty. As coaching psychologist Alison Clarke commented in a recent conversation: 'Research evidence is important but more and more practice can be based on the evidence of what is demonstrably workable' (Clarke, 2020).

A book about change goes out of date quicker than a book about stasis: if it doesn't, it probably isn't about change. This issue affected the content of certain chapters. For instance, it needed some care before naming particular assessments and publishing companies in the chapter on testing: companies regularly go out of business or are taken over. Areas such as technology and diversity, both of which are treated here, are changing under the influence of innovation in one case: of social pressures in the other.

Coaching is a diverse activity, an issue considered in Claudia Filsinger's chapter. Such diversity is as evident in the backgrounds and experience of the people who practice coaching as of those people who are coached. We hope the readership of this book will reflect this variety of viewpoints and backgrounds but this wish has affected how this book has been planned. For instance, coaches from a business background might not have easy access to large libraries or be comfortable with the framework of academic discourse. Coaches from a charity or public service background might, in turn, be put off by too much business language. While some chapters do address and extend academic arguments, we hope that this does not preclude practitioners finding them interesting. Just as the readership may come from diverse backgrounds, we were keen that the authors should have varied viewpoints. This is reflected in the tone and style of the chapters: some are more informal and light-hearted; others use more academic language and structures.

Why do human disciplines change?

The previous section begs questions. Is coaching really changing? If it is, why? Is all this change actually impacting practical issues in coaching or are we experiencing a storm in an academic journal teacup?!

It's generally accepted that coaching is a flourishing practice – growing in size and value. To take one rather old estimate at random, Ann Scoular quotes a 2003 article in the Economist as estimating that coaching was worth $1 billion, a figure which was doubling every 24 months (Scoular, 2011, 1) There are some issues that worry practitioners (the number of unqualified people delivering coaching, for instance) but a gradual move to professionalisation is seen as one possible solution to this. Mary Watts discusses this in the context of coaching ethics. One can argue that coaching method is standardising on certain foundations. These include acronymic models (such as GROW); unconditional positive regard; specific communication tools (active listening, open questioning, reframing etc) and specific insights gathered from psychology, analysis, therapy, sports and techniques like neuro-linguistic programming. But there are unanswered questions and perhaps the most fundamental is finding evidence backing the claims made for coaching's effectiveness. Simmy Groves and Adrian Furnham discuss this in a very useful paper (Groves and Furnham, 2016). Jonathan Passmore and Yi-Ling Lai raised the issue more recently: 'The evidence for investment in coaching interventions will continue to be a major concern for scholars in relevant domains as well as for organisational stakeholders . . . more rigorous research is required to inform practice' (Passmore and Lai, 2019, 80). Rob Briner's paper raises very useful questions about coaching's effectiveness from an outside perspective (Briner, 2012)

Many business thinkers and practising business leaders understand that the moment of greatest success is exactly the point where you need to start changing a human institution: a commercial business, a sports team or even a discipline. In his book *Always Change a Winning Team* (Robertson, 2007), Peter Robertson uses the S curve – a model whose shape describes the growth and inevitable decline of natural systems such as prairies and species – to describe why this is. Robertson applies the model to human institutions – which he typifies as particular kinds of natural systems – and shows that they start declining precisely at the point where their growth has reached its fullest extent. However, unlike purely natural systems, human institutions can be remade: just before they reach the point of greatest growth they need to rethink or reimagine their future and 'jump' to a new S curve. This is a simplification of a detailed and stringent argument. But it seems the S curve can be applied to coaching as a human activity. Put simply, coaching is flourishing: it is precisely now that we should be focusing on a vision for its future and rethinking it.

How did coaching get to this point?

At the risk of over-simplifying, there seem to be three strongly linked accounts of how coaching got to where it is now: a point at which it may need to question itself.

Coaching is a natural human activity

People throughout recorded history have coached, and present-day coaching is just a professionalisation of what we naturally do. Examples offered to back up this thesis almost invariably mention Plato's dialogues as early examples of someone using questioning to facilitate truth-finding in someone else. Philosophers are often used as examples, as are the arts. Drama and cinema often use this technique. A chapter in *The Trainee Coach Handbook* (Watts, Bor, and Florance, 2020) on the coaching relationship uses the character of Natasha from Tolstoy's *War and Peace* to illustrate coaching (Schnell, Searle, and Stoneman, 2020). Spiritual movements have long traditions of coaching type techniques (Buddhist koans, Christian parables and the text of the Talmud are obvious examples)

It is hard to argue with this account, but it's worth pointing out that many examples used to illustrate this idea seem to reduce coaching to the act of asking open questions. This is just one of the many techniques in the coaching skill set.

Nonetheless, the human race does seem to have practised forms of coaching for millennia and we still use it, without so identifying it, in relationships, hobbies and work. We recognise it when it occurs, even if we don't always give it a name.

Coaching sources in the 1960s counterculture

Leni Wildflower (Wildflower, 2013) gives a fascinating account of the countercultural – and sometimes abusive – roots of coaching, starting with best-sellers such as *How to Win Friends and Influence People*, first published in 1936 (see Wildflower, 2013, 6–8), and moving through the practice of certain cults and new age movements. Werner Erhardt's est is a prime example. It was active under that name from 1971 to 1984. Leni Wildflower's book gives a good description of est, its relation to other movements and its influence on coaching (Wildflower, 2013, 30–37) These streams solidified in the activities (occasionally antics) of the psychologists who developed aspects of humanist psychology and the human potential movement.

Wildflower's book makes a compelling case and it seems that Esalen, an influential source of '60s thinking, is also central to the development of humanist psychology and coaching (see Kripal, 2007 for more information on Esalen).

Coaching as a developing profession in the late 20th century

An interesting and comprehensive source of information for this account (and indeed a range of sources describing the history of coaching) is *The Sourcebook of Coaching History* (Brock, 2014) though it is somewhat out of date. To choose at random from the key moments Brock's book documents:

- UK and USA Companies started to offer business coaching and training courses in coaching in the 1980s.
- The inner game work of Gallwey and Whitmore became more widely available at the same time.
- Professional coach associations developed largely in the decade between 1995 and 2005. For instance, The International Coaching Federation was founded in 1995; the Special Group in Coaching Psychology of the British Psychological Society was founded in 2002 at the same time as the Australian equivalent.
- The first coaching psychology course started at the University of Sydney in 2000.

If this account is looked at in more detail, it suggests coaching is in some ways an outcrop of psychology, therapy and analysis. Originally a species of psychology-lite which non-psychologists could practice, it developed its own systems, bodies, practices and, increasingly, methods. One can argue that coaching is a separate profession in all but name, and that latter omission may soon be rectified as calls for professional status grow, a movement implicit and, at times, explicit in this book. But will we end up with two disciplines – coaching and coaching psychology – or do they overlap too much? This raises an important emerging conversation considering the historic, current and potential relationship between psychology and coaching.

Discussion

Rob Briner sums this up: 'While interactions and relationships that look a bit like coaching have probably been around for as long as there have been human groups and organisations, it is only in the last 30 years that formal coaching appears to have emerged' (Briner, 2012, 4). Jenny Rogers comments that coaching must be 'as old as human society' (Rogers 2016, 7).

These three accounts seem to outline one process: that a natural human tendency to coach was picked up in the Western countercultural revolution of the '60s and '70s (when 'jaw-jaw' was seen as preferable to 'war-war' and the anti-psychiatry movement was in full swing). An evidential base and professional standards were developed because, while the outcomes of early humanistic methods were seen as valuable, some of the methods were deeply questionable. This is not just a serial process: people still coach each other in an informal way; counter-cultural activities rooted in the '60s and '70s still flourish in certain environments – for good or ill; and some coaches are post-retirement hobbyists without professional training.

Other ingredients have been added to the coaching dish, particularly in recent years: labour, economic and work theory and practice; the influence of sports management and training, as sport has professionalised and become a global obsession; concerns over the use of drugs in healthcare and the rise of alternatives, including talking cures; the democratisation of debate through social media; the consequent collapse of certain authorities who had the public trust to be able to set rules. The chapter by Andreas Kleinschmidt with Mary Watts in this book discusses some of these issues.

How have these developments shaped coaching? As we have suggested, it is now a very successful, human activity. But it has become complex: with a huge range of influences, drawing on many different disciplines. Jenny Rogers typifies coaching as 'a pragmatic trade drawing on borrowed theory' (Rogers, 2016, 6). Some of its sources are creative, risky, unstructured and lack research. Rob Briner comments from an outside perspective that 'the plausibility of coaching is dangerous' (Briner, 2012, 11). Relatively recently, however, it has started to solidify and professionalise (see Brock, 2014 for detailed documentation on this). Add to this that throughout history it's often been technological innovation that facilitates (if not causes) genuine revolutions in human thought and behaviour, and it's no surprise that coaching faces some stark choices as technological change gathers pace.

In Tor Levin Hofgaard's keynote address at the 2019 European Congress of Psychology in Moscow (Hofgaard, 2019) he argued that the profession of psychology had failed to live up to its side of a bargain with society in a number of ways; not least the fact that it did not reach the majority of its possible beneficiaries for reasons including over-pricing, and lack of numbers. He suggested that psychology faced its Kodak moment: it would either reinvent itself or would become irrelevant in ten years' time. Sasha Webster's chapter in this book suggests some similar criticisms – and solutions – in the area of leadership coaching. Although coaching is not a formal profession, Hofgaard's point could equally be applied to coaching as much as to psychology.

Given all of this, it seems coaching is ripe for change.

This book

Our conclusion will look in more detail at the implications of the issues discussed by the authors. Before starting the authors' chapters, it's worth highlighting the dangers of concentrating solely on within-coaching issues as the engines for change. Certainly, there is a lot of self-questioning within the discipline. But it's important to look outside its confines. Change seems to source from three general areas: within coaching itself; from a range of health-related disciplines such as psychology and neuroscience; and from trends within wider society.

Within coaching issues

Mary Watts' chapter on Reflective Learning, Louise Shepherd's on supervision and Andreas Kleinschmidt's and Mary Watts' on ethics consider topics central to how coaching works more or less well. They draw on other professions' practice but if coaching is to improve its effectiveness, these three areas are critical to its quality control. Sarah Corrie's chapter on research touches on a key issue which casts a shadow over the whole discipline: how do we find evidence on whether it works in the way that we often claim. Tim Walker's chapter on pluralistic approaches to coaching draws heavily on his experience as a psychologist and so straddles the divide between this and the next category.

Issues from health-related disciplines

Changes in psychometric assessment and advances in neuroscience could profoundly affect the process of coaching but there are dangers in both areas, pointed out in chapters on these topics. Sarah Corrie's and Andrew A. Parson's chapter on mental health draws on an area which traditionally was the domain of psychologists but straddles all three of these categories; should coaching address this area at all or does it need specialist training; how far can psychology and health professions meet a need which is growing in part, at least, because of far greater mental health awareness in society. Noreen Tehrani and David A. Lane's chapter on trauma coaching shares this wider relevance.

Issues from wider society

Changes in education, not least a perception of the increasing importance of education for our future; the exponential growth in the use of and innovation in technology and changes in business practice and the role of leaders all source in wider societal movements and are discussed in chapters in this book. While business has recently tended to lay claim to be the VUCA environment, the term originally applied to the increased volatility, uncertainty, complexity and ambiguity of all aspects our world. This must be reflected in coaching.

In Our Conclusion we will discuss these three types of engines for change but now it is time for our 'colloquy of voices' discussing some of the questions which might affect coaching profoundly in the future.

Bibliography

Briner, Rob. (2012). *Does Coaching Work and Does Anyone Really Care?* OP Matters. 16. 4–12.

Brock, Vikki G. (2014). *Sourcebook of Coaching History*, 2nd ed. Ventura, CA: CreateSpace Independent Publishing.

Clarke, Alison. (2020). *Interview by Ian Florance*. The Psychologist. 33. 48–50.

Ellam-Dyson, V. (2012). *Coaching Psychology Research: Building the Evidence Base, Developing Awareness*. OP Matters. 16. 13–15.

Gardner, Howard E. (2006). *Multiple Intelligences*. New York: Basic Books.

Gratton, Lynda and Scott, Andrew. (2016). *The Hundred Year Life*. London: Bloomsbury.

Groves, Simmy and Furnham, Adrian. (2016). *Coaching as a Developmental Intervention in Organisations: A Systematic Review of its Effectiveness and the Mecanisms Underlying It*. https://org/10.1371/journal.pone.0159137

Hofgaard, Tor Levin. (2019). *And then Everything Changes: The Future of the Psychologist Profession in a Post 4th Industrial World*. Keynote Presentation. 2019 European Congress of Psychology, Moscow, July 4th.

Kline, Nancy. (2002). *Time to Think: Listening to Ignite the Human Mind*. London: Cassell.

Kripal, Jeffrey J. (2007). *Esalen: America and the Religion of No Religion*. Chicago: The University of Chicago Press.

Passmore, Jonathan and Lai, Yi-Ling. (2019). *Coaching Psychology: Exploring Definitiions and Research Contribution to Practice*. International Coaching Psychology Review. 14(2).

Robertson, Peter. (2007). *Always Change A Winning Team*. London: Times Editions.

Robertson, Peter. (2012). *De Ecologische Leider: De Natuurlijke Cyclus van Kernwaarden en Orgnisaties*. Amsterdam: Business Contact.

Rogers, Jenny. (2016). *Coaching Skills: The Definitive Guide to Being A Coach*, 4th ed. Maidenhead: McGraw Hill Education.

Schnell, Sabine, Searle, Jonny and Stoneman, Richard. (2020). The Coaching Relationship. In *The Trainee Coach Handbook*, edited by Robert Bor, Mary Watts and Ian Florance, 27–46. London: Sage.

Scoular, Anne. (2011). *Business Coaching*. Harlow: Prentice Hall Financial Times.

Watts, Mary, Bor, Robert and Florance, Ian (Eds.). (2020). *The Trainee Coach Handbook*. London: Sage.

Wildflower, Leni. (2013). *The Hidden History of Coaching*. Maidenhead, UK: Open University Press/McGraw Hill.

Chapter 2

Reflective learning
Increasing personal agency through challenge

Mary Watts

Overview

The focus of this chapter is on reflective learning. More broadly it is about reflective living, and the impact this may have on both learning and change throughout our lives. Coaching may often take the form of fostering transformative and emancipatory learning of a kind that enables our clients to take greater control over their lives and the choices they have in life. Coaches are in a unique position to adopt ways of working with their clients that enhance their learning for living and associated 'performance' in personally meaningful ways. Personal agency occurs when one has the capacity to initiate and direct purposeful action. It is enhanced when one has self-belief in one's ability to achieve chosen goals. It could be argued that a primary goal of coaches is to 'give their knowledge and skills away', thereby enabling their clients to become effective 'self-coaches'. This implies that through coaching the client gains improved reflection and change skills, and has the confidence to use these in self-coaching to support them in achieving their goals.

It is widely considered that building reflective capability has the power to enhance the coach's professional practice. Development of the same reflective skills and mindset could therefore be assumed to enhance the practice of the client and empower them within their 'everyday living'. I suggest that coach and client are *both* engaged in a process of meaning making, learning and change.

Introduction

Expectations and predictions are often implicitly made and frequently not reflected upon. Where this occurs, personal learning from our actions is likely to be limited, resulting in reduced opportunity for self-selected and self-directed change. Action becomes an experience when we reflect upon it and a learning experience when we review and evaluate it in relation to our expectations and predictions.

Implicit in the statements in the preceding paragraph is the notion that it is possible for us to initiate life changes, mediated through critical reflection and associated personal learning. It doesn't say what such changes may be, elaborate on the processes at the heart of initiating such change, nor detail the many things that might interfere with self-selected and self-directed change. This chapter considers some of the ways one can address these issues and enhance personal empowerment. Throughout our lives we are likely to be faced with opportunities and constraints. Many will pass us by in a somewhat unremarkable way. On other occasions we will become immersed in them – often expending considerable energy in worrying about possible future change, exploring missed opportunities or, more optimistically, generating and embracing new future opportunities and possibilities. Learning to negotiate our way through life, with its many ups and downs, could be described as 'learning for living'. Such learning combines different types of 'knowing', including that which relates to factual/hard data; that derived from primary experiences (those that I have personally experienced); and those derived from secondary experience (that which I have experienced vicariously through observing others, hearing their stories or reading). Our capacity for enhancing our 'learning for living' is likely to go up and down throughout our life and be influenced by many things including our energy levels, mood, the situation we find ourselves in and our motivation for both generating and embracing change.

Coaching scenario

Ingrid is the head of a team of hospital-based cardiologists. On a daily basis she and her team make decisions and carry out clinical interventions with very real life and death implications for patients. These are closely regulated by detailed research-based protocols for practice. In her coaching sessions Ingrid seeks to enhance her reflective learning skills. Her particular focus is the everyday aspects of her leadership and managerial roles, for which there are no clear guidelines and protocols. She realizes that her reading about leadership is not sufficient to equip her to deal with everyday issues relating, for example, to staff tensions and stresses, motivation, organizational change, and her own fluctuating energy levels. A theme running throughout is personal empowerment through learning.

Before the popularization of coaching (Whitmore 2017) the theme of personal empowerment through learning was a significant topic for those engaged in adult education. The themes and agendas were not so different to those in coaching today – personal empowerment, personally meaningful learning, achievement of goals, and ability to initiate and manage change. Reflection was a core theme within much of this writing, as was learning through experience, termed 'experiential learning' (Schön 1983, 1987; Kolb 1984; Mezirow & Associates 1990, 2018). Experiential learning, with reflective practice at its heart, became increasingly popular in many areas of professional education, especially those that were essentially people-focused such as the caring professions. Experiential learning, and linked reflective practice, is now a core-learning requirement in many areas of professional training. For example, those working in psychotherapeutic domains are required to keep reflective learning journals during their training and also beyond. This is not only intended for evidencing learning but is also an approach to fostering reflective learning. The same now applies in coaching where it has become core to professional learning and its assessment.

A rich review of literature on reflective practice has been provided by Kovacs and Corrie (2017), who draw attention to how it might be used to enhance coaching. In particular, they focus on how it may be used by a coach to enhance his/her coaching interventions. In support of this they present a number of questions that may be used by a coach to prompt reflective thinking about their coaching. For example:

1)   *What worked well? What does working well mean in this context?*
2)   *What hypotheses was I holding in mind and how did I go about testing these?*
3)   *How are my emotions, beliefs or assumptions influencing my ability to work with the client at this point?*
4)   *Am I applying the theories in which I am trained or just going with the flow and my gut feel? What are the implications of this?*
5)   *What different assumptions or beliefs would help me act differently next time? What would be the potential impact on the client?*

(Kovacs & Corrie 2017, p. 10)

The table of questions, which includes many more than those illustrated above, and the wider review of reflective practice provided by Kovacs and Corrie, are a very useful introduction to how a coach might build reflective capability. Though the emphasis is on assisting the *coach* in her practice, the *client* may also engage in self-empowered, reflective learning. Accordingly, in this chapter each of the coach and client is viewed as an active meaning maker, striving to learn from and for living, with multiple goals and intentions, values and beliefs, expectations, predictions and goals. Each is an agent, an influencer and has experience of being influenced. Their personal biographies and social and cultural circumstances will be shared in certain respects with others, and also be uniquely theirs.

Coaches and clients together create a shared world as well as remaining a part of their individual worlds. Each is a learner and learned, influencer and influenced, reflector and predictor, supporter and supported. In life beyond coaching they each take on multiple roles and these will be reflected in a variety of ways within the coaching relationship. A coach may, with the client's consent, move between different coaching roles, such as being a mentor coach, a skills coach and even a supervisory coach. Likewise, the client may be leader, learner and vulnerable job seeker, within the same client/coach relationship.

The reflective learner

Several key assumptions and perspectives underpin this section. Some of these are listed next:

- There are many different types of learning and knowing (for example, knowing published facts about Parkinson's and knowing what it feels like to have it; and learning what treatments are available and learning how, in everyday living, strategies may be adopted to better manage it).
- Not all learning involves learning to do (for example, learning that some of what I do gives me great satisfaction whilst other things cause me stress).
- Reflections can contribute to our personal meaning making and understanding of self and others (for example, through her reflections, Ingrid, the cardiologist in the vignette on p. 9, started to understand the impact of her behavior on others and think creatively about the type of leader she wanted to be).
- Critical/questioning reflections can lead to *transformative thought* and action (for example, recognizing and challenging some of my core assumptions about myself and my goals has caused me to have a major rethink and change the direction of my life).

You may pick up others as well as become aware of some of your own assumptions and perspectives, particularly if they are in opposition to those I have just articulated. Jarvis (1992) suggests that it is from recognition of and reflection on such tensions and disjuncture that new learning may emerge.

Returning to the sample of reflective questions for the coach from Kovacs and Corrie, listed on p. 10, it is interesting to consider how they might be re-framed to relate to the reflective, learning, client – and also to all other people interested in learning from and for living. If they are useful to the coach they are useful in equal measure to others who wish to take control, and enhance aspects, of their learning and action. This learning may be achieved in a variety of contexts including in education, coaching, supervision and self-directed and self-supported learning.

Kovacs's and Corrie's questions are re-presented in what follows with small changes to extend the focus beyond the coach.

1   What worked well? What does working well mean in this context?

This question is relevant to all adults and children who wish to understand the relationship between their thinking, actions and outcomes, and allows and encourages curiosity and a questioning approach to life. Its regular use reflects an approach to life that could be described as a particular kind of mindfulness – one where self-challenge and the questioning of personal assumptions is at the heart of reflective, learning from living (Chaskalson 2011; Dalton & Dunnett 2005; Illeris 2018; Jarvis 1999).

2 What hypotheses was I holding in mind and how did I go about testing these?

This question takes the first question a stage further. It is relevant to all of us, whatever our role or position in life. It acknowledges that we hold beliefs and assumptions about what has been, what is, and what may be in the future. It links closely to the statement near the start of the chapter, which suggests that 'Expectations and predictions are often implicitly made and frequently not reflected upon'.

We all carry around expectations and predictions and much of our behaviour is based upon these – even when they are not within our conscious awareness or made explicit in our thinking and verbalizing. We hold hypotheses, often implicitly, and we act upon these. Kelly (1955) refers within his very detailed and fascinating theory of personal constructs, to the person as similar to a research scientist, who holds hypotheses and engages in testing these. However, we often hold hypotheses that we take for granted and that could be proven inaccurate and unhelpful if we were to question and test them. As suggested towards the start of the chapter, hypotheses we hold that are never reflected upon and questioned may have the effect of reducing our learning and related change.

A key question for us all is 'how do we decide which hypotheses to test, and when and how to do this'. We rely on our beliefs and the accuracy of our hypotheses in every day living. It would be enormously time consuming and most likely very stressful to question everything. How do we become a skilled and discerning questioner and tester of hypotheses?

3 How are my emotions, beliefs or assumptions influencing my ability to be effective at this point?

The original question 3 refers to 'my ability to work with the client at this point'. When we take out the notion of working with the client and insert instead the more general notion of being effective, we again see that the question has relevance to us all – child, adult and senior adult, in any context. It is not meant to imply that there are no constraints upon our effectiveness, but suggests that emotions, beliefs and assumptions may have an impact on our thoughts and actions. To consider the impact of these requires an opening up to what they are – to reflecting upon them and considering within our reflections what their possible impact may be. There is a place for the coach doing this when they review their coaching, for clients to do it within coaching, and for all of us to develop skills in doing this, so that it becomes a common, but very significant, life skill.

4 Am I applying knowledge and understanding from previous learning and experience or just going with the flow and my gut feel? What are the implications of this?

In this question 'the theories in which I am trained' has been broadened and replaced with 'understanding from previous learning and experience'. The questions now have meaning and relevance in a broader context. They suggest that reflecting on previous learning and experience can have implications – and so too can going with my 'gut feel'. Acting on gut feel, or instinct, is an important area, as demonstrated in the work of Mercier and Sperber (2017).

5   What different assumptions or beliefs would help me act differently next time? What would be the potential impact on those around me?

In this question, reference to those around me has been inserted instead of reference to 'the client', thereby generalizing and broadening the question. The focus of the question has moved explicitly to action and a consideration of the impact of 'my action on others'. Implicit in this fifth question is a sense that reflection can lead to change, both in my thinking and my actions, and that in turn this may impact on and, in some way, change others.

There are many more reflection-focused questions that might be asked, however, those presented are sufficient to demonstrate that reflection can be engaged in by all of us; that asking certain types of question can be the trigger for reflecting; that when we engage in reflecting we may find ourselves challenging former beliefs, assumptions and ways of behaving; and most significantly, that reflection can lead to change on the part of the reflector and those around them. George Kelly, when elaborating his psychological theory of personal constructs, drew attention to the importance of asking questions, even if at some point in the past those same questions may have seemed to be satisfactorily answered and acted upon. As life changes, so do the issues and questions relating to it, and even where a question is still relevant the previous answer to it may not be. Kelly suggested that 'the function of an answer is not to make further questioning unnecessary but to hold things together until a round of better questions has been thought up' (1969, p. 115). He suggested that 'a pat answer is the enemy of a fresh question'. It prevents us from reviewing what we think we know, the sense we make of things around us, including our own personal, often implicit understandings and beliefs. If we allow no space for 'doubts and issues', asking no questions that will allow these to surface and be explored, we limit the degree to which we may knowingly and insightfully explore and initiate changes in our way of living and being.

Learning and experience

The reflective questions presented earlier, along with others that you, the reader, will readily identify, can be used to support and enhance the process of experiential learning outlined by Kolb (1984). He depicts the individual as having a concrete experience upon which the individual reflects, and based upon these reflections they generate general and abstract conceptualizations relating to the experience. From this, Kolb suggests, we then move on to a stage of active experimentation prior to starting the process again

The work of Argyris and Schön (1974, 1978) and Argyris (1993) explores the nature of actionable knowledge, drawing a distinction between espoused theories and theories in use, and between applicable knowledge and actionable knowledge – suggesting that the latter requires the identification of specific and relevant behaviours. Attention is also drawn to the distinction between reflection-on-action and reflection-in-action, the former occurring after an event and the latter whilst one is in the process of acting.

One cannot explore the nature of reflective practice for long before one is presented with issues of inconsistency, incongruence, contradiction, disjuncture and paradox. Learning from experience isn't simple and straightforward but complex and often contradictory. We may combine elements of unreflective following of routine with deliberative thought and action or espouse personal theories but act in contradiction to them. We may recognize paradoxes in our experience of living and learning or we may not. Indeed, Jarvis (1992) dedicated a whole text to pursuing the theme of 'paradoxes of learning' in which he referred to learning as the process of transforming everyday experience into knowledge, skills, attitudes, values and beliefs. One of the main arguments within the book is that:

> Learning begins with a fundamental disjuncture between individual biography and the socially constructed experience. This disjuncture leads people to ask questions and thus sets the learning process in motion. . . . Individuals can learn from the experience of life or learn to take life's experience for granted. Learning, then, is not straightforward but complex and even contradictory.
>
> (Jarvis 1992, p. 4)

It is often at the point of recognizing disjuncture or paradox that an individual might seek the help of a coach. Alternatively, an individual may not recognize, or choose to ignore, incongruities in his/her experience. Such a person may be referred for coaching by another and be at a completely different starting point to the person who has personally chosen coaching as a means to changing something in their circumstances and behaviour. To complicate matters further, when we reflect upon experience and translate this into personal learning and behaviours for change, one cannot separate out the impact of culture and ideology. These may often be implicit and invisible influencers (Watts et al. 2020).

From this short account a number of key issues emerge relating to learning from experience, with perhaps the most powerful being the significance of not only reflection, but also engagement in the kind of reflection that enables dilemmas, contradictions and paradoxes to emerge. Certain types of questions may help to surface these, and also facilitate their subsequent exploration. As Kelly suggested, a pat answer may shut down reflective exploration and debate, and restrict a potential learning opportunity, and with it, the creative ideas and momentum for personally driven change.

Within the context of exploring transformational adult learning Mezirow and Associates (1990, 2018) engaged in a detailed analysis of the concept of reflection and its theoretical foundations. His associates elaborated upon them in relation to a range of practice contexts. I draw attention to some of these in what follows, linking them with the world of current day coaching.

Reflection may be situated within not only a personal, interpersonal and psychological context but also changes to broader social, cultural, organizational and socioeconomic systems:

> Changing social norms reinforce our need to critically examine the very paradigms through which we have been taught by our culture to understand our experience. This process of critical self-reflection has the potential for profoundly changing the way we make sense of our experience of the world, other people, and ourselves. Such transformative learning, in turn, leads to action that can significantly affect the character of our interpersonal relationships, the organizations in which we work and socialize, and the socioeconomic system itself.
>
> (Mezirow & Associates 1990, p. xiii)

Coaching may be used as one route for fostering this type of reflection. It is easy to slip into the way of assuming that this type of reflection is for adults. However, the cultural paradigms that we are exposed to as children influence the way that we understand and learn from our experience. There is therefore scope in adulthood for introducing and supporting the key elements of questioning reflection that naturally occur within young children – and that are so often 'trained' out of them by an adult's unreflective and pat answers. Considering a child's approach to the world may help foster a mindset that is prepared for the sometimes challenging, critical self-reflection that Mezirow refers to.

A distinction may be made between reflection, critical reflection, and critical self-reflection. Reflection describes 'the examination and justification for one's beliefs, primarily to guide action and to reassess the efficacy of the strategies and procedures used in problem solving' (Mezirow & Associates 1990, p. xvi). This type of reflection is commonly used in coaching and is perhaps at the heart of what many coaches refer to when they use reflective practices in their coaching. Engaging in reflective practice of this kind enables us to stop, step back, and take stock of habitual and maybe mindless thoughts and actions that may be interfering with us becoming more effective in our problem solving in a particular area. A good coach can facilitate us in using reflection to enhance particular areas of activity in our lives.

Critical reflection Mezirow describes as involving a critique of the presuppositions on which beliefs have been built, recognizing that errors in presuppositions will inhibit effective problem solving. This type of reflection is likely to be more challenging than taking a more general reflective but less critical stance. The concept of "critical self-reflection" is even more challenging. Here the focus is very much on the individual's own meaning perspectives and how we pose and formulate problems in the first place. Not only are we to look at how our beliefs might interfere with effective problem solving, but we are challenged to consider where and how these beliefs might have originated, to question their validity and consider possible alternatives. Our values, beliefs, and a whole range of interconnected constructs, influence the way we pose a question, and indeed the very issues we choose to focus on. An individual's personal constructs influence the lenses through which they see and make sense of the world and are in turn influenced by their personal experiences and interpretations of that world. It takes great skill on the part of the coach to support and facilitate a client in the process of critical self-reflection. Timing, style of coaching, and a strong coaching relationship are all essential – not only for effectiveness, but also to ensure that no harm is done to the client.

Recently, two coaches I was supervising and I wrote a chapter on supervision (Watts et al. 2016). We envisioned supervision as being primarily a reflective learning process. We made several statements that for us were at the heart of our perspectives and understanding of the supervision process. These were that:

- Supervision is about learning.
- We can engage in it alone and with others.
- It benefits from creative and flexible thinking.
- Learning is ongoing and never ending.

Our premise was that 'We are all, whatever our role and personal history, engaging in a process of learning, albeit it in distinctive, individual, ways' (Watts et al. 2016, p. 213).

These points seem hugely relevant to coaching and also to the broader endeavour of 'learning from living' that we all engage with to a greater or lesser degree. This type of active learning is very different to that which is so often described and researched in psychology, where the learner is depicted as a passive recipient of things that happen to them (Olson & Hergenhahn 2016).

This more active, personally led, reflective form of learning can be defined as 'the process of making a new or revised interpretation of the meaning of an experience, which guides subsequent understanding, appreciation, and action' (Mezirow & Associates 1990, p. 1). Mezirow's three types of reflection each contribute to a more active and personal form of learning. Coaching and supervision are ideal forums for supporting and facilitating them. The skills involved in engaging in this type of learning may be supported by another person but may, more importantly, become core to a person's way of being and of living so that they can initiate and sustain their own reflective learning process. Perhaps a key aspect of this way of being, relates to the notion of 'not knowing' or 'un-knowing' as described by Spinelli (1997). Allowing oneself to be in a state of 'unknowing' is the first step towards having an open and enquiring mind that recognizes that there is much that we don't know, and that what we do know is still only partial knowing. Learning to recognize the discomfort that may go with this, staying with it, and working with it rather than avoiding it, are all important steps in challenging ourselves to learn from experience. So, to the four statements on page 16, I would now add a fifth:

- Being open to not knowing, and becoming un-knowing, are essential to transformational learning and change.

The in depth analysis by Mezirow and his associates (1990) brings to life the many ways in which critical reflection can trigger transformative learning. The chapter titles alone indicate they are as relevant to coaching today as they were in education in the 1990s – especially when one considers the increasingly broadening remit that coaching is now embracing. They include:

Liberation Through Consciousness Raising

(Hart 1990, pp. 47–73)

Challenging Habits of Expectation

(Roth 1990, pp. 116–133)

Using Critical Incidents to Explore Learner's Assumptions

(Brookfield 1990, pp. 177–193)

Reflective Withdrawal Through Journal Writing

(Lukinsky 1990, pp. 213–234)

Repertory Grids: Playing Verbal Chess

(Candy 1990, pp. 271–295)

Consciousness raising is an important step towards finding one's voice and becoming empowered to act in self-directed ways. Habits of expectation may have utility but can also come to define who we are, thus making it difficult for us to evolve from one identity to another. We all hold assumptions and exploring critical incidents may help us to surface these and their impact, as well as consider alternative ways of thinking and acting. Keeping a reflective journal may help us to 'step back' from our world, reflect upon it, and re-enter it with a different attitude. Repertory grids, initially introduced by George Kelly (1955) when he developed his theory of personal constructs, are a conversational tool for helping us surface our acts of thinking, our judgments, values and expectations, so that we may reflect on these, review them, and choose whether we wish to make changes (Stojnov et al. 2011).

The chapters in Mezirow's book, written in 1990, each encapsulates an area of learning and change as relevant for the coach and her client today as they were for educators 30 years ago. We may learn the skills of reflective learning for engaging in living research whilst working collaboratively with another, but these skills will serve us well if practiced and further honed throughout our lives – enabling us to become our own coach, our own supervisor and our own learning guide and facilitator. Personally managed reflective and transformative learning and change will become an integral part of our lives.

As we learn these important skills, at one level we will appear to need coaches less. However, on another level the role of the coach will become greater through their engagement in an ever-widening range of activities designed to educate the client in the knowledge and skills necessary to become their own coach. Coaches will give away their skills – but to do this requires that they understand what it is they are giving away; how the process of reflective learning works; how they might help an individual learn how and when to use it; and when it is appropriate and advisable for the client, and indeed themselves also, to seek support and further guidance from another. The key message at the heart of this process is that just as leadership skills may be considered relevant for everyone (Watts & Corrie 2013), so too may reflective learning skills be considered relevant for everyone!

Psychological perspectives on reflective coaching, learning and change

I want to share some psychological perspectives developed during my career so that I can link them to my newer, and ever-developing perspectives – and also to show how they link to reflective coaching, learning and change.

In the 1970s I joined a team working in a specialist cognitive and behavioural therapy (CBT) unit at the Middlesex Hospital in London. Until this time, I had given very little thought to the topic of learning in its own right. Learning was something that I did at school and university. I soon learnt that learning, and in particular conditioned learning, was considered to be at the heart of much psychological distress. I learnt, for example, how conditioned learning experiences could play a significant role in the acquisition, maintenance and resolution of phobias, obsessions and other stress related problems.

As a team we became adept at generating case formulations to guide our therapeutic interventions. We recognized the power of combining cognitive and behavioural approaches for understanding and changing behaviour. Among other things we had heated debates about the impact of the client/carer relationship and also upon the relative weights of behavioural and cognitive change on therapy outcomes.

At a personal level I held, and still hold, a great respect for the power of conditioned learning, but close relationships with patients and colleagues taught me additionally about the power of relationships, personal insights, self-determination, and self-belief. My introduction at this time to the works of George Kelly (1955), Martin Seligman (1975), Seligman et al. (1979), and Albert Bandura (1977) reinforced for me the importance of the lenses through which we see and interpret the world. It was heartening to be reminded that there were psychologists who believed that we could alter the course of our learning and our lives and these three people have had a major impact on my own learning from living and the direction and quality of my own personal and professional life. Their insights, coupled with those of adult education writers and researchers (in particular Jarvis and Mezirow) have inspired me to look more closely at the power of a personal, reflective type of learning. Newer work in psychology is enabling closer connections between my experience of these diverse worlds of theory and practice, especially in terms of how they link to learning through and for living and how this may be applied within coaching.

To illustrate the psychological dimension, I turn firstly to the more recent work of Albert Bandura. For instance, in his article Social Cognitive Theory: An Agentic Perspective (2001), he says 'The capacity to exercise control over the nature and quality of one's life is the essence of humanness'. This capacity he characterizes as "human agency" (Bandura 2001, p. 1), which he says operates through 'intentionality and forethought, self regulation by self-reactive influence, and self-reflectiveness about one's capabilities, quality of functioning, and the meaning and purpose of one's life pursuits'. Bandura recognizes the power of social systems but sees people as both producers as well as products of these systems.

The ideas elaborated by Bandura fit very comfortably with those earlier elaborated within adult education. For example, the notion of self-reflectiveness is totally compatible with the work of Mezirow and others referred to earlier. What Bandura's work does is to lend the weight and insights of psychological theory and research to earlier work. Skill in engaging in personal and shared reflective activity, as elaborated earlier by Mezirow and Associates (1990), and in the style of questioning illustrated by Kovacs and Corrie (2017), can legitimately be considered a core psychological skill for both coach and client.

The second area of psychological contribution I draw attention to is that driven by Seligman (2018). Together with colleagues he has had the courage, stamina, creative insight, scientific rigour and art of communicating, to constructively challenge the external validity of much traditional experimental psychology. In turn he has introduced us to an exciting new 'positive psychology' with its focus on well-being, flourishing, and empowerment of the person and institutions. Positive psychology has a very natural affinity with coaching (Green & Palmer 2019) In particular, I draw attention here to the work of Seligman and colleagues (2013, 2016), which explores research-based arguments linked to the question of whether we navigate our way into the future, or we are driven by the past. Seligman et al. suggest that

> viewing behavior as driven by the past was a powerful framework that helped create scientific psychology, but accumulating evidence in a wide range of research areas suggests a shift in framework, in which navigation into the future is seen as a core organizing principle of animal and human behavior.

They propose building a new framework for psychology that explicitly acknowledges the ways in which we draw on experience to select action in pursuit of needs and goals, saying 'this is not remotely a novel idea. It is a feature of common sense' (2013, p. 1).

Psychology has traditionally paid little attention to people as active meaning makers, creatively taking a hand in prospecting and crafting their own futures. This new 'common sense' framework for psychology takes account of values and goals, and the mental simulation of events that have an impact on future prospection and navigation. It sees people as active meaning makers who through their mental simulations and 'if then' prospections, play a significant role in determining key elements of their own futures.

The notion of behaviour being goal-driven is not new, especially within coaching. What is new is the very strong argument for a new dominant framework for psychology. One that is based on the explicit premise that our behaviour is predominantly driven by our needs and desire to prospect and manage our future, rather than being driven by past events.

It is this balance of external versus internal drivers of behaviour that coaches and their clients find they are so often juggling with, the major question being how to reduce the external power and increase internal power. One might argue that it is exactly this activity that coaches seek to enhance with their clients. Intuitively it is an implicit and often explicit underpinning belief of many coaches that prospection can be useful for clients, and anyone else who wishes to engage in purposeful, self-directed action. Being more explicit in respect of these ideas is important for the further development of effective coaching practice.

Coaches taking this approach must ask the all-important question 'how can each of us, individually and collaboratively, become good prospectors, effectively navigating our way into the future'? To become a good prospector, we need to draw on our experience, and also our memories and constructs relating to that experience. We also need to draw upon our reflections and our capacity for challenging and re-visioning our reflections and understandings. An approach to reflecting upon experience such as that elaborated by Mezirow is likely to be as relevant today in coaching, as it was when it was first introduced in adult education. What I have shown here is the strong psychological voice advocating the transformational power of reflective learning and the associated activities of prediction and prospection. What we don't have yet is an equally strong body of knowledge, experience and research elaborating its use within coaching.

Summary of key points emerging so far in this chapter:

- Expectations, predictions and rationale for action may be implicit.
- Reflection may help to surface what is implicit, including our thoughts, beliefs and values.
- Certain types of self-questioning may be a prompt for 'critical' reflection which plays a part in fostering learning and change.
- Learning and change may be initiated through the recognition of tension, paradox and incongruity in our lives.

- Through imagining and simulating images of possible futures we may navigate and prospect our way into the future rather than being driven by the past.
- The capacity for exercising an element of personal choice and control over our lives is at the heart of 'humanness'.

These points suggest that one way to managing our personal future is to surface implicit assumptions via skilled reflection, in order to open the door to creative simulation and prospection of future possibilities. An interesting question that follows relates to the place of explicit reason and decision-making in reflection and the achievement of goals (Kahneman 2011), and in contrast to this the increasing importance being attributed to the role of intuition (Mercier & Sperber 2017; Railton 2016). New work in this area suggests exciting new conversations and applications for coaching, which I turn to next.

Looking forward

It is generally recognized that coaches have a role in helping people navigate life at times when it is stormy or they wish to chart a new route through it. One could argue, however, that there is a very large somewhat untapped role for coaches, which involves working with a much wider population than at present. This would include working with both adults and children, helping them become better navigators, become more creative in terms of identifying potential routes and destinations, and even more importantly, helping their clients think about and refine their own processes of learning and change – enabling them to become their own coach. For after all, even if we have an excellent coach for a period of time, most of the time we rely on our own decision-making and actions. As Bandura observed, even in these situations there are ways that we can have greater personal agency and become more empowered. We can for example collaborate with others, become more aware of where sharing of learning can assist us, create situations where proxy agency may operate, and also engage in collective forms of learning and change (Bandura 2001).

In respect of each of these areas of activity there is scope for a coach to support individual and group learning. This may occur in all walks of life and in respect of all roles that we may engage with including, for example, work life, politics, business, parenting, the performing arts, in maintaining health, and also in living with chronic ill health.

In whatever area we may be coaching to support learning from and for living there is scope for looking first at our own personal approach to doing this.

My own reflections frequently reveal incongruities and tensions, often too many to deal with in detail. Some I may jot down to return to later. Often I discuss them with a colleague or supervisor. At times I need to make a rapid workable decision. It makes sense to me that much of my decision-making is based on intuition and I search to bring 'the tip of the iceberg of my intuition' within my conscious awareness (Mercier & Sperber 2017).

Much of my behaviour appears to be a mixture of habit and guesswork (Railton 2016). When examined, my reasoning may appear to be flawed (Kahneman 2011), but I like to draw upon the thesis of Mercier and Sperber who argue that 'The main role of logic in reasoning . . . may well be a rhetorical one: logic helps simplify and schematize intuitive arguments, highlighting and often exaggerating their force' (p 7). I realize that there is more of my thinking that could helpfully become explicit – but not all I think, or I would grind to a halt. I rely on my intuitions! But I also value the ability to reflect on my thinking and actions, allowing this to help me navigate my future. I may do this alone but frequently I engage in this activity with others as part of a shared learning endeavour.

Whether honing our skills as a reflective coach or helping a client to develop their own reflective learning skills, there is a place for skills to be learned and practiced. The application of core coaching skills is central to successful engagement with all types of reflective learning. They are as important to our client when they are self-coaching as they are to us when we coach a client or engage in our own self-coaching. I use the mnemonic LEARN as a reminder of these essential skills for coaching, whether working with an individual, an organization, or in self-coaching and supervision (Watts 2017).

The first of these skills is *Listening*. This may be listening to ourselves, listening to others, listening to our instincts, our gut feelings, and very importantly listening to and becoming aware of disjuncture and incongruence as discussed earlier in this chapter. Then follow the skills relating to *Engagement*. Knowing when and how to engage, recognizing for example, that in self-coaching we can't give equal engagement time to each of life's disjunctures and areas of tension; knowing how to actively listen and engage and when and how to go that step further – engaging in further exploration, experimenting with ideas and at some stage evaluating them; knowing that timings are of the essence and at the heart of what we do as coaches, whether engaging in self-coaching or coaching with others. Evaluating too soon, or even attempting to identify the areas to evaluate can close down creative thinking and experimentation.

The skills of listening and engaging are complemented by the skill of being able to consider how one might *Apply* a whole range of emergent thoughts and ideas. This is a very different stage of activity and skill set to how one chooses *Actions* and enacts these. There may be an enormous number of potential applications relating to what one is hearing and exploring, but action is more specific, contextual and has real consequences for real people. There may be potential tensions between the vast number of possible applications and actions and those we consider as real options for ourselves in a particular situation. It's easy to close our options down too soon, maybe drawing too heavily on negative or limited past experience.

Knowing how to safely revisit these is an important skill, not so that we allow our future to be driven by our past, but so that we may more effectively prospect and choose our future. This is where the power and skill of *Reflection* comes in: we allow ourselves to re-engage with something, even if for years we may have

Personal LEARNing Cycle

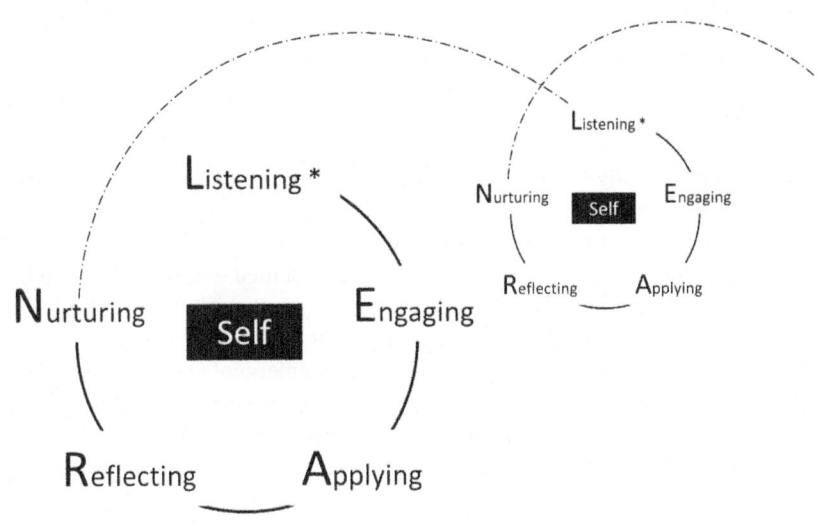

* Listening with all of your senses   (c) Mary Watts, Personal LEARNing Cycle 2014

Figure 2.1

thought we had answered all of the questions and issues to do with that thing. But if we remind ourselves of Kelly's suggestion, that as life changes, so do the issues and questions relating to it, then we can see that there is a place for re-engaging, re-examining, re-evaluating, re-applying and re-acting, maybe in a new and very different way to previously. Reflection thus becomes core to our future, not so that we are driven to it by the past (and are using reflection to understand this and reconcile ourselves to our powerlessness) but exactly the opposite, so that we may take an active role in choosing our future and actively prospect and enact it. The R of LEARN is also a reminder of the power and importance of relationship, the relationship with self, the relationship with others, and in coaching the relationship between the client and the coach (Van Nieuwerburgh & Love 2019).

At the centre of learning and reflecting is the self, or maybe more appropriately put, our many selves. It is I, for example, as mother, wife, coach and researcher who is learning, reflecting, changing. Sometimes there is tension between my different selves as I reflect, listen to my inner voice and my intuitions and consider my options and actions. The final skill linked to my Mnemonic is *Nurturing*. Nurturing my well-being, my developing skills, my new ways of knowing, and recognizing that my various selves and roles in life may sometimes be in conflict, and engaging with this – which returns me to the Listening skills at the start of

LEARN, but now I've moved on, I'm a different person and listening from a different place. I construe LEARN as a moving, open cycle (Watts 2017, p. 421). I never return to the same place. My learning changes me and I listen with new ears; my situation, options and potential have changed, along with my changing self. As I develop my own LEARNing skills it is equally important that I help my clients develop theirs.

Conclusion

There is a potentially significant role for coaches in promoting and supporting the reflective learning skills of their clients and also in applying these to their own learning in ways that enhance their coaching and wider learning from living. This chapter has focused on the power of reflection as a medium for substantial learning and change that may in many cases be transformational. It draws in particular on literature originating in adult education, psychology and also emergent work in coaching. In addition to furthering these still emergent conversations, there is scope for conversations on how learning in its broadest sense might be applied to advancing our understanding, practice and research in coaching.

A core theme running through this chapter relates to giving coaching skills away – empowering and enabling people, whomever they may be, to prospect and determine their futures. This requires coaching as a profession, and us as individual coaches, to reflect on the issues involved in this, exploring and researching how best this might happen; being open to new ways of construing our role as coaches and new contexts for practice; reviewing and revising coach training; and above all exploring how we might empower an ever broadening population of clients through the development of mindsets and skills that perhaps we implicitly consider sacred to ourselves as professional coaches. The time is ripe for pursuing these important but still emergent conversations.

Acknowledgements – with many thanks and much appreciation to Robert Bor, Esther Cavett, Sarah Corrie, Ian Florance and Kevin Swindin for reading earlier versions of this chapter and providing me with such insightful and helpful feedback.

References

Argyris, C. (1993) *Knowledge for Action: A Guide to Overcoming Barriers to Organisational Change*. San Francisco, CA: Jossey-Bass.

Argyris, C., & Schön, D. (1974) *Theory in Practice: Increasing Professional Effectiveness*. San Francisco, CA: Jossey Bass.

Argyris, C., & Schön, D. (1978) *Organisational Learning: A Theory of Action Perspective*. Reading, MA: Addison-Wesley.

Bandura, A. (1977) *Social Learning Theory*. London: Prentice Hall International, Inc.

Bandura, A. (2001) Social Cognitive Theory: An Agentic Perspective. *Annual Review of Psychology*, 52, 1–26.

Brookfield, S. (1990) Using Critical Incidents to Explore Learners' Assumptions. In Mezirow & Associates (Eds.), *Fostering Critical Reflection in Adulthood: A Guide to Transformative and Emancipatory Learning*. San Francisco, CA: Jossey Bass.

Candy, P. (1990) Repertory Grids: Playing Verbal Chess. In Mezirow & Associates (Eds.), *Fostering Critical Reflection in Adulthood: A Guide to Transformative and Emancipatory Learning*. San Francisco, CA: Jossey Bass.

Chaskalson, M. (2011) *The Mindful Worklace: Developing Resilient Individuals and Resonant Organisations with MBSR*. West Sussex: Wiley Blackwell.

Dalton, P., & Dunnett, G. (2005) *A Psychology for Living: Personal Construct Theory for Professionals and Clients* (2nd Edition). London: John Wiley.

Green, S., & Palmer, S. (2019) *Positive Psychology Coaching in Practice*. London & New York: Routledge.

Hart, M.U. (1990) Liberation Through Consciousness Raising. In Mezirow & Associates (Eds.), *Fostering Critical Reflection in Adulthood: A Guide to Transformative and Emancipatory Learning*. San Francisco, CA: Jossey Bass.

Illeris, K. (2018) *Contemporary Theories of Learning: Learning Theorists in their Own Words* (2nd edition). London and New York: Routledge.

Jarvis, P. (1992) *Paradoxes of Learning: On Becoming an Individual in Society*. San Francisco, CA: Jossey Bass.

Jarvis, P. (1999) *The Practitioner Researcher: Developing Theory from Practice*. San Francisco, CA: Jossey Bass.

Kahneman, D. (2011) *Thinking, Fast and Slow*. New York: Farrar, Straus & Giroux.

Kelly, G.A. (1955) *The Psychology of Personal Constructs Volume One: A Theory of Personality*. New York: W. W. Norton & Company Inc.

Kelly, G.A. (1969) The Strategy of Psychological Research. In B. Mayer (Ed.), *Clinical Psychology and Personality: The Selected Papers of George Kelly* (pp. 114–132). New York: John Wiley.

Kolb, D. (1984) *Experiential Learning*. Englewood Cliffs, NJ: Prentice-Hall.

Kovacs, L., & Corrie, S. (2017) Building Reflective Capability to Enhance Coaching Practice. *The Coaching Psychologist*, 13(1), 4–12, Leicester, BPS.

Lukinsky, J. (1990) Reflective Withdrawal Through Journal Writing. In Mezirow & Associates (Eds.), *Fostering Critical Reflection in Adulthood: A Guide to Transformative and Emancipatory Learning*. San Francisco, CA: Jossey Bass.

Mercier, H., & Sperber, D. (2017) *The Enigma of Reason: A New Theory of Human Understanding*. London, UK: Allen Lane/Penguin Books.

Mezirow, J. (2018) Transformative Learning Theory. In K. Illeris (Ed.), *Contemporary Theories of Learning*. Oxon & New York: Routledge.

Mezirow, J., & Associates (1990) *Fostering Critical Reflection in Adulthood: A Guide to Transformative and Emancipatory Learning*. San Francisco, CA: Jossey-Bass.

Olson, M.H., & Hergenhahn, B.R. (2016) *An Introduction to Theories of Learning*. Oxon & New York: Routledge.

Railton, P. (2016) Intuitive Guidance: Emotion, Information and Experience. In Seligman et al. (Eds.), *Homo Prospectus*. New York: Oxford University Press.

Roth, I. (1990) Challenging Habits of Expectation. In Mezirow & Associates (Eds.), *Fostering Critical Reflection in Adulthood: A Guide to Transformative and Emancipatory Learning*. San Francisco, CA: Jossey-Bass.

Schön, D.A. (1983) *The Reflective Practitioner*. New York: Basic books.

Schön, D.A. (1987) *Educating the Reflective Practitioner: Toward a New Design for Teaching and Learning in the Professions*. San Francisco, CA: Jossey-Bass.

Seligman, M.E.P. (1975) *Helplessness*. San Francisco, CA: Freeman.

Seligman, M.E.P. (2018) *The Hope Circuit: A Psychologist's Journey from Helplessness to Optimism*. London & Boston: Nicholas Brealey.

Seligman, M.E.P., Abramson, L.Y., Semmel, A., & von Baeyer, C. (1979) Depressive Attributional Style. *Journal of Abnormal Psychology*, 88, 242–247.

Seligman, M.E.P., Railton, P., Baumeister, R.F., & Sripasa, C. (2013) Navigating into the Future or Driven by the Past. *Perspectives on Psychological Science*, 8, 119–141.

Seligman, M.E.P., Railton, P., Baumeister, R.F., & Sripasa, C. (2016) *Homo Prospectus*. New York: Oxford University Press.

Spinelli, E. (1997) *Tales of Un-knowing: Therapeutic Encounters From An Existential Perspective*. London: Gerald Duckworth & Co. Ltd.

Stojnov, D., Džinović, V., Pavlović, J., & Frances, M. (Eds.) (2011) *Personal Construct Psychology in an Accelerating World*. EPCA: Belgrade.

Van Nieuwerburgh, C., & Love, D. (2019) *Advanced Coaching Practice: Inspiring Change in Others*. London: Sage.

Watts, M., & Corrie, S. (2013) Growing the 'I' and the 'We' in Transformational Leadership: The LEAD, LEARN & GROW Model. *The Coaching Psychologist*, 9(2), 86–99, Leicester, BPS.

Watts, M.H. (2017) The Reflective Practitioner: Some Personal Reflections. In R. Bor & M.H. Watts (Eds.), *The Trainee Handbook: A Guide for Counselling and Psychotherapy Trainees*. London: Sage.

Watts, M.H., Cavett, E., & Dudney, S. (2016) Learning Through Supervision. In C. van Nieuwerburgh (Ed.), *Coaching in Professional Contexts*. London: Sage.

Watts, M.H., Kleinschmidt, A., & French, D. (2020) Ethics Challenges – Challenging Ethics: Keeping an Open Mind on Ethics and Professionalism During Coach Training and Beyond. In M.H. Watts, R. Bor, & I. Florance (Eds.), *The Trainee Coach Handbook*, 249–263. London: Sage.

Whitmore, J. (2017) *Coaching for Performance: The Principles and Practice of Coaching and Leadership* (5th Edition). London & Boston: Nicholas Brealey.

Chapter 3

New perspectives on how psychometrics and coaching can inform each other

Ian Florance

In the past testing and coaching have influenced each other less than they might; that's unfortunate since both areas (psychometric testing in some applications, coaching at its core) seek to help people develop self-awareness and understanding to improve their lives. Both areas are also evolving, and their respective changes are bringing them closer together. To create a richer interplay between them, practitioners in both areas need to understand the other area better. For instance, many coaches need to be familiar with the advantages and disadvantages of more models of personality measurement than the *type* approach, if they are to get the most benefit from personality psychology. Equally test publishers and developers need to create more reports informed by in-depth understanding of what's unique about coaching, rather than treating it as psychology-lite. I've tried to make reasons for this lack of in-depth conversation clear in this chapter, as well as to show how developments in testing could aid or, in certain cases, inhibit closer understanding. I've observed a few guidelines in writing it.

First, since testing is undergoing a very fast and fundamental transformation, references to specific tests and publishers are liable to go out-of-date very quickly, especially around on-line delivered testing. I've only been specific where it is unavoidable.

Second, testing can be a technical area, often unnecessarily so in my view. This chapter is not a primer of testing statistics. One of the points to make is that the statistical methods by which you analyse data to gain reliable, meaningful information have changed, and will change, much less than how and where you obtain the data in the first place. The statistics coaches need to understand are covered in good test training. I've therefore simplified ideas, tried to make them practically relevant and avoided numbers, while stressing that numbers are one of the types of evidence that testing supplies.

Thirdly, I concentrate on formal psychometric testing tools rather than assessment in general. There are several reasons for this but the most compelling one is that it's precisely the relationship between formal psychometrics and coaching that needs discussion. Many coaches are used to using informal methods of evaluation: strengths inventories; 360° tools; structured interviews with co-workers and managers; and self-authored surveys, for instance. They have worried less about the difference between formal tests and informal assessments than psychometricians and psychologists. I use words such as 'testing' and 'assessment' where they make a sentence readable, rather than to make minute – and in coaching terms – irrelevant discriminations.

Finally, since all the other chapters in this book paint a detailed picture of how and why coaching is changing, I've focused here on changes in testing and how this might make it a more useful, acceptable technique within the coaching armoury.

Coaching and assessment

The origins and approaches of testing and coaching were and, in some cases still are, different (see Table 3.1).

However, the view of assessment detailed in this table, has begun to look out-of-date. In certain countries and applications, assessment has moved from being a more academic, research-based area of psychology, applied by experts to 'subjects', to becoming a more practical tool used to underpin positive action in schools, hospitals and clinics, business and sports teams. In other words, assessment has become more like coaching.

Despite some statements that assessment is central to coaching (Chapman, Best, and van Casteran 2003, 51) coaches have only dipped their toes into the huge range of formal tests available. In conversation, Professor Adrian Furnham suggested that there are now around 50,000 tests measuring different psychological aspects, yet most coaching primers only reference a very narrow and focused selection. This usually comprises more formal tests of personality and one or

Table 3.1 Contrasting coaching and assessment models

Coaching	Assessment
Equalises power: 'equalisation of power has become a mantra' (Rogers 2016, 45)	**Power / expertise on tester's side:** there has been a constant emphasis on the very specific knowledge required to use formal tests, conferred by initial or professional training (British Psychological Society 2000; Smith and Smith 2005, throughout).
A process done between people: coaching methods are specifically designed to create relationships in which power is equalised; expertise is less critical than attention and the key work is done by the 'client' rather than an 'expert'.	**A process done by someone to someone else:** this perhaps reflects the roots of testing in academic research but has been reinforced by the emphasis on test users learning high level skills in order to accurately describe, categorise or diagnose a lay person.

Coaching	Assessment
Future-focused: fundamental coaching models, such as GROW, are feedforward systems: they facilitate moving forward to a future vision.	**Past-focused in three ways:** 1 Testing's grounding in clinical and educational contexts tends to focus it on the past causes of present behaviour 2 Evaluating whether a test is measuring what it's supposed to often involves comparing its results with those of earlier tests – using earlier technologies as a present validating reference point. 3 Future-oriented predictive studies are frequently honoured by their rarity. They're expensive and need a continuity which is difficult to arrange.
Action-oriented: as many other contributors to this book imply, coaching is focused on increasing the likelihood of beneficial action by basing it on personal realisation rather than external orders or instructions.	**Categorisation / description oriented:** the roots of testing are in categorisation. Examples include: – Alfred Binet's original educational tests set out '[to identify which French children he felt were not worth schooling' (Roseveare 2017, 252). – Clinical testing often categorises people by the DSM system (American Psychiatric Association 2013). – Even developmental tests, while suggesting action will implicitly consign individuals to binary categories (for instance 'warrants training' vs 'does not warrant training').
Emphasises possibilities: coaching is, at its base, a strengths-based practice.	**Seeks out deficits:** this is not always true and has changed under the influence of developments such as positive psychology. But as some of the issues raised indicate, much educational and clinical testing was designed to identify problems that could be solved or, at least, dealt with.
Rests on words and gestures: coaching training emphasises active listening, body language, the unacknowledged implications of words. It is possible to become a coach without touching on very basic statistics.	**A numbers-based discipline:** testing is underpinned by complex statistics and training emphasises this.
Either a-theoretical or drawing on several different disciplines. Jenny Rogers discusses this briefly (Rogers 2016, 6).	**Based on a developed theory of psychology and measurement.** For a good if technical discussion of this see Rust and Golombok, 1999.

two related areas (emotional intelligence and increasingly, values, resilience and motivation) rather than those of ability, attainment or other aspects of human behaviour. *Psychometrics in Coaching: Using Psychological and Psychometric Tools for Development* (Passmore 2012) is an exception because its core subject is assessment.

Even when it comes to formal personality measures, coaches tend to use a limited number of titles. A very good introductory text, the one I trained with, has a section on psychometrics which evaluates two tests – MBTI, FIRO-B – and two strengths inventories, while mentioning representative titles in three other linked areas: dark-side assessment, entrepreneurship and leadership (Scoular 2011, 108–122). It is generally accepted that the type model of personality is the most popular one among coaches and has given rise to an excellent recent one-volume introduction to the whole area (Rogers 2017). If coaches know only one test it will usually be the Myers-Briggs Type Indicator. This may be a good entry point offering a simplified, easy-to-use and discuss set of reports (Florance and Moyle 2018) but many coaches go no further in investigating the whole testing area.

External issues, not least the revolution in digital technology, are transforming both assessment and coaching. Carol Braddick's chapter in this book paints a more detailed picture of how technology might change coaching. I'll treat it as one of a range of influences affecting both coaching and assessment practice.

Why and where tests are used in coaching now

Whether they like it or not, coaches assess at the start of a coaching relationship: either explicitly and formally via test use or implicitly and informally; for instance, chemistry sessions (Scoular 2011, 36) are precisely intended for coach and coachee to 'check each other out' and decide whether they want to work together.

There's general agreement about many of the purposes of assessment in a coaching context. The coach may get 'useful insights' into the development task and how this might be achieved (Chapman et al. 2003, 52). For the individual being coached, assessment brings increased self-awareness which underpins change and improvement. In addition, assessment introduces people to psychological insights that will be useful in dealing with others. Testing feedback is a form of developmental training, particularly useful to new people managers.

But I'd add a few more functions assessment fulfils now, whether the participants realise it or not (see Table 3.2).

Why tests are used less than they might be in coaching

The issues outlined in Table 3.1 answer this question in part. There are, I think, other reasons. *The Hidden History of Coaching* (Wildflower 2013) recounts the non-academic – often counter-cultural – roots of coaching (see also the Introduction to this book). This history is one reason why many coaches see their practice

Table 3.2 Additional reasons for using tests in coaching

Measuring progress	Coaching is about change. Assessments can be used to measure what changes in human characteristics, such as personality and values.
Helping coaches improve	Some tests, whether self-administered, administered by coaches or coach's supervisors, give insights into a coach's style which will help him or her improve the service he or she offers and avoid blind spots and prejudices.
Coaching professionalisation	Training in tests may provide coaches with reassurance that they do have a transferable set of tangible skills to 'sell'. Fellow students in my initial coaching training course confessed to imposter syndrome (see Watts, Swindin, Al Khalil, and Cavett 2020) at the very least insecurity, about not having a definable and explicable expertise or knowledge base related to coaching. Reassurance provided by technical test training might help coach's well-being.
Increasing engagement in the coaching process	While ability and knowledge tests often cause anxiety, my experience as a test publisher confirmed that people enjoy tests of personality and other personal characteristics. In this they serve a function akin to active, focused listening, increasing engagement, enjoyment and a sense of being valued, reactions which seem to improve the chance of coaching's success as detailed in *Time to Think: Listening to Ignite the Human Mind* (Kline 2002).
Gathering focused information quickly	'How many times do my seminar delegates need to see me to make a decision about my honesty? The answer is at least 10–15, maybe as many as 25–30, observed over six months'. This is a quote from the original English manuscript of a fascinating book published in Dutch (Robertson, 2012) It takes us much longer to get to know critical aspects of other people -such as values – than we think. Psychometric tests gather very focused, objective information in a very short time.

as syncretic; dealing with existential experience and 'what works' rather than what research recommends as robust. Another reason is that coaches come from many different backgrounds; from schools and clinics; from commercial organisations and not-for-profits; from new age, experiential and professional backgrounds. Many will have had no grounding in research practice; others will have an initial qualification in the arts. This diversity may explain the huge variety of approaches used by coaches: put simply, I've only occasionally met a coach who initially volunteers that their practice is a research-based science when asked to describe it.

Coaches have thus tended to pay less attention to numbers than other 'mind sciences' such as psychology. Hence the paucity of basic research on whether coaching works (Groves and Furnham 2016). Psychometrics, which is highly numbers-oriented, makes claims to scientific stringency and often delivers judgements rather than mutual insight, so may not have appealed to coaches in the past, hence the relative lack of test use. (For further discussion of the nature of coaches see Rogers 2016, 186–205.) But this suggested bias against numbers in coaching is changing, particularly in leadership and other work-related applications. Here, the need to provide a return on investment (ROI) for coaching moves the process away from a purely humanistic/verbal approach to efficiency/economic models and research underpinning. Organisations demand numerical proof that coaching works and is worth the money: anecdotes and case studies no longer suffice. Assessments can provide numbers; the digitisation of assessment further strengthens this trend.

Influences on testing

There are new and vigorous conversations going on within testing. Much of the basic work that underpins widely used personality tests took place between the 1930s and 1960s, and many of the tests that we use are later editions of tests developed then. While some were changed fundamentally during translation to digital and on-line delivery, others are still paper and pencil tests translated onto screen without utilising the capabilities of digital environments to make them more attractive and/or accurate in their predictions. Testing, until the early '90s at least, remained pretty unchanged from its early to mid-20th-century roots. Meanwhile the world changed dramatically. Table 3.3 suggests some of the obvious recent influences that have created the need for new sorts of tests and new ways of testing. It is no coincidence that they are also behind some of the rethinking of coaching that is going on now.

Present and future developments in testing

Given all of this what are the emerging trends and conversations in testing? As this section heading suggests, some new trends have already started and may continue in the future. Others are more speculative.

Changes in what is measured

Some practices and areas of application in testing are long-established. For instance:

- business test use has long been focused on leadership, not least for economic reasons since leadership tests can have a higher price and, often, expensive add-on consultancy services.
- personality testing tends to be based on one of a small number of theoretical approaches (typically factor-analytic, type, ipsative and, to a lesser extent, projective).
- certain aspects of educational and clinical testing have been based on a model in which specific sorts of ability are measured as surrogates for, or more focused applications of the robust, but often criticised, practice of IQ testing.

Table 3.3 Some top-level influences on testing

Changes in technology	As mentioned earlier, Carol Braddick's chapter gives a good summary of technological changes that might influence both coaching and testing. A by-product of technological innovation is the generation of huge amounts of manipulable data. This can be analysed in many ways. Thus, the need for a tool (a test) to generate psychological data is reduced: the need is for ways of analysing that data, creating valid, reliable and useful psychological information and using that to create action plans.
Life span	*The Hundred Year Life* (Gratton and Scott 2016) gives an excellent review of this area. It draws out the implications of longer lives in a number of areas, not least the shape of careers. The implications for testing range from the need for more testing (and coaching) in increasing life and work transitions, to the need to measure different sorts of skills and human characteristics, comparing results to different norm groups.
Developments in psychology as a discipline	In particular it is claimed that the neurosciences (especially the use of high-powered scanning technologies) allied to advances in genetics are doing away with the need for some sorts of testing. But Hamira Riaz's chapter in this book suggests some concerns about claims made on behalf of the neurosciences.
General awareness of psychological issues	Bestselling novels, books, films and magazines often take psychological issues as a core theme. It can be argued we live in a psychologised society. Often informal tests and quizzes are one way of taking part in this and psychological language is used freely outside traditional settings.
Changes in testing	Over the past 20–30 years, technology has influenced the theory and practice of testing, reintroducing techniques like item banking and item response theory to create a more flexible set of tools which, to some extent, adapt to the individual test taker. One other influence on testing is similar to that on coaching. The question 'Does testing truly predict future behaviour?' may be better researched than 'Does coaching work?' but, in both cases, users are commenting that given the amount they spend on these two techniques, they'd like to be more certain that they 'do what they say on the tin'.

However, new areas to be measured are developing all the time. As an example: Howard Gardner's book on Multiple Intelligences (Gardner 2006)) underlay the publication of many tests of emotional intelligence, a concept which has been accepted enthusiastically in business and educational contexts. This area and its link to positive psychology seems more compatible with many coaching approaches, engages coaches and has generated interest in some new sorts of test. Gardner's book also fuelled interest in other sorts of 'intelligences', ranging from the though-provoking (kinaesthetic and musical) to the bizarre (sexual intelligence anyone?). This sort of development, coupled with the seemingly annual remodelling of what leadership is, suggests that many of these new areas of assessment may be driven by management fads and media stories, rather than genuine psychological insights.

All this said, new areas of assessment are developing. These are often simply more focused areas within personality or ability. Some of them need little explanation. Some are less relevant to coaches: those which aid recruitment in business, diagnosis in clinical practice and measure attainment in education for instance. Others, however, do seem to fit in to coaching more easily.

It should be obvious that at least some of these newer testing areas – and this is just a selection – would be useful in coaching. Most of these tests investigate

Table 3.4 Some new and developing subjects for assessment which may be of interest to coaches

What's measured	Discussion
Situational judgement	Tests of situation judgement measure responses to realistic scenarios rather than a more rarefied, not contextual decision-making ability.
Service orientation	Became more important when service industries were seen to be taking over from manufacturing. Particularly used in telesales and service centres. A development/adaptation of these assessments might be the creation of care-orientation given the growth of care roles in Western society (Gratton and Scott 2016).
Creativity and values	Seen as a gap in the present range of assessments.
'Game changing'	The question 'How do you identify very young people who have no track record but whose natural ability (in areas such as IT) allows them to think "outside the box"?' is exercising a lot of companies. In a sense this returns assessment to one of its starting points – identifying prodigies.
Integrity	Integrity tests have long been popular in the USA but there has been some resistance to them in Europe due to cultural and legal issues.
Trainability/ flexibility	Given huge numbers of work transitions in any life and the constant pace of change, how easily will individuals find it to learn new skills or adapt to new situations (Gratton and Scott 2016 throughout).
Prejudice/bias	This is a controversial area as there are huge dangers in labelling someone (rightly or wrongly) as prejudiced. This is also a very difficult area to assess. Harvard's work in this area has highlighted possibilities and problems (Implicit Project 1998).

What's measured	Discussion
Resilience	There is much debate about the definition of this.
Developmental differences	Given longer life spans and the fact that younger people may have 'game changing contributions' to make in organisations (see earlier) and older people are active longer, one would expect more assessments to look at differences created by life-long development.
Clinical and quasi clinical areas	There has been a very gradual breaking down of the barrier between clinical, work and educational assessment. There are still very specialist tests which can only be used by medical and other professionals. But the growing understanding of child mental health issues and reports on the incidence of mental health problems among the general, working population have created tests which begin to cross the boundaries. Good examples are tests of derailment and dark side behaviour.
Team assessment	Assessment has focused on individual differences and measurement of team compatibility and effectiveness has tended to add together the qualities of individual team members. A renewed interest in social psychology may lead to more sophisticated assessments of the characteristics of groups of people.

characteristic behaviour or the basic motivations and values that underlie life and work choices.

Changes driven by digital technology

Over the past two decades, the increasing delivery of assessments in digital formats has changed several features of the practice. For instance, rather than giving every test taker the same content to measure something, technology and measurement theory enables us to change the questions we ask while measuring the same thing. Newer developments like automated item generation (a computer generates questions on the fly, based on a psychometric rule base) and item banking (creating a huge number of questions or items whose properties are known, a unique selection of which is used in any particular testing session) underpin these uses. These developments can prevent cheating where there are right or wrong answers. While this benefit will not impinge on coaching to any great extent, another one – shortening the time to take a test – might. This can be achieved by comparing someone's responses on a few questions to how others have responded, generating a hypothesis of the final results and then asking a smaller number of questions to confirm or deny this hypothesis.

Other benefits of digital delivery which might encourage coaches to use tests include the creation of more involving test items. Generations bought up on

DVDs, video games and the internet are not going to be satisfied with verbally based, multiple choice questions, ink blots or geometrical matrices. So, there has been a move from words to pictures (sometimes moving) as the stimulus to which a test subject responds. I deal with the implications of this in the next section of New Ways of Delivering and Structuring Tests

Changes in reports

Test reports have changed dramatically. They've shortened, placed more emphasis on action rather than description, downplayed statistics and translated technical psychological terms into more natural language. They've tended to emphasise maximising potential rather than identifying problems and, as such, have started to directly influence training and consultancy (such as coaching) that follows on from testing. The underlying algorithms that generate reports from test-takers' answers have grown exponentially more sophisticated. Increasingly tests – particularly personality titles – generate a wide range of reports for different purposes (for instance coaching, selection. succession planning) and for different users (the test taker, his or her manager, the specialist test user etc). The emphasis has moved away from expert interpretation of tests to the test taker reaction to how their answers have been analysed – in other words it's moved in a more coaching direction. But there is still a lot to be do, not least explaining the basis on which 'expert reports' have been constructed.

Changes in where testing is done

Tests are increasingly administered in many different environments. How you administered a test used to be a major element in test user training, but this is no longer true. Certain sorts of tests are now delivered on-line, anywhere from someone's home to an internet cafe. Trends suggest that mobile phones will be the increasingly dominant way of delivering assessment (as they already are for so many techniques) and this must have an impact on how tests are designed, scored, reported (McHenry 2017).

New ways of delivering and structuring traditional tests

Gamification

Gamification is the application of game-design elements and game principles in non-game contexts. These are early days for this development though several publishers are both pioneering their use and, it would seem, theorising and researching their future development.

Several generations have grown up with increasingly sophisticated digital games as one of their primary means of entertainment. Games require gamesters to make choices, evaluate evidence, show preferences, learn from the past and react to change, as well as exhibit a variety of different reasoning skills. Many implicitly force gamesters to exhibit personal preferences, typical behaviours and even prejudices. Whereas games used for entertainment may offer situations involving killing zombies, building worlds and defeating Orcs, new *serious* games (as they're sometimes called) can offer environments built round leadership situations, the experience of family dynamics or psychological syndromes, sports matches and games. With a sophisticated statistical underpinning and a focused design, tests can therefore be used to measure psychological qualities in an environment which is visually and narratively rich and which can be made to seem much more relevant to the choices to be made on their basis.

Video reporting

As a logical conclusion to these points, IT capabilities could inform test reports as well as tests. For instance, a film of someone acting in a way that suggests he or she scores very high on a preference for Introversion and very low on Openness to Experience would be more engaging (and arguably, would be understood better, more often) than a bar chart reporting percentile scores on those two personality scales.

b2c

Increasingly test publishers and providers talk about the growth of a potential direct-to-consumer (b2c) market for tests. Whereas at one time tests were only used by trained professionals, improved access via Smartphones, tablets and other devices means tests can be delivered directly to consumers (McHenry 2017). While the dangers of access to very personal, sometimes technical information by untrained people have been pointed out, developments in reports outlined earlier reduce the dangers of misinterpretation. Social and work changes suggest that, just as coaching will increasingly be bought by individuals to help them navigate through increasingly complex and numerous life choices, the same is true of testing (see Gratton and Scott 2016 for a general treatment of these complex life changes).

New ways of accessing data

While these innovations have been affecting and updating traditional tests, designed to generate reliable and valid data on human beings, a more fundamental change has been taking place which is causing a lot of discussion.

We often believed we needed (and sometimes still believe we need) psychometric tests to generate data about people's psychological states on which to base plans, treatment, job offers, education, life-changing decisions etc. One prediction of the future is that soon we either won't need such tools. Personal data is everywhere. Michal Kosinski (2014) argues that in analysing social media data we are analysing psychology in action – we are observing people making real choices rather than the artificial ones tests create. So, the issue of how you get psychological data becomes almost irrelevant next to the techniques that underlay traditional tests: how you draw accurate inferences from the data; how you ensure the resulting information is valid and reliable; and how you accurately translate this information into actions, plans and treatments. So, as I wrote at the beginning of this chapter, 'the principles of how you analyse data to gain meaningful information have changed much less than the way you get the data in the first place'.

What are some of the sources for this sort of data? It's worth taking the points about the influence of technology on coaching Carol Braddick makes in her chapter, and applying them to testing. For instance, Alexa, Siri and other virtual AI assistants could use more sophisticated natural language analysis to hypothesise enduring psychological traits and temporary psychological states from the language someone is using, the tone of his or her voice, her or his speed of articulation

There are beginning to be robust and proven correlations between physical states as measured by devices such as Fitbit and wearables manufactured by Garmin. This is not a new idea: biodata has long been an entry point for understanding someone else's (and one's own) mood. Pulse rate, sweating, increase or decrees in weight have always been data from which we extract psychological descriptions. The new wearables just make the process quicker, easier and, once more research has been done, more accurate. (McHenry 2017) for an excellent introduction to this.

The most controversial source of data which can be analysed psychometrically are social media. The Cambridge Analytica scandal continues to raise questions about privacy, influence and disclosure in social media. As Kosinski has argued. this method of analysing people's data has huge advantages, but also attendant dangers and it must be used professionally and ethically. (Kosinski 2014).

Some warning voices

As the previous sections show, change brings threats as well as opportunities. Increased access to psychometric analysis, the use of different sorts of data from a variety of sources – all the issues I have mentioned – have potential downsides.

Claudia Filsinger-Mohun's chapter on diversity implicitly raises several of them. The use of psychometric tests in a non-coaching area such as selection may tend to psychologically 'clone' someone who has previously done a job. Rather than seeking to employ someone who will meet the challenges of a changing market or industry, the recruiter uses tests to find someone like the person who did the job before. Tests can be used to find people who are 'like us' – who fit our culture. This reduces diversity and Claudia's chapter argues the critical importance of diversity in any team or organisation. Coaches are not involved in selection, but these examples highlight a tendency to simplify test results and fit them into pre-conceived patterns. This tendency can range from the Barnum Effect in which someone will agree with a test report whatever it says, to the way some test users give undue weight to extreme scores or certain scales and fit these into a precon-ceived, often pathologising model. If coaching is about working as an individual, with an individual, the perceived tendency of tests to simplify individuals makes some coaches suspicious of tests' increasing use.

What might be the emerging conversation between testing and coaching: a summary

Many of the commonalities and potential increasing interactions between coach-ing and testing are implicit in the previous sections. In this concluding section I want to suggest my topics for conversation, though you may have spotted others.

First, coaches need to get more involved in the design of assessment systems (tests or ways of analysing pre-existing data) which generate reports and ques-tions specifically for coaching use. Equally, test developers need to involve coaches when working on such systems. Coaching has its own insights, theories, techniques and requirements. Tests rarely seem to factor these issues in.

Coaches should also try to know, and possibly get trained in, a much wider variety of tests rather than using the one they liked in their initial training as a one-size-fits-all solution. Testing is purposive and different tests should be used for different purposes. There is a real danger of over-testing: many coaches will know clients have been tested several times previously one popular personality test and view one more attempt to define their type or profile with barely concealed bore-dom. Having different tests at your disposal is on one of the solutions to this problem. In particular, coaches should consider tests beyond general personality tools to look at some of the areas I outlined in Table 3.2. But this is easier said than done as test training is expensive and to train in even a few tests often strains newly qualified coaches' budgets past breaking point. This has wider implications (more on this later) but test training providers should (and in one or two cases are) providing more flexible and economically viable training routes which aren't simply a function of cutting out competitors' products.

That coaches subconsciously downgrade the importance of numbers is a huge generalisation but is often the case. At least understanding basic statistics would really help coaches focus their services, justify them and interpret tests more sub-tly. Coach training should recognise this.

Tests offer a way of shortening coaching engagements by gathering focused psychological information quickly and, once initial investment is written off, cheaply. And as many of the testing initiatives I've described grow more sophisti-cated, this information will be more accurate and individualised. As is mentioned in other chapters of this book (especially Carol Braddick's) and as I imply in my comments on a growing b2c market, the economic basis of both coaching and testing may change. Offering services to individuals for life and career tran-sitions rather than to companies for leadership development suggests a funda-mental change to the pricing of coaching. Testing can provide exactly the sort of quickly sourced information which will make lower-priced, widely available, more diverse coaching possible. Despite this comment, coaching at senior organ-isational levels will continue for the foreseeable future. Here increased testing provides two key kinds of information. First it can provide numerical informa-tion which is easier to translate into ROI financial analysis. Is coaching worth the money? Test data makes it easier to answer the customer and potential customer's question. Equally test data makes it easier to look at individual progress, using well-established test-retest models. Here test data provides underpinning for strin-gent, quantitative efficacy research.

A lot of coaches shy away from technology applications which smack of sci-ence fiction. This is, I believe, a mistake in the case of testing. Whether the coach is a technophobe or not (and I share many coaching prejudices in this respect), many clients will be enthusiastic users of wearables and social media. There are opportunities to engage clients even more than in the past by entering their world and using these sorts of technology. Equally coaches can get involved far more in the way these sorts of technologies are applied and developed.

Some of these topics for conversation tap into as wider issue. In my conversa-tions with many coaches and coaching psychologists. a lot of them express a view that what they do is very different from the reductionist, scientific model that drives many sorts of psychology, and much health policy. Testing is sometimes seen as an (perhaps the prime) example of reductionist thinking applied to human being, resulting in damaging over-simplification. To many coaches therefore, testing rep-resents a technology with no place in their practice. I hope it's clear that I don't necessarily agree with this view, but I do think testing has to change and improve to meet new challenges, to reflect the complexity of human individuals in more detail and to meet the needs of an increasingly active and innovative coaching profession.

The key issue in all these is to break down barriers between topics, profes-sions and specialisms and concentrate on goals. The goals of testing and coach-ing overlap, involving as they do what Mary Watts writes about elsewhere in this volume – reflective practice and self-knowledge as a key to decision-making. At the risk of appearing naive, both areas seek to help people improve their own lives. A more in-depth conversation between these two disciplines would further this goal.

Bibliography

American Psychiatric Association. (2013). *Diagnostic and Statistical Manual of Mental Disorders-5*, 5th ed. Washington, DC: American Psychiatric Publishing.
Bentall, Richard. (2003). *Madness Explained: Psychosis and Human Nature*. London: Penguin Books.
Bluckert, Peter. (2006). *Psychological Dimensions of Executive Coaching*. Maidenhead: Open University Press.
British Psychological Society. (2000). Retrieved June 14, 2018 from http://ptc.bps.org.uk/bps-qualifications-test-use.
Chapman, Tony, Bill Best, and Peter van Casteren. (2003). *Executive Coaching: Exploding the Myths*. Basingstoke: Palgrave Macmillan.

Cook, Mark and Barry Cripps. (2004). *Psychological Assessment in the Workplace: A Manager's Guide*. Chichester, UK: John Wiley and Sons.

Darby, Jayson and Ian Florance. (2018). *Trends in the Testing/Assessment Market and Industry*. Presentation, De Vere Cotswold Water Park, February 26.

Florance, Ian and Penny Moyle. (2018). *Why Use Assessessments in Coaching: Which Ones? When?* Presentation, Berkeley Partnership, London, May 15.

Furnham, Adrian. (2017). Interview with one of the editors on 'New Techniques in Assessment', May 5.

Gardner, Howard E. (2006). *Multiple Intelligences*, New York: Basic Books.

Gratton, Lynda and Andrew Scott. (2016). *The Hundred Year Life*. London: Bloomsbury.

Groves, Simmy and Adrian Furnham. (2016). *Coaching as a Developmental Intervention in Organisations*. https://dol.org/10.1371/journal.pone.0159137

Implicit Project. (1998). Retrieved June 15, 2018 from https://implicit.harvard.edu/implicit/.

Kline, Nancy. (2002). *Time to Think: Listening to Ignite the Human Mind*. London: Cassell.

Kosinski, Michal. (2014). *Measurement and Prediction of Individual and Group Differences in the Digital Environment*. PhD Diss. Cambridge: Downing College.

McHenry, Robert. (2017). The Future of Psychometric Testing. In *Psychometric Testing: Critical Perspectives*, edited by Barry Cripps, 269–281. Chichester: Wiley Blackwell.

Palmer, Stephen and Alison Whybrow (Eds.). (2007). *Handbook of Coaching Psychology: A Guide for Practitioners*. Hove: Routledge.

Passmore, Jonathan (Ed.). (2012). *Psychometrics in Coaching: Using Psychological and Psychometric Tools for Development*. London: Kogan Page.

Peltier, Bruce. (2010). *The Psychology of Executive Coaching: Theory and Application*, 2nd ed. Hove: Routledge.

Robertson, Peter. (2012). *De Ecologische Leider: De Natuurlijke Cyclus van Kernwaarden en Orgnisaties*. Amsterdam: Business Contact.

Rogers, Jenny. (2016). *Coaching Skills: The Definitive Guide to Being A Coach*, 4th ed. Maidenhead: McGraw Hill Education.

Rogers, Jenny. (2017). *Coaching with Personality Type: What Works*. London: McGraw Hill Education.

Roseveare, Jay. (2017). A Practitioner's Viewpoint: Limitations and Assumptions Implicit in Assessment. In *Psychological Testing: Critical Perspectives*, edited by Barry Cripps, 251–262. Chichester: Wiley Blackwell.

Rust, John and Susan Golombok. (1999). *Modern Psychometrics: The Science of Psychological Assessment*, 2nd ed. London: Routledge.

Scoular, Anne. (2011). *Business Coaching*. Harlow: Prentice Hall Financial Times.

Smith, Mike and Smith, Pam. (2005). *Testing People at Work: Competencies in Psychometric Testing*. Oxford: BPS Blackwell.

Watts, Mary, Robert Bor & Ian Florance (Eds.). (2020). *The Trainee Coach Handbook*. London: Sage.

Watts, M., Swindin, K., Al Khalil, C., & Cavett, E., (2020). The Reflective Trainee Coach. In *The Trainee Coach Handbook*, edited by Mary Watts, Robert Bor & Ian Florance, 67–88. London: Sage.

Wildflower, Leni. (2013). *The Hidden History of Coaching*. Maidenhead, UK: Open University Press/McGraw Hill.

Chapter 4

Developing coaching through research

Sarah Corrie

Introduction

Imagine that some years ago, you coached someone who achieved transformational results through the work you did together. This client never forgot your impact and one day you receive a call from a solicitor who explains that your former client has left you a gift in their will. The solicitor tells you that your inheritance is a substantial sum of money – more than enough to be able to take a year out of your regular work and cover all of your salary needs and expenses. However, the terms of this gift are that during this year out you will devote yourself to undertaking a specific piece of research. The topic and focus of the research are entirely down to you – you can investigate whatever you like and use the methodology of your choice. The project could be a large-scale multi-centre research trial or a small-scale, in-depth analysis of aspects of your own practice, but regardless of its focus you can rest assured that there is sufficient money available to fully fund the project and to pay for any additional resources that you need. Putting aside for a moment any practical or ethical sensitivities, how would you react to such a proposition? Would it feel like the opportunity of a lifetime, or a sentence to endure? Would you know exactly what you wanted to research, or would you be left floundering, wondering where to start? Would you ultimately accept the gift or decline it, and what are the factors that would inform your choice?

Research is central to establishing the integrity of all professions concerned with enabling human change. The thoughtful and judicious application of research findings has the potential to benefit all levels of coaching delivery, from the services that coaches provide to their clients, to the commissioning of coaching and perhaps, ultimately, to public policy. Thus, research has a vital role to play in supporting the advancement of coaching and in shaping perceptions of its credibility.

At the same time, for many of us, research can often feel remote or even daunting – an activity separate from practice carried out by individuals and communities whose interests, priorities and skills differ significantly from our own. If, then, you responded with a degree of anxiety (or even horror!) to the fictitious scenario at the start of the chapter, know that you are not alone. For some, the concerns of the practitioner and those of the researcher seem to exist in two separate worlds.

However, when research and practice become polarised, everyone loses. As coaches we lose because we are deprived of access to creative and robust knowledge that can support, challenge and refine our practice. Our clients lose because they are working with coaches who are not stimulated in their thinking by the varied ideas, perspectives and findings that research offers. Equally, researchers lose because they are disconnected from the wealth of context-specific knowledge that typifies professional practice including the myriad procedural rules through which coaches bring knowledge to life for the benefit of their clients. Thus, research has much to learn from practice in the same way that practice has much to learn from research. Where the two work together as complementary endeavours, both are enriched, and our clients are more likely to receive the best of what coaching has to offer.

The aim of this chapter is to facilitate a thoughtful engagement with the many ways in which we can investigate our practice, learn from experience, and vitalise our work. In order to achieve this, we shall explore some of the challenges involved in creating a seamless partnership between coaching research and practice in an era dominated by the notion of evidence-based practice. We then explore how research might be conceptualised more broadly as a context for learning and discovery, taking account of the role that coaches have as both producers and consumers of knowledge. Finally, in the spirit of this broader conceptualisation, the chapter introduces a visual representation of some of the factors that shape our enquiries. This is offered in the hope that it might enable you, the reader, to arrive at a personalised, contextually astute and reflexive response to the many contributions that research has to offer our discipline.

Whilst reading this chapter, I would like to invite you to remain open to re-examining your own relationship with research as both a consumer of others' work and as a producer of your own. I also invite you to consider whether, in the light of the ideas presented, it would be beneficial to you to revise any prior beliefs about research in order to support your learning and development. Ultimately, by engaging in this journey of exploration, my hope is to nurture a refreshed understanding of research that can help you create more effective contexts for discovery of your own, and to equip you to ask the questions that matter most – to you, your clients and the coaching community.

Why research matters: the accountability agenda

The field of coaching is at an important point in its development. In recent years, the popularity of coaching has grown substantially – both as a service requested by clients[1] and as a career choice for practitioners. At an organisational level, many managers now see coaching as a necessary competence. Coaching skills are also increasingly expected of professionals including occupational, clinical and health psychologists. Coaching, it would seem, is a flourishing industry.

However, the growing demand for, and availability of, coaching tells us nothing about its effectiveness. Indeed, historically the field has been criticised for making fervent pronouncements about effectiveness that exceed the evidence which supports such claims (Briner, 2012). Although the coaching industry has developed exponentially since the 1990s when life coaching courses were in abundance and coaching-specific research was virtually non-existent (Grant & O'Connor, 2019), there is no room for complacency. Coaching is still an emerging discipline, an unregulated profession and as yet has no nationally agreed standards or training routes. Thus, if coaching is to maintain its credibility, and to assert confidently its place alongside more well-established helping professions, being able to make claims through recourse to something more robust than enthusiastic anecdotes is vital.

Critics such as Briner draw our attention to one very important function of research – namely, its ability to hold us accountable for the claims that we make. Conceptualising research as a vehicle of accountability and thus, justification has been increasingly privileged in recent years, gaining ascendancy through the movement of evidence-based practice. Introduced originally into healthcare by Sackett et al. in 1996, the principle that practice should be evidence-based has become so central to how the professions establish their credibility and how collectively we think about 'best practice' that it warrants consideration as a phenomenon in its own right. This is considered next.

The ascendancy of evidence-based practice

As perhaps the clearest and most well-developed manifestation of how research holds practitioners accountable for their work, evidence-based practice has been defined as:

> the conscientious, explicit and judicious use of current best evidence in making decisions about the care of individual patients . . . integrating individual clinical expertise with the best available external clinical evidence from systematic research.
>
> (Sackett et al., 1996, p. 71)

In extending this definition to coaching, Grant and O'Connor (2019) define evidence-based coaching as:

> the intelligent and conscientious use of *relevant and best current knowledge*, integrated with professional practitioner expertise in making decisions about how to deliver coaching to coaching clients and in designing and delivering coach training programmes.
>
> (p. 4; italics in original source)

Both definitions, although originating from within different professional contexts, capture a value which lies at the heart of evidence-based practice – namely, a commitment to ensuring that the services we deliver to our clients are based on the best available knowledge about what works for whom. This commitment also signals to the professions the moral necessity of basing our work on robust data, systematically gathered and impartially interpreted (Corrie, 2003, 2010; O'Donohue & Henderson, 1999). For an emerging profession such as coaching, therefore, the pursuit of an evidence-base affords significant advantages. These include:

- Ensuring that we keep our knowledge up to date for the benefits of our clients;
- Improving the quality of the services we offer through developing our work;
- Maintaining standards;
- Increasing confidence in the services that we deliver (our own and those who buy or otherwise commission coaching services) and because of this:
- Enhancing credibility;
- Protecting clients against the uncritical application of method, technique or intuition and
- Providing an ethical basis for providing a service for which we charge fees.

On initial examination, it can feel difficult to even question such a seemingly obvious and valuable innovation. After all, who could truly argue *against* the idea that our clients deserve anything but the expert application of the latest evidence of what works? Who would *not* want a conscientious coach who is striving to underpin their work with state-of-the-art knowledge? Evidence-based practice, then, is an inherently plausible idea. Yet, as the Italian Marxist and political activist Antonio Gramsci observed, ideas that are plausible to the point of seeming beyond question are precisely those that require scrutiny.

Towards an understanding of evidence

As Grant and O'Connor (2019) observe, despite the rhetoric, using the research literature to inform practice in the way that evidence-based practice advocates is no easy task. First, a number of research methodologies are complex. Making sense of statistical data and the premises that underlie their correct application, for example, requires specialist knowledge that may be inaccessible to many coaches. Second, if we are to draw on evidence to justify our claims or shape our practice, we need to be clear what is meant by evidence and how we can recognise 'good' evidence especially if we are not trained in research methodology.

Attempts to define and categorise the multiple forms of evidence available to us have tended to result in hierarchical representations of different types of data. Consider, for example the widely adopted classification proposed by the Department of Health (1999):

- Type I evidence: at least one good systematic review including a minimum of one randomised controlled trial.
- Type II evidence: minimum of one good randomised controlled trial.

- Type III evidence: at least one well-designed study without randomisation.
- Type IV evidence: minimum of one well-designed observational study.
- Type V evidence: opinion of experts, service users and carers.

Hierarchies of this kind provide an important insight into the implicit assumptions that underpin the notion of research as accountability. For example, although hierarchical position is not synonymous with usefulness and the type of evidence required depends on the nature of the enquiry, Sackett et al.'s (1996) original definition of, 'integrating individual clinical expertise with the best available external clinical evidence from systematic research' (p. 71) does seem to encourage us to cast our vision to the upper levels. This is perhaps because with each move up the hierarchy, the evidence is believed to become more compelling as a function of its greater objectivity and decreasing bias. Thus, types I and II evidence have come to represent the gold standard for the professions and therefore, that to which coaching has also aspired. Indeed, knowledge that takes the form of types I and II evidence is often what scholars and buyers of coaching look to in order to appraise the standing of the field. Equally, Briner's (2012) critique stems in part from the fact that historically, there has been a lack of randomised controlled trials demonstrating the efficacy of coaching interventions. However, as an emerging discipline that is still developing its own distinct knowledge-base, a dearth of randomised controlled trials in coaching (at least relative to other fields of practice) is not perhaps surprising. So what type of research has coaching produced so far and how has coaching research fared when examined through the agenda of accountability?

The body of research that underpins coaching has grown substantially in the last two decades (Fillery-Travis & Corrie, 2019). Alongside an expansion of studies overall as well as a diversity of contexts in which these studies are conducted, the journals and books devoted to coaching research have increased considerably. As coaching research has established itself, several scholars have provided summaries of the research that currently characterises the field.[2] In looking across the literature in its entirety Fillery-Travis and Corrie (2019), for example, identify three distinct strands of coaching research: (1) coaching outcomes (e.g. early studies looking at return on investment, randomised controlled trials, customised surveys incorporating multi-rater feedback), (2) process studies (e.g. Fillery-Travis and Lane's (2006) identification of three core clusters of relevant factors: coach attributes, client attributes and coaching practices) and (3) the more recent body of research investigating the coaching interaction (i.e. the relational elements of coaching and how these influence the outcomes obtained). Along similar lines, Grant and O'Connor (2019) have also identified three dominant strands of coaching research: outcome studies, coach-coachee relationship studies and the characteristics of effective coaches and studies investigating how coaching works. Taken as a whole, although there is still some way to go, our research shows promise in enabling the development of a distinct knowledge-base and in demonstrating its credibility through mapping its claims against the type of evidential hierarchy outlined earlier. However, in positioning our research in this way, we also confront some challenges.

First, as noted earlier, the 'evidence' of evidence-based practice is believed to become more compelling as a function of its decreasing bias and greater objectivity. However, objectivity is a tall order for all social sciences where multiple confounding variables are ever-present (see the British Psychological Society, 2016, for a detailed exploration of these issues). Moreover, evidence is not fixed. What 'works' in one setting may not translate to other populations, social contexts or historical moments. This is of particular relevance given that we are now living and working in a volatile, uncertain, complex and ambiguous (VUCA) world (Barber, 1992) where simple, linear cause-effect relationships rarely apply (Cavanagh & Lane, 2012).

Additionally, in making sense of the different forms of evidence to which we are exposed and through which we are expected to justify our claims, it is necessary to remember that we live in a culture that is heavily invested in numerical data (Wheatley, 1999). In the context of commissioning and evaluating coaching, numbers and measurement still tend to be equated with status and authority. However, an uncritical allegiance to numerical data may have some unintended consequences in that it (1) decontextualises the evidence-gathering endeavour; (2) encourages us to seek simple measures to capture complex experiences and (3) runs the risk of polarising science and practice as opposed to seeing them as complementary activities within the same cycle of discovery. Thus, the belief that it is possible to build an evidence-base for coaching that is stable, constant, objective, decontextualized and reassuringly numerical is inherently problematic.

One potentially useful 'lens' through which we might better understand, critique and debate the pursuit of evidence-based coaching comes from the 20th-century Italian Marxist and political activist Antonio Gramsci (see Hoare & Sperber, 2016). Imprisoned for his political beliefs and activism during Mussolini's fascist dictatorship, Gramsci wrote the now celebrated 'prison notebooks' which may offer us a way of making sense of our own historical context.

Gramsci understood that political power was ultimately achieved not through controlling the economy or the institutions that govern society but rather through transforming the cultural beliefs that go towards creating what he termed *senso commune* (loosely translated as 'common sense'), a collective body of assumed, unquestioned knowledge about the nature of the world through which we navigate our way through life. Once a political stance, creed or idea becomes part of a society's common sense it acquires the status of 'normal'; that is, it becomes a reality that is so obvious to any sensible, fair-minded person that it ceases to become a legitimate topic for reflection, discussion or debate. In essence, by making a belief or perspective 'normal' it becomes immune to challenge.

Although Gramsci's context was very different from our own and indeed from the political and historical contexts in which both evidence-based practice and coaching have emerged, his insights may have something valuable to teach us about the rapid absorption of evidence-based practice into our society. Specifically, it could be argued that the importance of pursuing an evidence-base has acquired the status of 'normal' and as such is so inherently plausible that it is beyond question and thus immune to critique or change. Examining the rise of evidence-based practice through a Gramscian lens may, then, help us fashion a more thoughtful response to our current ways of accumulating coaching-specific research, as well as helping us consider afresh what we want and need our knowledge to do for us.

Along similar lines, Corrie (2010, 2014) and Sturdee (2001) have argued that it is vital to understand evidence-based practice as a social phenomenon that has emerged in a specific political, economic and historical context where evidence has an investment value to those that produce it. For these reasons Sturdee (2001) encourages us to give serious consideration to the following types of question as we seek to make sense of the knowledge that is produced by others and generate our own:

- Who decides what counts as evidence?
- Who owns the evidence (and is therefore entitled to make statements and set precedents on the basis of it)?
- What is the best way to use the information obtained?
- What is the likely impact?
- Who gains and who loses from this information?
- Who are the stakeholders who have an investment in the data we gather?

Thus, seemingly clear, logical and straightforward questions about the effectiveness of coaching, or the effectiveness of one intervention relative to another, can serve complex and unspoken agendas which we need to understand in order to avoid being disadvantaged.

Expanding the research agenda: beyond the call for accountability

In positioning research as a socially embedded and politically informed endeavour, rather than one that produces objective data, the intention is not to undermine the value of research or to question the need for accountability. Rather, it is to encourage a more reflective approach to the knowledge that underpins coaching, to raise our awareness of the complex factors that sit behind the framing of research as a means of evidencing our claims and to become attentive to the many agendas that coaching research might serve, including who might benefit or be marginalised by those agendas. Indeed, if evidence is not immutable and objective but crafted and contextualised, we might be inclined to consider some novel and potentially illuminating questions including:

- How do we want to define research for the purposes of our discipline?
- What is the range of activities that we might consider as falling under the umbrella of research – how narrow/focused vs broad/inclusive do we want our research to be?

- How does coaching develop a research agenda that matches the needs of the field at this point in its development?
- To what extent do we want to replicate the approaches to evidence-based practice that have dominated other fields.

  - Are there other options and if so, what might these be?

- Should we understand research primarily as bringing greater objectivity to our practice, with a strong emphasis on the rational or do we want to see research also as harnessing our imaginative capability?

  - If the latter, what types of methods would we need to create to enable this?

- What would an innovative, ground-breaking mutually informative relationship between research and practice look like?

In considering our responses to these questions it is important to appreciate that research is not a singular activity. In order to consider what might be optimally fit for purpose for the development of our field, we need to be clear about how we are defining research – the range and scope of enquiry that falls within this activity, and the types of methodologies that are permissible to use in progressing the field.

Nutley et al. (2007) have defined research as, 'any systematic process of critical investigation and evaluation, theory building, data collection, analysis and codification' (pp. 298–9). This broad and inclusive definition implies that research legitimately encompasses a very wide range of activities, perspectives and methods of investigation. Of course, not every coach – researcher or practitioner – will engage in every type of research, for reasons of interest or opportunity. Nonetheless, Nutley et al.'s (2007) broad and inclusive definition is likely to appeal to the priorities of practitioners who always need to balance rigour with relevance. Consider, for example, du Plock's (2004) positioning of research where, from within the field of psychotherapy, he embraces forms of investigation as diverse as (1) helping a trainee access literature that is relevant to their studies, (2) being asked to facilitate an awayday for a group of professionals, (3) analysing part of a therapy session and drawing on relevant literature to support this, (4) reading about a medical condition after a family member has received a diagnosis, (5) taking an issue from therapy to supervision and (6) writing a paper on a topic that attempts to fill a gap in the current literature.

Although not everyone would agree with du Plock's way of conceptualising research, the investigative endeavours of coaches do and arguably should take multiple and varied forms given the vast amounts of data which we routinely collect to inform our work. Moreover, his examples highlight the need to attend more closely to what has been termed 'practice-based evidence' (Barkham & Mellor-Clark, 2000) in order to access the types of knowledge that are most compelling to coaches themselves. This is important because perceptions of relevance and resonance will likely impact how we respond to and use research (Corrie &

Callanan, 2001). In attempting to better understand the types of evidence that are particularly persuasive for coaches, Fillery-Travis and Corrie (2019) drew upon Bartunek's (2007) use of the system of rhetoric developed by Aristotle. Taking the domain of academic writing as the focus of her analysis, Bartunek identifies three different domains of knowledge – *logos*, which appeals to logic and clarity of argument; *pathos*, associated with an appeal to our values, beliefs and affect and that often inspires us to action, and *ethos*, which is concerned with credibility and trustworthiness. Whilst Aristotle argued that all three were necessary for a text to be persuasive, Bartunek observed that practitioner audiences place great store by pathos, an observation with which Fillery-Travis and Corrie (2019) concur, especially given the emotional investment that practitioners typically have in their work.

Perhaps then, one way of understanding the disconnect that can occur between research and practice is where practitioners experience studies as paying insufficient attention to *pathos* in relation to the questions asked, the methodology selected or implemented or the way the data are reported. However, a privileging of pathos does pose certain challenges. Specifically, it requires us to consider how we differentiate what resonates with us because it is trustworthy from what resonates for less valid reasons (e.g. the results confirm what we already believe or because we like the writing style of the author who has conducted the study). This brings us to another kind of relationship that we have with research – namely, our role and responsibilities as consumers of research.

From producers to consumers: establishing a knowledge-management strategy

If evidence-gathering is a contextualised and socially embedded activity we need to recognise that coaching research has an audience and as consumers of research, we are part of that audience. As consumers, we may draw upon coaching research as a systematic route into a reflexive engagement with our work. For example, if current thinking is progressing in one direction and our individual practice is progressing in an entirely unrelated direction, knowledge of the literature can help us consider whether we are highly innovative in our thinking or simply off track. However, as noted earlier in the chapter, becoming a skilled consumer of the work of others is a complex undertaking. How do we consume wisely? How do we discern what is sound? What criteria do we apply to decide when and how to modify our practice in response to the findings of a particular study?

As the range, type, scope and quality of studies expands, being a skilled consumer becomes more of a challenge. Each of us needs to develop a robust knowledge management strategy. In formulating a response to this need, Grant (2016) has developed the Research Relevance-to-Coaching model – a simple and accessible way of helping those working in practice take the best of what coaching research may have to offer in their distinct domain. Briefly, this model comprises two intersecting axes: (1) an axis concerning relevance to coaching

(coaching-specific or coaching-related) and (2) an axis related to degree of strength (whether the research is weak or strong). Coaching-specific research is that which focuses *directly* on coaching, such as effectiveness studies that attempt to quantify coaching outcomes or in-depth qualitative analysis of specific events occurring within a coaching session. Coaching-related research refers to studies that have *indirect relevance* – for example, knowledge arising from disciplines such as psychotherapy, neuroscience, management and leadership – where the study might illuminate aspects of coaching practice. Strong evidence refers to well-designed studies whose methodology and outcomes are peer-reviewed and ideally replicated by other scholars. Weak evidence in contrast is where the studies are limited in number, involve small numbers of participants, are poorly designed and, in the case of quantitative studies, have low statistical power.

Grant's (2016) model of classification is offered as an aid to those who seek a more robust approach to developing their understanding of coaching research. Although he cautions against its use as a definitive system of categorisation, it is a potentially useful way of bringing a clarity of purpose and perspective to a complex terrain that can otherwise feel difficult to navigate. However, with its consideration of strong and weak evidence, we can recognise the echoes of the type of hierarchy described previously: one that emphasises objectivity, seeks to minimise bias and favours wherever possible, a knowledge-base that is formed from within the discipline of coaching itself. We need to consider whether this is a sufficient basis for developing the field, particularly given the realities of delivering coaching in a VUCA world.

Creating knowledge fit for a 'wicked world'

Despite the challenges of uniting research and practice, fruitful, seamless collaborations have arguably never been more essential. The challenges confronting us are changing. Brown et al. (2010) have conceptualised our era as increasingly characterised by 'wicked problems'. Wicked in this context does not denote immorality but rather how such problems are diabolical in their resistance to our usual approaches to problem solving. For Brown et al. (2010), a wicked problem is:

> a complex issue that defies complete definition, for which there can be no final solution, since any resolution generates further issues, and where solutions are not true or false or good or bad, but the best that can be done at the time.
>
> (p. 4)

Examples of wicked problems include climate change, terrorism, poverty, the welfare system, health care, immigration, and organisational growth in the context of global competition, cost-containment and a downward trending economy. Our relationship with technology might also fall within this category: on the one hand its increasingly dominant role in our lives provides many opportunities, including new ways of connecting with our clients (see Stokes, 2021). However, it also poses new challenges including how we engage with and navigate the digital world, the extent to which our personal data is being harvested without our consent and questions concerning the ownership, use and archiving of the massive amounts of data that social media generates.

Wicked problems have been noted by Brown et al. (2010) to have the following characteristics:

- They occur in a context of continual change/unprecedented challenges;
- They involve multiple stakeholders who have different/conflicting priorities, values and expectations;
- The factors driving the problem are complex and enmeshed;
- The nature of the problem shifts with each attempt to resolve it;
- There is no existing precedent that can inform how to proceed;
- There is no 'right answer' (and any solution implemented will have unintended consequences that create new dilemmas).

These characteristics pose significant challenges for our existing research methods, many of which were developed in the 20th century or even earlier. It is far from clear whether the body of coaching research needed to address the priorities of tomorrow can be developed from the research methods of today, and a brief examination of the literature within coaching and beyond would seem to suggest the need to expand and in some case replace the ways of conducting research that have characterised many of our enquiries to date.

One obvious example of this changing methodological landscape is the emergence of so-called 'big data' – that is, those datasets that are too vast or complex to be managed by traditional methods of data-processing and software programmes. Datasets of this size and scale are forcing a reconsideration of how we collect, store, analyse, share and update our knowledge. As a distinct field of enquiry, big data has the potential to transform our understanding of what is meant by evidence and the ways in which we use it to inform how we work.

Other developments are emerging through philosophical challenges, with some scholars advocating the need for knowledge derived from epistemological and ontological perspectives that differ from the empirical worldview dominant in current representations of evidence-based practice. Whilst advocates of qualitative research have long championed the repositioning of psychological science away from a positivist ideology, a growing interest in critical realism is enabling novel contributions from within coaching and beyond. In clinical psychology, for example, Pilgrim (2018) has argued that a critical realist perspective is a means of '(rescuing) us from the rock of implausible positivism and the hard place of post-modernism' (p. 12). Williams et al. (2016) have applied a critical realist approach to research aimed at enhancing professional practice in nursing. In coaching, Kovacs (2016; Kovacs & Corrie, 2017) applied realist evaluation to investigating the role of case formulation in complex coaching assignments arguing that the knowledge-base of coaching is optimally developed through seeking to uncover the generative mechanisms that produce different outcomes.

A further response to the investigative challenges of wicked problems has been transdiciplinarity (Nicolescu, 2002). Transdisciplinarity is concerned with complex and heterogeneous forms of knowledge and knowledge production, transcending the concerns and methods of any single academic discipline. Its fusion of the cross-disciplinary perspectives champions both local context and uncertainty and 'includes the practical reasoning of individuals with the constraining and complex nature of social, organisational and material contexts' (Lawrence, 2010, p. 18).

Finally, the growing popularity of professional doctorates should also be considered. Professional doctorates are practice- rather than institutionally-based and located specifically in the candidate's own work context. This 'brand' of doctorate aims to produce original contributions to practice and generates a form of knowledge that leads to professional or organisational change (CRAC, 2016). These advanced programmes of study also attest to the increasingly creative ways in which scholars are seeking to better unite the worlds of research and practice in order to generate knowledge that has relevance for the world around us.

Whilst it is beyond the scope of this chapter to examine these initiatives in depth, the aim in headlining them is to highlight that what we mean by research and 'doing research' is changing in potentially unprecedented ways. Taken collectively, these perspectives and approaches on what research might look like offer exciting and innovative ways of supporting the field of coaching in creating, critiquing and refining the types of knowledge that befit the evolving needs of our clients and our communities (local, national and global). In looking across disciplines as diverse as behaviour analytics, philosophy, and transdisciplinarity and practice-based evidence, we can appreciate how such emerging trends might also open up new types of conversation between practitioners and researchers that enable the identification of common concerns and complementary knowledge-gathering endeavours.

Emerging conversations: new connections, new horizons

So far in this chapter, the focus has been on how coaches might position themselves as producers and consumers of their own knowledge-base, but is there potential for coaching to adopt an additional role as innovators in research methodology? At the 5th European Conference of Coaching Psychology (2015) Professor Jamie Hacker Hughes, a former President of the British Psychological Society, described coaching psychology as setting an example for the Society in terms of its cross-disciplinary relevance, and its creative approach to inter-disciplinary activity. What unites us as a community of practitioners and scholars is an interest in being at the vanguard of human change interventions, a desire to find innovative ways to enable individuals, organisations and communities to flourish, and a commitment to extending psychological knowledge and practice to new stakeholder groups (as noted at the start of this chapter, coaching is a rapidly expanding field). Is there the potential, then, for coaching to be at the forefront of research innovation rather than attempting to demonstrate respectability by reproducing what has gone before? Could coaching even lead the way in helping other disciplines re-examine their relationship to research and how they produce and consume evidence?

It would be naïve to assume that in the current climate of accountability we could side-step the dominant agenda of evidence-based practice. Nonetheless, it could be argued that with its broad knowledge-base and cross-disciplinary relevance, coaching is uniquely placed to reach across professional groups and facilitate what Nutley et al. (2007) have described as research enhancement strategies that 'encourage greater variety of voices in opportunities for dialogue' (p. 298). Seen in this light, it may be useful to conceptualise our research activities as providing an 'organising context' through which we can develop good investigative habits and acquire principles and methods that provide an optimal context for learning and discovery (Corrie, 2014).

In the spirit of capturing this broader positioning of coaching research, I offer the following visual representation of some of the factors to which it would seem imperative to attend (see Figure 4.1). Derived from work originally conducted in

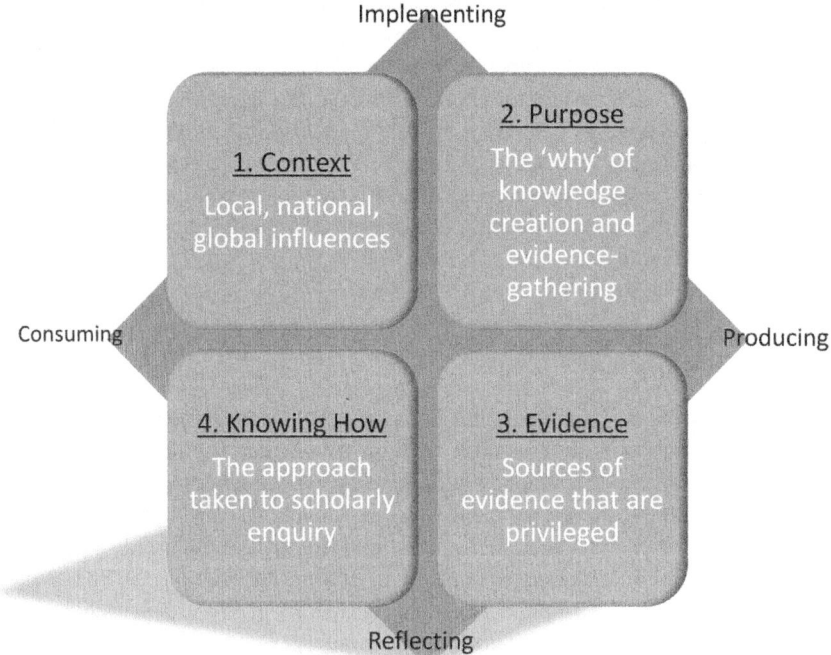

Figure 4.1 Lenses through which to understand coaching research

2014 (Corrie, 2014), this representation of coaching research draws our attention to some of the issues, themes and perspectives highlighted in this chapter as a way of (1) aiding understanding of our individual positioning as both producers and consumers of knowledge and (2) becoming more collectively aware of the multiple agendas that our research can serve.

The foreground of Figure 4.1 identifies four core areas or 'lenses' through which we can, individually and as a community, examine our investigative endeavours in order to better understand what we have achieved so far and where we might now need to be headed. For example, questions arising from the first position, that of 'Context', might include the following:

- What are the 'hot topics' in your particular area of coaching?
- Who determines what good evidence is in your specific context?
- Who is currently producing the evidence that influences you (i.e. who is shaping your actions as a consumer of research)?

    - Who else is using this research?

- Who has a claim on your evidence?
- Who might use or misuse your evidence?
- For whom is your research good or bad news?

Questions arising from the second position, that of 'Purpose', might include the following:

- What purposes do you want your research to serve?
- What purposes do others want it to serve?
- What will 'success' look like?
- Who has the power to define success in relation to the research that you produce?

Questions arising from the third position, that of 'Evidence', might include the following:

- What type of knowledge or evidence most resonates with you? This might be:
    - Dialogues with other scholars and stakeholders;
    - Professional guidelines;
    - Your values, attitudes, beliefs, and/or those of your clients;
    - Theories, models and frameworks;
    - Research studies;
    - Externally imposed requirements such as organisational or professional codes of conduct, national policy, etc.;
    - Your own reflective practice;
    - Feedback from clients and other stakeholders.

- Why is this type of evidence so impactful for you?
- What do you gain and lose by privileging these sources of knowledge over others?
- Who defines good evidence in your specific context?

Questions arising from the fourth position, that of 'Knowing How', might include the following:

- What is your knowledge management strategy?
- How will you synthesise current evidence with your own practitioner-based evidence?
- What will your response be if the available evidence and your own professional experience conflict?
- What types of conversation and with whom would help you advance your knowledge at this point in your career?
- What are the most important questions you need to ask right now?
- What are the under-valued questions that as a coaching community we need to champion?

The background in Figure 4.1 indicates how at any point in time we can align ourselves more closely with the role of consumer or producer (horizontal axis) and position ourselves as reflector on, or implementer of, any knowledge to which we are exposed (vertical axis). Within this broad terrain we might choose to locate ourselves at any point along these two axes as a function of the nature of the question in hand, our working context or the way in which our careers are configured. Thus, depending on how we position ourselves as consumers, producers, reflectors and implementers, we may find it useful to engage with the following questions:

- What issues and questions are most pressing for me in my practice right now?
  - What methods of investigation would help me answer those questions?
  - Do I have the knowledge to apply those methods or do I need assistance?
- What methods of investigation are most likely to help me grow in my learning and development more generally?
  - What skills would I need to implement those methods of investigation to best advantage?
- To what extent can my approach be driven by my own agenda for myself and my career and to what extent do I need to take account of the concerns and priorities of others?
- What types of research, produced by others, do I think should inform my practice and why?

- What type of research strategy is needed to optimally advance the field of coaching?

  - What are the strengths and limitations of this current research strategy?

- Who is currently most influential in deciding what counts as evidence in coaching?

  - What might their agendas be?

- Who gains and who loses from the way collectively we have conceptualized, conducted and disseminated coaching research to date?

This is as yet an untested approach to landscaping some of the themes raised in this chapter and only time will tell if it has any value to those who wish to shape coaching through the enterprise of research. As such, it would fall short of the standards imposed by those who have a strict allegiance to current ways of thinking about evidence-based practice. Nonetheless, if we are to cultivate curiosity and creativity in our pursuit of novel perspectives and methodologies a willingness to share emerging ideas about how to make sense of our changing world would seem to be vital. It is in the spirit of this pursuit that this representation of coaching research is presented.

Conclusion

The field of coaching has witnessed an exponential increase in both supply and demand, and high-quality research is needed to inform all stages of its commissioning, creation, delivery and evaluation. However, helping the field establish its effectiveness is only one of the benefits that research has to offer. When we conceptualise research as concerned *primarily* with justification and accountability, we can lose sight of other roles that it can play in helping us learn and grow in a climate of discovery.

In this chapter, it has been argued that far from being an objective and impartial endeavour, research is always embedded in specific political, social and historical contexts, even though these contexts can be difficult to discern. By adopting a broader, more inclusive definition of the range of activities that can be encompassed under the umbrella term of 'research' we can better appreciate how investigative endeavours of all kinds have a role to play in advancing the knowledge that underpins our discipline. The need to learn and grow within a VUCA world that increasingly confronts us with wicked problems opens up a wealth of opportunity for scholars everywhere to share their vision of how practitioners and researchers can work together to create a body of knowledge that can shape our exciting, dynamic and emerging field. Identifying some of the myriad ways of pursuing such an agenda really *would* be a conversation worth having.

Notes

1 For ease of reading in the context of this chapter the term 'client' is used to refer to both the direct recipients of coaching and those who may have commissioned coaching, such as in the case of an organisation commissioning coaching for one of its executives. The term 'coachee' is used only where citing the work of an author who has specifically used this label.
2 It is beyond the scope of this chapter to provide a comprehensive summary of the different forms of research activity and these categorisations should not be considered a systematic literature review. For a more detailed review, the interested reader is referred to Fillery-Travis & Corrie, 2019; Fillery-Travis & Passmore, 2011; Grant & Cavanagh, 2007; Jarvis et al., 2006).

References

Barber, H.F. (1992). Developing strategic leadership: The US Army war college experience. *Journal of Management Development, 11*, 4–12.

Barkham, M. & Mellor-Clark, J. (2000). Rigour and relevance: The role of practice-based evidence in the psychological therapies. In N. Rowland & S. Goss (Eds.), *Evidence-based Counselling and Psychological Therapies: Research and Applications* (pp. 127–142). London: Routledge.

Bartunek, J.M. (2007). Academic-practitioner collaboration need not require joint or relevant research: Toward a relational scholarship of integration. *The Academy of Management Journal, 50*, 1223–1333.

Briner, R.B. (2012). Does coaching work? *OP Matters, 16*, 4–11.

British Psychological Society (2016). *The Replicability and Reproducibility of Psychological Science*. Available at: www.youtube.com/watch?v=tTuZ-IEc0Eg.

Brown, V.A., Harris, J.A. & Russell, J.Y. (2010). *Tackling Wicked Problems Through Transdisciplinary Imagination*. London: Earthscan.

Cavanagh, M.J. & Lane, D.A. (2012). Coaching psychology coming of age: The challenges we face in the messy world of complexity. *International Coaching Psychology Review, 7*, 175–190.

Corrie, S. (2003). Keynote paper: Information, innovation and the quest for legitimate knowledge. *Counselling Psychology Review, 18*(3), 5–13.

Corrie, S. (2010). What is evidence? In R. Woolfe, S. Strawbridge, B. Douglas & W. Dryden (Eds.), *Handbook of Counselling Psychology* (3rd ed., pp. 44–61). London: Sage.

Corrie, S. (2014, February). *Deconstructing the Concept of Evidence: Diverse Perspectives on the Quest for Legitimate Knowledge*. Invited address as part of the Expert Seminar Series at the Institute for Work Based Learning, Middlesex University, London.

Corrie, S. & Callanan, M.M. (2001). Therapists' beliefs about research and the scientist-practitioner model in an evidence-based health care climate: A qualitative study. *British Journal of Medical Psychology, 74*, 135–149.

CRAC (2016). *Provision of Professional Doctorates in English HE Institutions. Report for HEFCE by the Careers Research & Advisory Centre (CRAC)*. Cambridge: Careers Research & Advisory Centre (CRAC) Ltd.

Department of Health (1999). *National Service Frameworks for Mental Health: Modern Standards and Service Models*. London: Department of Health.

Du Plock, S. (2004). What do we mean when we use the word 'research'? *Existential Analysis, 15*(1). Available at: www.metanoia.ac.uk/media/1452/sdp-what-do-we-mean-when-we-use-the-word-research.pdf.

Fillery-Travis, A. & Corrie, S. (2019). Research and the practitioner: Getting a perspective on evidence ass a coaching psychologist. In S. Palmer & A. Whybrow (Eds.), *Handbook of Coaching Psychology* (2nd ed., pp. 68–79). Abingdon, Oxon: Routledge.

Fillery-Travis, A. & Lane, D. (2006). Does coaching work or are we asking the wrong question? *International Coaching Psychology Review*, *1*, 23–36.

Fillery-Travis, A. & Passmore, J. (2011). A critical review of executive coaching research: A decade of progress and what's to come. *Coaching: An International Journal of Theory, Research and Practice*, *4*(2), 70–88.

Grant A.M. & Cavanagh, M.J. (2007). Evidence-based coaching: Flourishing or languishing? *Australian Psychologist*, *42*, 239–254.

Grant, A. & O'Connor, S. (2019). A brief primer for those new to coaching research and evidence-based practice. *The Coaching Psychologist*, *15*(1), 3–10.

Grant, A.M. (2016). What constitutes evidence-based coaching? A two-by-two framework for distinguishing strong from weak evidence for coaching. *International Journal of Evidence Based Coaching & Mentoring*, *14*(1), 74–85.

Hoare, G. & Sperber, N. (2016). *An introduction to Antonio Gramsci: His Life, Thought and Legacy*. London: Bloomsbury.

Jarvis, J., Lane, D.A. & Fillery-Travis, A. (2006). *The Case for Coaching: Making Evidence-Based Decisions on Coaching*. London: CIPD.

Kovacs, L. & Corrie, S. (2017). Executive coaching in an era of complexity. Study 1: Does executive coaching work and if so why? A realist evaluation. *International Coaching Psychology Review*, *12*(2), 194–209.

Kovacs, L. (2016). *Enabling Leaders to Navigate Complexity: A Model for Executive Coaching amid Ambiguity, Uncertainty and Change*. DProf thesis, Middlesex University. Unpublished manuscript.

Lawrence, R.J. (2010). Beyond disciplinary confinement to imaginative transdisciplinarity. In V.A. Brown, J.A. Harris & J.Y. Russell (Eds.), *Tackling Wicked Problems Through Transdisciplinary Imagination* (pp. 16–30). London: Earthscan.

Nicolescu, B. (2002). *Manifesto of Transdisciplinarity*, translated by K.-C. Voss. New York: SUNY.

Nutley, S.M., Walter, I. & Davies, H.T.O. (2007). *Using Evidence: How Research Can Inform Public Services*. Bristol, UK: Policy Press.

O'Donohue, W. & Henderson, D. (1999). Epistemic and ethical duties in clinical decision-making. *Behaviour Change*, *16*(1), 10–19.

Pilgrim, D. (2018). Paying the price of positivism. *Clinical Psychology Forum*, *309*, 12–15.

Sackett, D.L., Rosenberg, W.M.C., Gray, J.A.M., Haynes, R.B. & Richardson, W.S. (1996). Evidence-based medicine: What it is and what it isn't. *British Medical Journal*, *312*, 71–72.

Stokes, A. (2021). Technology, social media and online coaching. In M. Watts, R. Bor & I. Florance (Eds.), *The Trainee Coach Handbook* (pp. 183–199). London: Sage.

Sturdee, P. (2001) Evidence, influence or evaluation? Fact and value in clinical science. In C. Mace, S. Moorey & B. Roberts (Eds.), *Evidence in the Psychological Therapies: A Critical Guide for Practitioners* (pp. 61–79). Hove, East Sussex: Routledge.

Wheatley, M. (1999) *Leadership and the New Science. Discovering Order in a Chaotic World*. San Francisco, CA: Berrett-Koehler Publishers.

Williams, L., Rycroft-Malone, J. & Burton, C.R. (2016). Bringing critical realism to nursing practice: Roy Bhaskar's contribution [online]. *Nursing Philosophy* [viewed 9 September 2018]. Available at: https://onlinelibrary.wiley.com/doi/full/10.1111/nup.12130.

Chapter 5

The contribution of coaching to mental health care

An emerging specialism for complex times

Sarah Corrie and Andrew A. Parsons

Introduction

Everyone experiences challenges to their emotional well-being at some point in their lives. Given that mental health[1] is central to both our quality of life and our ability to function, we can be confident that as coaches we will, at some point in our careers, encounter issues relating to emotional well-being in the requests that our clients make of us. This might be directly (i.e. the client sitting in front of us), indirectly (e.g. coaching a manager who is supporting staff with mental health problems), or systemically (e.g. working with the senior leadership team of an organisation that wishes to address high levels of sickness and staff turn-over or who wish to promote mental health awareness within their company culture). And of course, we may well, at some point, confront a mental health issue in ourselves.

Working with emotional well-being has long been a feature of life coaching. In other areas, including business coaching, the domain of mental health and emotional well-being is still something of an emerging conversation with many unanswered questions concerning the role that coaches could or should adopt, if any. This chapter turns a spotlight on some of the questions, concerns and opportunities that arise from moving into this domain. We examine the collective state of our mental health by drawing on relevant statistics and the questions for coaching to which these statistics give rise. We then make the case for coaching in mental health and offer ways of conceptualising and responding to our clients' emotional well-being needs when we find ourselves confronted with them. We also propose that the time is ripe within mental health care for a paradigm shift and argue that coaching has a critical role to play in this regard. In support of this paradigm shift we present two specific propositions: (1) that mental health can be usefully conceptualised as an example of what has been termed a 'wicked[2] problem' that requires transdisciplinary innovations in thinking and practice and (2) that an approach known as 'salutogenesis' (we explain this in more detail later in the chapter) provides one potentially valuable framework for enabling coaches to move into this domain with greater confidence and clarity about their contribution.

Why coaches need to know about mental health

Mental health problems are widespread. Statistics from the World Health Organization (WHO) indicate that approximately 450 million people are living with a mental health problem (World Health Organization, 2001). In England, approximately one in six adults has a common mental problem (McManus et al., 2016). Further, it has been estimated that 20 percent of adolescents experience a mental health problem in any given year (World Health Organization, 2003), with 10 percent of children and young people (aged 5–16 years) having a clinically diagnosable mental problem (Green et al., 2005). In excess of 20 percent of adults aged 60 and over are living with a mental or neurological disorder (World Health Organization, 2019).[3] In summary, these statistics build up a picture of why mental health problems have been identified as one of the main disease burdens worldwide (Vos et al., 2015) and there can be little doubt that mental health is a growing public concern. Thus, it is reasonable to infer that coaches cannot easily side-step mental health issues even if they wished to. However, coaches are not mental health specialists and so the current rates of incidence and prevalence raise questions including, should coaches have a role in working with mental health problems? If so, what might this role be? What knowledge, skills and competences are needed to ensure that coaches are able to make informed decisions about how to work with clients where a mental health issue features in their presentation? How can coaches know when and how to sign-post clients to other services? Additionally, if coaches do have a role to play in working with clients with mental health issues what implications might this have for the training, development and supervision of the workforce?

Given that we will almost certainly encounter them in some of our clients, it seems reasonable to propose that every coach needs at least a foundational level of knowledge of mental health issues if for no other reason than to be able to detect their presence and determine when coaching may not be appropriate. However, the question of detection is neither simple nor easy. Consider, for example, the case of Maureen, a client whom we ask you to imagine you are coaching and whose interactions with you give rise to unanticipated questions and dilemmas about how to proceed.

Box 5.1 Conceptualising Maureen's situation

Three months ago, Maureen[4] was promoted to the role of service manager within a large multinational service company. She is 46 years old. The company is eager to develop a 'coaching culture' and Maureen's line manager suggested that Maureen take up the opportunity of coaching provided by an external coach, to help her transition into her new role.

Your first meeting with Maureen goes well and you agree some specific areas to work on, in conjunction with her line manager. These include supporting the team in working cohesively during a period of organisational restructuring and supporting Maureen in developing her new role. You notice that Maureen seems a little agitated at times but overall the meeting feels positive and you are confident that you have agreed a clear contract for the coaching that is to follow.

At each session, Maureen indicates that she is finding coaching helpful. However, at your fourth coaching session, you notice that Maureen appears quite hot, fidgety and a little dishevelled. She begins to reveal concerns that she says she has felt able to tell no one else. She tells you that she has been feeling increasingly low over the last three months or so and is not enjoying her work. She says she is prone to bouts of tearfulness that have no obvious trigger, that her concentration and memory are poor, and that she is concerned she could make a mistake that proves costly for the organisation.

Maureen has no idea why she is feeling the way she is – she has a good life, finds her career rewarding and was looking forward to the promotion for which she has worked so hard. She is worried that her difficulties with concentration and memory might be symptoms of early onset dementia (she is currently the main carer for her elderly mother who has Alzheimer's disease). She says she has begun to wonder whether she should have been promoted and is not sure what to do about her concerns. You are someone she trusts and feels able to confide in and so she asks your advice . . .

As her coach, how should you make sense of, and respond to, the type of information that Maureen has disclosed? Her willingness to share her distress is a sign of trust in you, but her disclosures do not directly fall within the remit of the agreed coaching contract. On the one hand, then, it is a detraction from what you have both agreed to focus upon. On the other hand, it may well be the very reason that Maureen needs support.

There are a number of different potential responses to this scenario. The first might be to continue with the coaching contract as agreed and see if you can work around the issues that Maureen is describing. An experience of psychological disruption is not uncommon during life transitions and she has, after all, just begun a new and more demanding role. A second response might be to temporarily halt the coaching and refer Maureen to her occupational health department or her GP, explaining that before you proceed, you both need to establish whether a medical intervention (such as medication or even a brain scan) is warranted. You may decide to talk with Maureen about accessing additional support, including her own line manager, especially if there are concerns about making mistakes that could prove detrimental to the organisation.

Alternatively, if you are a dual-trained coach and already have a working knowledge of common mental health problems, you might decide to engage in some further information-gathering to determine whether her difficulties are consistent with a presentation of depression or anxiety. Armed with this information, you could then discuss with greater confidence whether coaching or therapy would be best suited to her needs and sign-post her to relevant services if necessary. Then again, you might decide you want to ask some further questions about her physical health. For example, when was the last time that she had routine blood tests? Would it be helpful to see her GP to talk about a blood test to rule out thyroid dysfunction (a potential cause of some of the symptoms she is describing)? You might also be mindful of her age – some of the difficulties she describes are consistent with the menopause and so you might decide that as part of being diligent in your efforts to help her, you need to enquire about changes relating to her hormonal health.

All of these are potentially legitimate courses of action and thus, when we work with a client who is experiencing emotional depletion, we need to decide what, in the context of the coaching contract and our role as coaches, we are entitled to ask about and what falls outside of that boundary. We also need to consider how wide-ranging our knowledge needs to be in order to help our clients with the issues that they are facing. And of course, we need to decide who is best placed to deliver the service that is needed – ourselves, a coaching colleague with a different skillset or a professional from another discipline altogether.

Ensuring that we are able to make an informed decision in each case is no easy task and will vary as a function of our individual preferences, resources, prior training and the client's own context and needs. Nonetheless, the accurate detection of a mental health problem is likely to afford a number of benefits. For example, we are less likely to be thrown off track by issues that our clients introduce that were not part of the original coaching contract (as in the case of Maureen) and will be better able to recognise when clients need sign-posting to a mental health service. A good level of foundational knowledge of common mental health problems also enables us to think through whether, when and how coaching might help and to design a more effective intervention plan. Finally, recognising the presence of a mental health problem in a client and being able to talk openly with them about your concerns for their well-being may ultimately prevent a looming crisis.

Towards an understanding of mental health

Mental health is neither dichotomous (i.e. present or absent) nor static. Although there are diagnostic criteria for specific, widely recognised disorders, mental health exists on a continuum with each individual having their own baseline level of 'wellness'. Moreover, each of us moves along the continuum as a function of a variety of internal and external factors as well as what we, personally, can manage. Depending on a client's overall resilience, repertoire of coping skills, general psychological problem-solving skills and other protective factors (e.g. a caring life partner and good level of social support), even high levels of distress over a temporary period might be managed effectively by the client and so pose no obstacles to any coaching contract that has been agreed. In such cases, the approach taken by the coach and client may be as simple as acknowledging the presence of a specific issue and then working around it in pursuit of the client's coaching-related goals. However, there will be other instances where a coach is likely to be left questioning whether more intensive input is needed. In these instances, it is important for the coach to have a set of criteria for informing their decision-making about how best to respond.

The emerging interest in mental health coaching (Bishop, 2018; Buckley & Buckley, 2006; Corrie, 2016, 2019a, 2019b; Szymanska, 2018) suggests the need to attend to a range of indicators when attempting to make sense of our clients' emotional well-being needs. In broad terms, indicators of problems that are more likely to require referral to a mental health professional are those where distress is having an obvious, demonstrable impact on the client or those around them. This might be because the client's distress (1) is occurring too frequently, (2) is too easily activated, (3) is too intense for the client to manage effectively, (4) takes too long for them to return to a state of equilibrium, (5) is too disruptive for the client or for those around them or (6) is related to issues of risk (to self or others).

Drawing on the six criteria outlined above, it has been suggested that in building up a picture of the client in front of us, there are three key areas that can usefully inform our decision-making about the type of intervention from which a client might optimally benefit (Corrie, 2019a, 2019b). These are as follows:

1   What do you see and experience when with the client?
2   How does the client describe their situation?
3   What is *not* said (and what you may want to ask about explicitly)?

In relation to what a coach might see and experience when working with a client, it is important to pay attention to how a client looks physically, how they present in the room and how we feel in their presence (Corrie, 2019a, 2019b). Obvious physical warning signs might include looking unwell, appearing unkempt, seeming out of breath or being markedly under- or overweight. Attending to a client's physical presence can also draw our attention to important non-verbal clues such as whether they are able to sit still, pause, and reflect as our conversation with them unfolds or whether there are signs of agitation, restlessness or pressure on speech (signs of agitation often manifest in a tendency to speak very fast whereas when mood drops significantly, speech can be significantly slowed as a function of reduced cognitive efficiency). Finally, it is important as part of this criterion to consider your own internal reactions to the client. How do you feel when you are with them? What types of thoughts and feelings are evoked in you (perhaps especially attending to reactions that would not be typical for you when working with other clients)? For example, do you find yourself feeling agitated or 'speeding up' in your interactions with them? Do you feel tired or irritated in their presence?

These types of reactions can represent important potential clues as to what a client might be experiencing and need.

A second criterion concerns paying careful attention to how the client describes their situation (Corrie, 2019a, 2019b). The client being able to provide a coherent account of their perceived needs and aspirations that can form the basis of a coaching contract is a cognitive skill in its own right. Corrie advocates that how the client tells their story is one means of establishing how well able they are to reflect on and articulate their internal world. For example, what is the form and flow of the person's communication? What is their capacity for sharing information? Does the narrative have a coherence and structure that makes it easy to follow or is their story fragmented or disconnected in some way? How a client tells their story can also provide clues as to their locus of control and their perception of any coping and rescue factors that are available to them in the situation. It is important to remember that many mental health problems are characterised by a temporary deterioration in cognitive functioning and problems with concentration and memory are common features of both depression and anxiety. It is useful, therefore, to explore any difficulties with attention, concentration or memory, especially if you are concerned that the client may not be aware of mistakes they are making in the workplace.

In relation to the third point earlier, what is *not* said (and which you may want to ask about explicitly), the coach is encouraged to reflect on those concerns that it may be difficult for the client to share out of a sense of embarrassment or shame (Corrie, 2019a, 2019b). Although some topics may not be appropriate to the coaching context, it can be useful to enquire about the client's typical approaches to problem-solving and methods of self-care (e.g. do they tend towards proactive methods of addressing life challenges or do they adopt avoidant methods of coping?), as well as commonly known impactors of mood such as the consumption of caffeine, alcohol and recreational drugs. As part of this, asking a client about signs that their emotional well-being is compromised or that they need support can reveal a great deal about self-awareness, self-reflective capability and general life skills that as coaches we may want to help our clients to acquire. Equally, asking about strengths and resources they have available to them and whether they are using them builds up an understanding of the client's approach to challenges and opportunities.

Having built up a clearer picture, the coach must then decide how to synthesise the information obtained into a coherent understanding of a client's needs that has implications for the type of service subsequently offered. In deciding when to work with a client and when to refer to another professional, we have found it useful to use the Health Awareness Tool (Corrie, 2019b) that is presented in Figure 5.1.

The purpose of this tool is to help a coach, in partnership with their client, consider the intersection of two broad domains – resources and functioning – and to consider whether the client is high or low on each of these as a basis for deciding whether coaching is the optimal first line intervention. Used as a framework for facilitating discussion, the coach and client can consider which of the four quadrants overall most accurately reflects the client's current position.

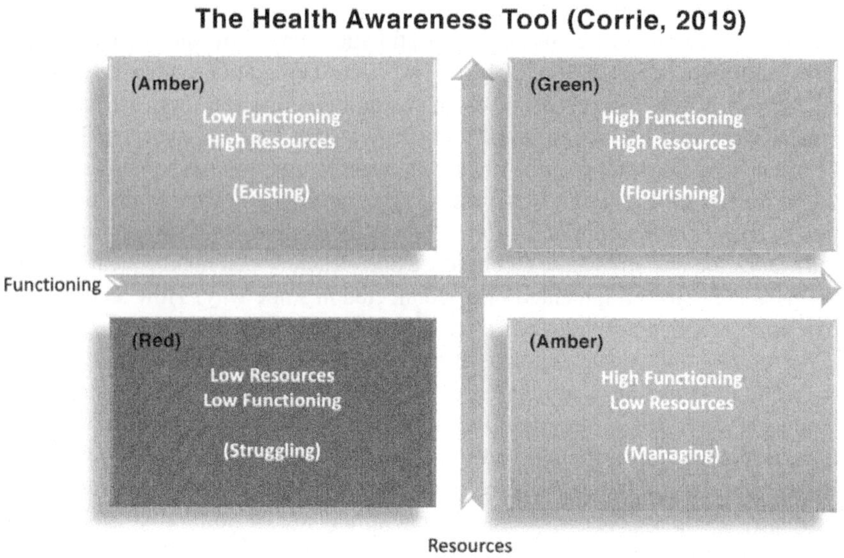

The Health Awareness Tool (Corrie, 2019)

(Amber)	(Green)
Low Functioning High Resources (Existing)	High Functioning High Resources (Flourishing)

Functioning

(Red)	(Amber)
Low Resources Low Functioning (Struggling)	High Functioning Low Resources (Managing)

Resources

Figure 5.1 The Health Awareness Tool, developed by Sarah Corrie (2019) and adapted for this book in monochrome

The original, colour-coded model draws on the analogy of a system of traffic lights. Thus, the quadrants are coloured red, amber or green as a function of whether the coach and client need to stop (red) in order to reflect on what is most needed, whether they can proceed with caution (amber) or whether the process of coaching can proceed (green). In the monochrome diagram above, the quadrant labelled 'Struggling' is the red zone; the quadrants labelled 'Existing' and 'Managing' represent the amber zones and the quadrant labelled 'Flourishing' is the green zone. Where a client is high in both resources and functioning, there is grounds for confidence that coaching is a potentially helpful intervention in relation to pursuing a coaching contract (the green light gives the go-ahead). Thus, as noted earlier, a coach may be working with a client who is experiencing quite high levels of emotional distress. However, given that they are functioning well (e.g. they are able to function effectively at work, are capitalising on leisure pursuits and are enjoying their relationships) and have a good degree of resources (e.g. their overall resilience is high, they have a good repertoire of coping skills, a caring life partner and good level of social support), they fall within the green quadrant.

In contrast, if a client is well-placed in neither their resources nor their functioning, this is likely to place them within the red quadrant, the zone of struggle, indicating a need to pause the coaching – at least until further avenues have been considered. It is likely that additional input and support will be needed for the client to reach a stage where they are able to benefit optimally from what coaching may provide.

When a client is high on one dimension but low on another, the coach and client are in the amber territory. Here, the client may be managing day-to-day or simply existing but will not currently be in a position to flourish. Attention may need to be given to ways of enhancing either functioning or resources before the original aims of the coaching contract can be pursued with confidence. Alternatively, both parties may decide to proceed with the coaching but build in additional checks along the way (e.g. there is an agreement that the client will consult with their GP or occupational health) to ensure that the work provided is meeting the client's needs optimally.

Of course, neither functioning nor resources are static. Using the Health Awareness Tool is not about diagnosing the presence of a mental health disorder but rather about building a picture of a client's level of well-being and need. Nonetheless, we have found it to be helpful in enabling a conversation about potentially sensitive areas of a client's experience as a way of helping clients take greater ownership of the decision-making process. Whatever system we use, by developing a set of criteria we can have greater confidence that we are using a systematic approach that can help us decide whether our particular coaching offer is best suited to a client's needs at a specific point in time.

Mental health as a wicked problem: why coaches are necessary for the mental health workforce

In Chapter 4 of this volume, Corrie makes the point that many of the critical issues confronting us as a society are taking the form of a new type of challenge. Conceptualised as 'wicked problems' (Brown, Harris, & Russell, 2010), these types of challenge share a set of features in that they are highly complex and enmeshed, occur in a context of continual change, are unprecedented in the obstacles they present and involve multiple stakeholders who have different priorities and needs. They are also resistant to traditional approaches to problem-solving and tend to shift with each solution implemented giving rising to unintended consequences that create new challenges.

Commonly cited examples of wicked problems include climate change, terrorism, poverty and immigration as well as challenges confronting the welfare and health care system. Features of contemporary life including the impact of modern lifestyles, an ageing population, expanding and disruptive technologies, institutions and economies facing upheaval as well as the changing ways in which our working lives are configured, all influence the issues with which our clients present us and represent the consequences of living in a 'wicked world'.

It is our view that the mental health needs of humankind also represent a wicked problem. Consider, for example, how in 2008 England introduced the 'Improving Access to Psychological Therapies' (IAPT) initiative aimed at increasing the accessibility of empirically supported psychological interventions for common mental health problems (Clark, 2011). Although these interventions are now more available than ever before, they have not appeared to stem the escalating emotional distress of the population, as evident from the statistics cited earlier in this chapter. Moreover, the requirement of IAPT services to meet pre-determined targets has necessitated the creation of an entirely new type of workforce trained not as psychotherapists, psychologists or counsellors but as practitioners who deliver empirically supported interventions for specific clinical presentations. This raises questions concerning the identity and positioning of this workforce relative to other mental health professionals, as well as questions about who will regulate them once they are qualified. As Corrie and Lane (2015) observed, the nature of the workforce delivering psychologically informed interventions and the context in which those interventions are delivered is changing, characterised by both tighter state expectation and regulation and the simultaneous deprofessionalisation of service provision.

Thus, there is now a greater range of empirically supported interventions for mental health problems than ever before and an expanding workforce being trained to deliver these interventions (enabled by public funding). Yet despite this, the statistics are not indicating improvements in global emotional well-being and as the workforce expands, questions arise concerning training, standards and credentialing. The opportunities and pressures that arise from introducing initiatives to tackle the mental health crisis are precisely those typical of wicked problems where a solution implemented to meet one type of need raises dilemmas in another.

However, the fact that the mental health workforce is changing and broadening to embrace the contribution of a wider number of professional groups suggests that coaches, too, might have a valuable role to play in working with mental health issues – directly or indirectly. In a world that is volatile, uncertain, complex and ambiguous (Barber, 1992), we need to be more creative in how we conceptualise and work with client issues of this nature. As Einstein stated, 'The significant problems we face cannot be solved with the same level of thinking that created them' (www.quotes.net/quote/9226). Working in a wicked world requires both commissioners and providers of health care to separate job title from professional competence, forcing us to look across traditional professional boundaries in order to create new partnerships in knowledge generation and service delivery. In this context the key question ceases to be, 'Does this person need coaching or therapy?' and becomes, 'What skillset, knowledge-base and competences are required to meet this client's needs?' This paves the way for a more fundamental re-examination and re-definition of the role for coaching in mental health care.

Reconceptualising the role for coaches: salutogenesis as a potential organising framework

So far, the focus of this chapter has been on recognising signs of depletion in our clients and how, as coaches, we might respond. By focusing on the type of issues that may characterise the presence of a mental health problem and that might signal the need to refer a client to another specialist, we have located the discussion within the currently dominant views of mental health and its 'treatment'. However, coaching has the potential to bring fresh perspectives to how we conceptualise working in this domain. In particular, the values and perspectives that coaching contribute may offer a timely challenge to authorised views of service delivery introducing novel ways of bringing the client 'centre stage' in the process of building relationships with mental health services. Moreover, in the context of a world characterised by wicked problems, a challenge to authorised views of service delivery that understand clients' needs as remedial in favour of interventions that are developmental would pave the way for what we believe is now essential – namely, a paradigm shift in mental health care in which coaching has a vital role to play.

Moving away from traditional thinking about the client receiving 'therapy' or 'coaching' allows us to think about the needs of the client in a different way. Instead of conceptualising the task as one of alleviating *dis-ease*, we can shift our focus to one of health (*saluto*) promotion (*genesis*). Salutogenesis, a term introduced in the 1970s–1980s by the medical sociologist Aaron Antonovsky, is focused on building generalised psychological, social and physical/material resources. The ability of an individual to build and access these resources enables the maintenance and promotion of their health, even in difficult states of 'tension' (Antonovsky, 1979). The salutogenic approach is consistent with the WHO definitions of health and mental health (World Health Organization, 2004, 2014). Furthermore, it has been proposed as a suitable framework for describing a complete state of health where approaches that prevent and treat disease can be viewed alongside those that also promote and protect the health of individuals (Keyes, 2014).[5]

At the heart of his model, Antonovsky described a 'sense of coherence' which fosters a global orientation of confidence that both internal and external environments are predictable and that things will work out reasonably positively. This orientation reflects the individual's view of life and their sense of capacity to deal with the situations in which they find themselves. A high sense of coherence, therefore, promotes 'good health' even where individuals have experienced traumatic life events. For example, Antonovsky's early work involved investigating the experiences of the menopause amongst different cultural groups in Israel including Jewish women who had survived the Holocaust (see Antonovsky, 1987). Over the last 40 years, sense of coherence measures have been developed in over 40 countries and languages. However, current thinking is now directed to the transdisciplinary nature of salutogenesis as an umbrella term to integrate many different theories and approaches that impact the ability of an individual to relate to self and others (Eriksson & Mittelmark, 2017). Sense of coherence is one of these, and potentially related to several others. How the individual learns to develop and utilise their resources to develop their sense of coherence is a continual and life-long learning process at the heart of salutogenesis (Eriksson, 2017).

Salutogenesis can be defined in narrow, broader and global terms (Mittel-mark & Bauer, 2017). Its narrow definition is consistent with the early interests of Antonovsky, with a focus on sense of coherence and its measurement as the key component of health. A broader definition encompasses an orientation to health promotion rather than reducing health risks and preventing disease. This orienta-tion provides a different language and set of assumptions for how both individuals and organisations approach situations. For example, instead of classifying health or disease, a salutogenic orientation conceptualises a health continuum which offers a novel way of thinking and of making inferences from observations. Thus, rather than emphasising the need to reduce risk factors and pathology, the empha-sis is on promoting the identification and use of resources to support health whilst focusing on the person as a whole (Antonovsky, 1996). The broadest sense of the definition encompasses the model of salutogenesis which outlines genetic, constitutional and psychosocial resistance resources that are shaped during life experiences. These resources can be characteristics of individuals and/or groups that offset the impact of stressors to maintain sustainable health (Antonovsky, 1979). Aligning the salutogenic framework with the Health Awareness Tool (see Figure 5.1) provides a means of further building the resources needed to enable the person to thrive.

The salutogenic framework highlights the interplay between personal, social and environmental resources and the learning through the experience of life stressors of how they can be utilised. The ability to develop and utilise these resources creates the sense of coherence through life. These resources could also be described as mental capital; that is, the sum of an individual's cogni-tive, emotional, genetic, early biological programming and life experiences (Jenkins et al., 2008). The salutogenic framework predates the development of the positive psychology movement but the integration of both approaches with the social constructivist viewpoint leads to better alignment and the gen-eration of health and well-being (Joseph & Sagy, 2017). It may also offer a different perspective on the role of intrinsic motivation (Deci & Ryan, 1985) in maintaining subjective well-being. Salutogenesis in its broader definitions could, therefore, act as a transdisciplinary framework to integrate multiple approaches to support health and well-being (Eriksson & Lindström, 2006; Eriksson & Mittelmark, 2017).

Adopting multiple and varied perspectives and exploring a wide range of potential solutions is an important aspect of tackling wicked problems. Embrac-ing the salutogenic framework creates an opportunity for coaches to play a significant role in supporting mental health and well-being. Coaches support the development of mental capital and the utilisation of the client's personal resources to promote health. Within this perspective, it is important to note that the coach's role is not remedial (i.e. to provide a 'fix' for a client's well-being). Rather, it is developmental in that coaching creates a context for learning that allows the client to become more aware of their environment and to actively participate in shaping it.

Coaching and mental health: the role of a specialist coach in supporting learning, self-development and relations with others

Coaching processes have developed over the last 30 years. Initially privileging the achievement of goals (the so-called first generation), subsequent perspectives have emphasised supporting the client in reaching their own solutions (second generation) and more recently a co-creative approach working with values, identity and integrating experiential and existential perspectives through reflection and application (third generation) (Stelter, 2014). Devising collaborative dialogues as part of a coaching process will provide an opportunity for the client to reflect, assimilate new learnings and apply these to their situation. A specialist third generation coach may, therefore, be able to support assimilation and development of new perspectives of self and others. Interestingly, this coaching approach has been observed in the development of workplace coaching over the last 30 years. Conversations that occupy this collaborative style of conversation produce a focus on both performance and well-being of the employee (Grant, 2017).

Coaching models have been developed that align to the salutogenic framework's sense of coherence (Gray, Burls, & Kogan, 2014) and utilised to develop resilience programmes with a small number of individuals that reported benefit (Gray, 2016). A salutogenic approach to coaching also appeared beneficial in a case study involving developing resilience in a senior manager (Gray, 2017). Despite the small numbers involved and the narrow focus on sense of coherence, these studies highlight the potential to develop a salutogenically oriented approach to clients' learning and development. The opportunity is to develop a wider learning perspective that captures not only the sense of coherence construct but also the salutogenic model and lifestyle orientation manifest in everyday situations. The third generation style coaching approach focusing on values and learning through discussion (Stelter, 2014) appears well-placed to develop the framework for coaching in this arena. Stelter (2014), for example, has proposed areas of practice that would be essential for specialist coaches. These include an understanding of organisational theories, the ability to expand the reflective space through use of questions, open narratives and metaphors, a focus on values, identity and motivations and their link to actions (Stelter, 2014; Stelter & Andersen, 2018).

Coaching approaches that explore cognitive, emotional, physical and spiritual perspectives which are linked to purposeful actions may also feature within this salutogenic orientation (Spence & Deci, 2013). Additional skills for the coach may include having the ability to access and share a life perspective that aligns with the salutogenic orientation. The availability of supervision would also be essential, as working in the arena of mental well-being will require the processing of potentially difficult information necessitating support and the development of appropriate learning and recovery strategies for the coach themselves.

The coach as mental health specialist: new horizons, new directions

Not every coach will want to work with mental health issues or concur with the stance taken by the authors of this chapter. Certainly, we are not advocating a 'one size fits all' approach. Nonetheless, there is evidence that some coaches are becoming increasingly confident about recognising and perhaps even working within this domain. For example, in a survey of members of the British Psychological Society's Special Group in Coaching Psychology (Corrie, 2017), 95 percent of respondents indicated that they were confident they could accurately detect a mental health problem in a client. In addition, 93 percent stated that they would be confident about what action to take if they suspected that a client had a concern of this nature. However, 88 percent of the sample also said that they would welcome an opportunity to undertake further training in this area. Although generalisation of the findings is restricted by sample size (the survey data were gathered from a sample of 96 respondents), they hint at a growing awareness that coaches will encounter mental health problems in their practice and an emerging willingness to engage effectively with an increasingly diverse range of needs. So, for coaches who do have an interest in moving into this area what are their options?

First, it is important to identify that mental health coaching is not established territory. Those wishing to work within this field will need to be comfortable with adopting the role of the pioneer, facing questions about the range and scope of their expertise and a need to innovate and justify emerging practices in the face of potential opposition. Second, if mental health does indeed qualify as a 'wicked problem' then we might anticipate the need for greater cross-disciplinary, collaborative and transdisciplinary models of working. Those who are drawn to working in this area are perhaps also likely to relish the opportunities (and challenges) that come from developing novel approaches to practice and service delivery. These novel approaches will also likely draw upon methods that enable the co-production of knowledge that brings together the voices of diverse stakeholder groups whose expertise originates from experiences and training quite different from that of coaching professionals.

Given that mental health is a multifaceted experience and multi-layered in its impact on self and others, we might reasonably assume that our offer of service can be equally multifaceted. A coaching approach may adopt both a prevent/treat orientation and a promote/protect orientation. Thus, we might conceptualise the role of coaching in mental health as occupying a range of potential positions along a continuum of involvement and influence. At one end of the continuum, coaches might adopt the role of advocate for mental health at a national level. The developmental agenda that underpins coaching along with the skills in facilitating conversations in which coaches are trained might enable dialogues that make a difference – amongst the public, in lobbying and pressure groups, in the media and at the level of policy development.

Moving along the continuum are opportunities for shaping the knowledge and responses of organisations who wish – or perhaps need – to embrace a culture of well-being and flourishing. Working with organisations, we might seek to enable conversations that promote a shift in culture in which emotional well-being increasingly becomes a daily, enacted value. Coaches may also seek to contribute their expertise specifically to health care systems, specialising in coaching clinicians and leaders in health care systems to move from expert to empowerer, building transparent and collaborative systems, supporting the development of relationships across health and social care and creating meaningful approaches for building staff resilience and well-being.

Those with an interest and specialist knowledge in this area could also contribute to the work of professional bodies who need to be invested in the well-being needs of their members. Although not a direct focus of this chapter, the statistics relating to the prevalence and incidence of mental health problems as well as the reality of living and working in a wicked world suggests that coaches will need to attend to these factors within themselves, not solely in terms of maintaining fitness to practice but also in terms of developing methods of self-care that will sustain them over the course of their lives and careers. There may be those who choose to specialise in researching and developing interventions that are tailored to the mental health and emotional well-being needs of coaches themselves.

However, the previous section on salutogenesis also suggests the potential for a more radical paradigm shift as health care increasingly embraces person-centred care over and above the notion of working exclusively with any diagnosed illness. Such a paradigm shift could open a variety of opportunities for coaches. In her scoping review of mental health coaching Bishop (2018), for example, suggests that coaching could have a role to play in medication withdrawal given the success of coaching in smoking cessation. Becoming experts in the delivery of mental health first aid would also be an avenue for influencing understanding and responding in others.

An even more radical departure from traditional thinking could take the form of a coaching workforce who are identified and registered as specialists in the field of mental health and who carve out a unique contribution alongside other mental health professionals. In some instances, this may take the form of delivering coaching as an adjunctive intervention alongside other, more traditional mental health interventions such as psychotherapy and medication, or delivering coaching interventions tailored for individuals living with mental health issues. Dual-trained practitioners (i.e. those trained as both coaches and therapists) are already an emerging group and are well-placed to participate in some of the innovations outlined earlier. However, over the longer-term coach training programmes may be commissioned to offer formal, certificated professional development opportunities that train experienced coaches in the specialist knowledge and qualifications they need in order to lay claim to an ultimately protected title of 'mental health coach'.

These are just some of the many ways in which the field of coaching and the professionals who make up this workforce might move into the mental health arena. Initially, it will be up to each of us to create a 'personal brand' in which we are able to make the claim for being specialists by practice and to create methods of learning and development that reflect the work we are increasingly called to deliver. This would introduce further diversity within the coaching community. However, coaching has always embraced diversity and so arguably, it is well-placed to champion new forms of practice at the cutting edge of human need. Any developments of this nature will, of course, have significant implications for the training, credentialing, supervision and continuing professional development of coaches and ultimately, progressing coaching within this field will require the full participation of both training institutions and the professional bodies. Challenging conversations will lie ahead. And yet this is also consistent with the spirit of our times – one in which we are coming to terms with the fact that the old ways of conceptualising and responding to our collective well-being needs are no longer sufficient. As a field coaching is uniquely placed to question, facilitate, challenge, collaborate, co-produce and empower all those who are trying to generate effective responses to what is one of the greatest challenges of our times.

Conclusion

Despite the advancements that the human race has made on so many levels, the number of individuals who are living with significant levels of emotional distress appears to be increasing. Innovative approaches to conceptualising and working with mental health issues are going to be essential if we are to find sustainable solutions to this complex area of human need. This chapter has been based on the potentially controversial premise that coaching has an important, emerging role to play in working with mental health issues. In particular, we have sought to raise awareness of how common mental health problem might present in our clients, how we can enhance our awareness of the warning signs of reduced well-being and how to increase our confidence in responding appropriately when a mental health problem becomes evident.

We have also argued that the time is ripe for a paradigm shift, one in which coaching has a potentially central role to play. The complexity and scope of issues emerging in relation to our collective mental health calls for responses from a range of disciplines working collaboratively rather than as silos. The solutions to wicked problems, of which we consider mental health to be one, will require the development of transdisciplinary relationships that can contribute novel approaches to knowledge generation from a willingness to draw upon a plurality of perspectives. As part of a transdisciplinary agenda, we believe that coaching has a unique contribution to make to the tapestry of services and service providers to which the wicked problem of mental health may be giving rise. We hope that this chapter might help start the conversations that are needed for this paradigm shift to come to fruition. The potential is enormous if we are willing to embrace it.

Notes

1 For the purposes of this chapter, mental health is defined as 'a state of complete physical, mental and social well-being' (World Health Organization, 2014). In recognising the absence of any universally agreed definition, we use the terms 'mental health' when referring to states of emotional well-being and 'mental health issue', 'problem' or 'disorder' when referring to states of emotional and psychological distress or widely recognised diagnosable disorders. This differentiation is used to optimally frame the ideas presented in this chapter and to help explore the roles that coaches might contribute to this broad and complex area of human need.
2 As explained later in the chapter, the term 'wicked' is used in a very specific way to capture the essence of particular types of problem that defy our existing problem-solving strategies through their complexity. In no sense does it imply a value-based judgement concerning the nature of the problem itself. That is, the term does not imply that the problem is bad or wicked in any moral sense of the term.
3 Rates of prevalence and incidence vary as a function of how mental health problems are defined, the methods used to measure symptomatology and cultural differences in the self-reporting of emotional distress. They also vary as a function of how recently the data were collected. These statistics are best understood, therefore, as illustrative rather than providing definitive statements on specific numbers of individuals directly living with a mental health problem at any given point in time.
4 This case scenario is fictitious and used solely as a basis for illustrating the themes presented in this chapter.
5 For the purposes of this chapter Salutogenesis refers to a transdisciplinary framework with three core components (Mittelmark & Bauer, 2017). These are (1) the model of salutogenesis proposed by Antonovsky (1979), (2) the measure of sense of coherence, the ability of an individual to mobilise internal and external resources for health and (3) the general worldview concerned with promoting health and utilisation of resources.

References

Antonovsky, A. (1979). *Health, stress, and coping*. San Francisco: Jossey-Bass.

Antonovsky, A. (1987). *Unraveling the mystery of health: How people manage stress and stay well*. San Francisco: Jossey-Bass.

Antonovsky, A. (1996). The salutogenic model as a theory to guide health promotion. *Health Promotion International, 11*(1), 11–18.

Barber, H. F. (1992). Developing strategic leadership: The US Army war experience. *Journal of Management Development, 11*, 4–12.

Bishop, L. (2018). A scoping review of mental health coaching. *The Coaching Psychologist, 14*, 5–15.

Brown, V. A., Harris, J. A., & Russell, J. Y. (2010). *Tackling wicked problems through trans-disciplinary imagination*. London: Earthscan.

Buckley, A., & Buckley, C. (2006). *A guide to coaching and mental health: The recognition and management of psychological issues*. New York: Routledge.

Clark, D. M. (2011). Implementing NICE guidelines for the psychological treatment of depression and anxiety disorders. *International Review of Psychiatry, 23*, 375–384.

Corrie, S. (2016). *Promoting self-care in a complex world: What every coach should know*. Paper presented at the SGCP Coaching Psychology Workshops and Conference, London.

Corrie, S. (2017). SGCP research network. What role do coaching practitioners have in working with mental health issues? Results of a survey. *The Coaching Psychologist, 13*(1), 41–48.

Corrie, S. (2019a). *Broadening our horizons: Why coaches should specialise in mental health.* Paper presented at the International Conference of Coaching Psychology 2019, London.

Corrie, S. (Producer). (2019b). *What do coaches need to know about mental health?* Webinar for the Special Group in Coaching Psychology.

Corrie, S., & Lane, D. A. (2015). Things to keep us awake at night: The challenges of being a psychologist in the UK. *Psychology Aotearoa, 7,* 140–144.

Deci, E. L., & Ryan, R. M. (1985). *Intrinsic motivation and self-determination in human behavior.* New York: Plenum.

Eriksson, M. (2017). The sense of coherence in the salutogenic model of health. In M. B. Mittelmark, M. Eriksson, J. M. Pelikan, G. A. Espnes, S. Sagy, G. F. Bauer, & B. Lindstrom (Eds.), *The handbook of salutogenesis* (pp. 91–96). Cham, Switzerland: Springer Nature. http://doi.org/978-3-319-04600-6_11

Eriksson, M., & Lindström, B. (2006). Antonovsky's sense of coherence scale and the relation with health: A systematic review. *Journal of Epidemiology & Community Health, 60*(5), 376–381.

Eriksson, M., & Mittelmark, M. B. (2017). The sense of coherence and its measurement. In M. B. Mittelmark, M. Eriksson, J. M. Peiikan, G. A. Espnes, S. Sagy, G. F. Bauer, & B. Lindstrom (Eds.), *The handbook of salutogenesis* (p. 97). Cham, Switzerland: Springer Nature. http://doi.org/10.1007/978-3-319-04600-6_12

Grant, A. M. (2017). The third 'generation' of workplace coaching: Creating a culture of quality conversations. *Coaching: An International Journal of Theory, Research and Practice, 10*(1), 37–53.

Gray, D. (2016). Developing resilience and wellbeing for healthcare staff during organisational transition: The salutogenic approach. *International Journal of Evidence Based Coaching and Mentoring, 14*(2), 31–47.

Gray, D. (2017). Developing leadership resilience through a sense of coherence. *Contemporary Leadership Challenges,* 15. http://doi.org/10.5772/64611

Gray, D., Burls, A., & Kogan, M. (2014). Salutogenisis and coaching: Testing a proof of concept to develop a model for practitioners. *International Journal of Evidence Based Coaching & Mentoring, 12*(2), 41–58.

Green, H., Mcginnity, A., Ford, T., & Goodman, R. (2005). *Mental health of children and young people in Great Britain 2004.* Basingstoke, Hampshire: Palgrave Macmillan.

Jenkins, R., Meltzer, H., Jones, P. B., Brugha, T., Bebbington, P., Farrell, M., . . . Knapp, M. (2008). *Foresight mental capital and wellbeing project.* London, UK: The Government Office for Science.

Joseph, S., & Sagy, S. (2017). Positive psychology in the context of salutogenesis. In M. B. Mittelmark, M. Eriksson, J. M. Pelikan, G. A. Espnes, S. Sagy, G. F. Bauer, & M.-L. Lindbohm (Eds.), *The handbook of salutogenesis* (pp. 83–88). Cham: Springer.

Keyes, C. L. M. (2014). Mental health as a complete state: How the salutogenic perspective completes the picture. In G. F. Bauer & O. Hammig (Eds.), *Bridging occupational, organizational and public health: A transdisciplinary approach* (pp. 179–192). Cham: Springer.

McManus, S., Bebbington, P., Jenkins, R., & Brugha, T. (Eds.). (2016). *Mental health and wellbeing in England: Adult psychiatric morbidity survey 2004.* Leeds: NHS Digital.

Mittelmark, M. B., & Bauer, G. F. (2017). The meanings of salutogenesis. In M. B. Mittelmark, M. Eriksson, J. M. Pelikan, G. A. Espnes, S. Sagy, G. F. Bauer, & B. Lindstrom

(Eds.), *The handbook of salutogenesis* (pp. 7–13). Cham, Switzerland: Springer Nature. http://doi.org/978-3-319-04600-6_2

Spence, G. B., & Deci, E. L. (2013). Self-determination theory within coaching contexts: Supporting motives and goals that promote optimal functioning and well-being. In S. David, D. Clutterbuck, & D. Megginson (Eds.), *Beyond goals: Effective strategies for coaching and mentoring* (pp. 85–108). Abingdon, UK: Gower.

Stelter, R. (2014). Third generation coaching: Reconstructing dialogues through collaborative practice and a focus on values. *International Coaching Psychology Review, 9*(1), 51–66.

Stelter, R., & Andersen, V. (2018). Coaching for health and lifestyle change: Theory and guidelines for interacting and reflecting with women about their challenges and aspirations. *International Coaching Psychology Review, 13*(1), 61–71.

Szymanska, K. (2019). Coachee mental health: Practice implications for coaching psychologists. In S. Palmer & A. Whybrow (Eds.), *Handbook of coaching psychology*, 2nd ed. (pp. 567–577). Abingdon, Oxon: Routledge.

Vos, T., Barber, R. M., Bell, B., Bertozzi-Villa, A., Biryukov, S., Bolliger, I., . . . Dicker, D. (2015). Global, regional, and national incidence, prevalence, and years lived with disability for 301 acute and chronic diseases and injuries in 188 countries, 1990–2013: A systematic analysis for the Global Burden of Disease Study 2013. *The Lancet, 386*(9995), 743–800.

World Health Organization. (2001). *Mental disorders affect one in four people.* World Health Report. Retrieved from www.who.int/whr/2001/media_centre/press-release/en/

World Health Organization. (2003). *Caring for children and adolescents with mental disorders: Setting WHO directions.* Retrieved from www.who.int/mental_health/media/en/785.pdf.

World Health Organization. (2004). *Promoting mental health: Concepts, emerging evidence, practice: Summary report.* Retrieved December 20, 2019 from www.who.int/mental_health/evidence/en/promoting_mhh.pdf

World Health Organization. (2014). *Basic documents.* Retrieved December 20, 2019 from http://apps.who.int/gb/bd/PDF/bd48/basic-documents-48th-edition-en.pdf#page=1

World Health Organization. (2019). *Mental health of older adults.* Retrieved from www.who.int/en/news-room/fact-sheets/detail/mental-health-of-older-adults

Chapter 6

The role for coaching in psychological trauma

Noreen Tehrani and David A. Lane

Introduction

Trauma is everywhere impacting on most people at some point either directly or through secondary impacts from people we know (Breslau, 1989). The concept starts to appear in literature from the time of the Trojan Wars. In Sophocles' "Ajax", the play follows the story of a combat veteran who slips into depression and attempts to kill his commanding officer. In John Arden's Serjeant Musgrave's Dance, toward the end of the play, Serjeant Musgrave exclaims "There used to be my duty: now there's a disease". The description of his night terrors maps across to PTSD (see Langley, 2004). Beveridge describes how Charles Dickens was involved in a serious rail accident and reported, a year later, "sudden vague rushes of terror even when riding in a Hansom Cab". In the nineteenth century neurologists started to describe post traumatic "railway spine" and there is brief mention of "traumatic neurasthenia" in Tuke's 1892 Dictionary of Psychological Medicine and early case examples refer to "mental parasites" following road accident. However, controversy about the term and the role of organic and functional elements occur very early in the literature Knapp (1897).

By the time of the First World War the concept of shell shock appeared which implied nervous damage caused by the impact of shellfire. After the Second World War the reference manual DSM coined "battle fatigue" and "gross stress reaction" with the recognition that even the most robust could suffer. It was following the Vietnam war that the concept of post-traumatic stress disorder became established. It entered the psychiatric lexicon in the form of DSM 111 (and ICD classification). This has been regularly updated as understanding increased. This was elaborated upon through to DSM-IV and connected with non-combatant forms of trauma, such as the capsize of the car ferry, The Herald of Free Enterprise.

What has been increasingly understood is that such trauma can emerge from any extreme condition and can become even more difficult to resolve where multiple traumas occur in the form of a complex trauma for example childhood abuse followed by abuse in adulthood or exposure to a life-threatening accident.

The descriptors indicative of psychological trauma are listed in the DSM and ICD guidelines (see DSM V for current descriptors: www.ptsd.va.gov/professional/treat/essentials/dsm5_ptsd.asp). However, it is important to note that the emergence of DSM V was highly contentious (www.nhs.uk/news/mental-health/news-analysis-controversial-mental-health-guide-dsm-5).

There is a tendency to think about interventions for trauma as solely an individual therapeutic endeavour. We contend that it is also an organisation level matter and that ways to work with individuals, teams and systems need to be part of the approach (Taylor and Lane, 1991; Tehrani, 2011). This creates a role for coaches. However, coaches need to understand trauma and the way in which current events can trigger memories from the long distant past. If coaches work in this area, they have a responsibility to understand the boundaries of their role, when and when not to intervene. This chapter explores the skills that coaches bring, guidance on when to refer on to a trauma therapist and briefly looks at preventing secondary trauma and compassion fatigue. We draw extensively upon ideas presented by Tehrani et al. (2012).

Why coaches and trauma, is that not just for therapists?

There has been much discussion of the boundary between coaching and parallel fields (e.g. psychology, therapy). In particular coaches have been warned to stay away from anything that might be therapy. It is the case that coaches should not attempt to be therapists, yet the complexity of our lives and the contexts in which we work mean that there are ways for coaches to intervene which are outside of therapy but nevertheless helpful. The argument that therapeutic areas should be off limits because coaches do not have the training for it and it could be dangerous is correct, but only if a narrow view of distress, disengagement, and trauma are adopted. The boundary discussion has prompted research into the differences between coaching and therapy (Turner, 2008; Bachkirova, 2007; Spinelli, 2008) The debate includes the concepts that other disciplines bring to coaching and the transfer of ideas between disciplines without a research base to support it. (Lane, 2010) The boundary debates exist not only within coaching but rage fiercely within the therapeutic disciplines. (House and Loewenthal, 2008). It is not only the boundaries between coaching and therapy that may be fuzzy but also those within therapy as practices and disputes about what is and is not appropriate are as tense as they appear across the coaching therapy divide.

When we turn to consideration of trauma Taylor and Lane (1991) in a Special Issue of the British Journal of Guidance and Counselling introduced a number of papers that made clear that invention is not just about therapeutic work. They argue that we have to address four stages to generate a comprehensive approach – preparation, response, recovery and mitigation. A similar case was made in a position paper from the British Psychological Society on Psychological Aspects of Disasters (1991). Intervention involves:

> **Preparation** to include design of environments to reduce causes of disaster or stress and burnout and the prevention and management of trauma in the workplace.

Response includes action taken in the immediate aftermath of a crisis or disaster.

Recovery is concerned with both assisting individuals and organisations through from initial victimhood, survival and then learning to thrive. Therapy has a role but so do coaching and organizational change processes.

Mitigation takes the longer-term view and looks at how organizations and individuals can generate new approaches to mitigate problems occurring in the future based on learning from past incidents or future scenarios.

This leads us to think about issues such as the influence of workplace culture, business continuity, mental health, organizational structures, the role of toxic organizational process, resilience, compassion fatigue and burnout and building organisations fit for a complex world. These are areas in which coaches have contribution to make. We explore in this chapter some of these issues.

Trauma and the workplace

When we think of the workplace, we have to recognise the wide range of factors affected by personal traumas (Tehrani et al., 2012):

- industrial accidents
- violence or bullying
- industrial exposure through a work role in high risk environments
- contexts in which professional and public meet in distressing circumstances, nurse, social worker, police officer, ambulance or fire and rescue personnel
- sudden death of a much-loved colleague
- slow demise of a close work colleague from cancer
- unexpected mass redundancies

Some workplaces have a higher exposure to traumatic events; indeed they are almost routine. This can be direct exposure in the case of fire-fighters, paramedics and police officers or indirect when dealing with victims of rape or child abuse. Organisational effectiveness is impacted. In a scoping review for Public Health England, The British Psychological Society and College of Policing, Richens et al. (2019) reviewed fifty studies on early intervention. They found that such interventions help emergency responders to manage post incident trauma with the proviso that they are delivered in a way that respects organisational culture, have the support of the organisation and senior management, and incorporate existing social cohesion and peer support within teams. This detailed report is required reading for anyone working in this field or considering setting up an organisational response. It carefully evaluates various studies and provides guidance on approaches.

Some of these would be within the capability of properly trained coaches. Coaches work with clients, as a result of events such as a redundancy, bullying, conflict or relationship breakdown. It can happen that the current issue triggers an underpinning issue which is trauma related. This makes it important for all coaches to have some understanding of traumatic stress – the similarities and differences from everyday stresses and strains of life.

Understanding psychological trauma?

It is important to understand that trauma can happen to anyone – it arises from our evolutionary past – it is not a sign of weakness. The key to how our brain responds is through a primitive part called the amygdala which is highly sensitive to danger. (see Diagram 1 from Tehrani et al., 2012) Because the amygdala is unable to discriminate the dangerous from signals associated with danger a past event can trigger it to react. In a project (known as the Raid Trauma Network) working with staff who were subjected to bank raids, it was found that long after the event someone, entering the bank, who shared features to the raider could generate a fearful response. It was necessary for the employer to recognise that recovery could be a long process.

The evolutionary benefit that the amygdala generates is the speed with which it can respond to danger signals. Essentially over time we develop templates of real and associated danger signals to which the amygdala reacts potentially causing anxiety, distress or fear. The hippocampus is the site of ways of coming to terms with these events, essentially through the creation of narratives. New memories are constructed which can be reconstructed to form more helpful stories that enable progress from a fearful state to an adjustment. Lying between the amygdala is a connection that metaphorically acts like a fuse which blows between the amygdala and the hippocampus, protecting the brain from being overwhelmed. Coaches need to understand the role of the amygdala its relationship to the hippocampus and the way traumatic events are processed. Useful theories for coaches to explore include the Dual Representation Theory of Brewin (Brewin et al., 1996). This proposes that traumas experienced after early childhood create two types of memory: (1) verbally accessible, e.g., narrative memories and (2) automatically accessible, e.g., situational

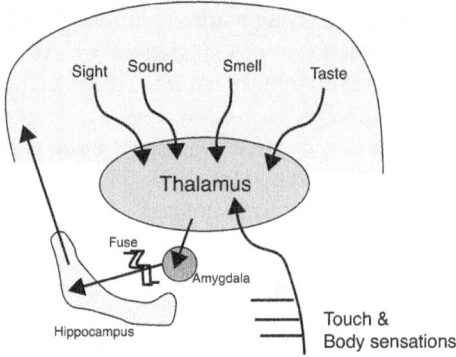

Figure 6.1 The Brain's response to trauma

or sensory images. The ways these interact give rise to different ways of processing trauma. Kleim and associates (2009) explore a number of theories and experimental studies on memory processing after trauma. Their findings are compatible with the dual representation theory but also offer support to other approaches. The different approaches certainly should inform any intervention by a coach.

It is important to recognise that given the opportunity to reflect and make sense of the experience (creating a meaningful narrative that can be constructed and reconstructed) most people will recover from a traumatic exposure. They may still experience flashbacks but can learn to recognise that this is the amygdala reacting to related sensory features of the trauma experience (see Brewin et al., 2017 for an account of developing thinking about diagnosis of PTSD).

As a coach working with a client who has experienced a traumatic event the emphasis is on issues raised by the client – listening to their story so that they feel heard. For example, Tehrani (Tehrani et al., 2012) provides a case to illustrate this:

> If a client was involved in a car crash it is important to focus on the features of the crash and not explore other times when the client may have feared for his or her life or felt out of control. Whilst in therapy it may be appropriate to explore the significance of the date, people involved or meaning of the crash or early life experiences and attachments, this is not helpful to a traumatised person, who needs to deal with the trauma in a more straight-forward way.

Tehrani makes the points that:

- Processing trauma memories, particularly when these memories are difficult to access as they have become embedded in the amygdala in a sensory rather than verbal form, can be a slow process.
- Teaching clients relaxation skills to help them remain calm during the retelling of their experience is helpful but may take time.
- The amygdala does not release the sensory memories to the conscious awareness on demand, sometimes waiting for opportunities to disclose the encrypted fear in flashbacks, nightmares, recurrent thoughts and behaviours.
- For a traumatised client these re-experiences of the traumatic event are regarded as frightening symptoms of a trauma disorder, rather than the key to help them regain well-being.
- Coaching clients need to recognise and accept these post-trauma responses as natural outcomes of their experience. This takes away fear and allows the meaning of the traumatic event to be created.

When might coaches help?

At the individual level the role of the coach is primarily to create a safe container for the client to tell their story. This can happen without the need to challenge or explore the emotional responses. It is about the opportunity to begin to create a

Table 6.1 Difference between trauma support coaching and counselling

Trauma Support Coaching	Counselling
• Structured	• Generally less structured
• Closing down	• Opening up
• Acceptance	• Challenging
• Limited focus	• Wide focus
• Client control	• Client risk taking
• Information provided	• Non-advisory

narrative that is open to reconstruction. As clients work with their narrative they can envisage movement from a victim status to someone who can learn from the experience and begin to thrive (Joseph, 2012, see Corrie and Lane, 2010 for an exploration of approaches to exploring narrative). However, coaches often bring other capabilities such as organisational development experience giving them the opportunity to contribute at the team and systems level. Table 6.1 shows the different skills and activities involved in dealing with an individual traumatised client (Tehrani et al., 2012).

According to Hawker, (Hawker et al., 2011) dealing with a traumatised client in an effective way requires a clear structure and an exploration, in a safe environment, of what happened. The focus should be on factual and sensory information, not the processing of thoughts and emotional responses. The process of acting as a psychological first aider is now widely established (see bulleted suggestions from the National Child Traumatic Stress Network and the World Health Organisation). PFA provides an opportunity to acknowledge and gain closure to traumatic experiences. A trauma supporter will accept the story and impressions of their client rather than challenging their recollection and provide the client with opportunities to dictate the speed and content of what they wish to describe. Unlike counselling which generally will not include providing information or advice, trauma support requires the supporter to provide information, education and exercises to help reduce the trauma symptoms. While some coaching psychologists reject an advice-giving role for others, it makes sense when appropriate to the client. This is one of those occasions. Suggestions from the National Child Traumatic Stress Network cover eight *PFA* Core Actions:

- **Contact and Engagement:** To respond to contacts initiated by survivors, or to initiate contacts in a non-intrusive, compassionate, and helpful manner.
- **Safety and Comfort:** To enhance immediate and ongoing safety and provide physical and emotional comfort.
- **Stabilization (if needed):** To calm and orient emotionally overwhelmed or disoriented survivors.
- **Information Gathering on Current Needs and Concerns:** To identify immediate needs and concerns, gather additional information, and tailor Psychological First Aid interventions.

- **Practical Assistance:** To offer practical help to survivors in addressing immediate needs and concerns.
- **Connection with Social Supports:** To help establish brief or ongoing contacts with primary support persons and other sources of support, including family members, friends, and community helping resources.
- **Information on Coping:** To provide information about stress reactions and coping to reduce distress and promote adaptive functioning.
- **Linkage with Collaborative Services:** To link survivors with available services needed at the time or in the future.

The essence of Psychological First Aid according to the WHO is:

- feeling safe, connected to others, calm and hopeful;
- having access to social, physical and emotional support; and
- feeling able to help themselves, as individuals and communities.

These provide a number of ways in which the experiences of coaches can be useful. However, coaches need to recognise:

- the limits to their knowledge and competence. This includes dealing with some of the deeper issues which may be present in a client experiencing significant levels of trauma symptoms or where the traumatic events are complex or go back to early life abuse or losses.
- that in order for them to work effectively with a client there has to be a reasonable level of self-awareness and willingness to work on those activities which will reduce their anxiety and levels of arousal.
- the need to enable social support, which is extremely important to someone experiencing trauma symptoms. Research has shown that where a trauma victim has the support of their family, colleagues or friends they have a much better chance of recovery (Bryant and Harvey, 2000).
- that in dealing with a traumatised client there is a need to work not just with the client but to ensure that effort is put into encouraging the building or re-establishment of social networks and support.

How can coaches help provide support?

Much of the discussion in the trauma field has been on the negative impact. However, there is an increasing body of evidence to demonstrate that trauma can lead to personal growth (Joseph, 2009, 2012). Helping clients to grow is a key part of the capability of the coach. In addition, many coaches have experience of undertaking skill assessments. (Linley and Minhas, 2011). The aim of such assessment in trauma is to help clients remember their inherent abilities and strengths which may be applied to the current situation. There are several toolkits available which contain material which will be familiar to coaches who have worked to develop skills or journeys towards growth. Of particular value is the roads to resilience project from the American Psychological Association (see The Road to Resilience, www.apa.org/helpcenter/road-resilience). This provides a ten-step guide.

There are also many resources available from the National Center for PTSD (www.ptsd.va.gov/professional/assessment/screens/tsq.asp). These include screening questionnaires and practical tools for assisting clients. These tools help to create new learning and as a result increase capacity to make sense of distressing experiences. The practical use of such tools to build capacity fits well with a coaching approach.

Of particular value to coaches are a number of approaches to looking at trauma in the workplace (Tehrani, 2011) provides a wealth of information and practical ideas for understanding the contexts within which trauma impacts and ways to deal with it.

Coaching can be a process for supporting clients to achieve a valued goal or objective. Coaches therefore employ a range of skills all of which are useful when dealing with a traumatised client or supporting an organisation. Table 6.2 (Tehrani et al., 2012) highlights some of the skills.

Table 6.2 Coaching skills and post trauma support at individual and organisational level

Individual coaching skill	Description	Example
Goal setting	Coaches need to be able to identify clear and well-defined goals	Traumatised people find it hard to focus on the future, the use of SMART goals gives a direction and sense of a future which can be influenced
Reframing	Taking perceived problems and presenting the problem in a different light/framework	The reframing for a client who is nervous about meeting people "That is really interesting – your reactions are helping you to think about how to deal with this meeting in a different way"
Observing	Being aware of body language and having an intuitive sense	Body language in people who have experienced trauma gives an insight to their inner experiences. Watch their posture, expression, skin tone and movements to help you understand
Active listening	Active listening which includes, open and closed questions, paraphrase and summary help to get into the client's world	A traumatised person can find the experience of being listened and responded to accurately and non-judgementally extremely helpful in the process of teasing out pre-conscious trauma memories from the Amygdala

(Continued)

Table 6.2 (Continued)

Individual coaching skill	Description	Example
Empathy	The ability to get into the trauma victims world and to respond accurately to their experiences	Empathy helps clients to feel less isolated and alone. There are some dangers for the coach in becoming emotionally empathetic as this can lead to burnout or compassion fatigue
Immediacy	Providing clear and specific feedback on the client's actions and responses in the session	This skill is used to test out hunches and intuition as well as to provide positive feedback on achievement. The feedback should be observational and non-judgemental
Respect	Checking out how the client is feeling and what they want shows respect and also gives the client some control over the session	For many victims of trauma control has been taken away. Showing respect and consideration gives back control and enables them to decide on how they would like to work with their coach
Supporting change	Making sure that targets are manageable, efforts are rewarded and support is available	Change is not easy for anyone, even more so for a trauma victim. Building in rewards, acknowledgement of effort and believing in your client's ability to recover is essential
Building organisational resilience	Understanding how organisations can be resilience to toxic events and build structures to support staff (and customers) to address them.	Having policies to deal with issues such as bullying provides an organisational response but does not address the way in which organisations can themselves be toxic. Organisational resilience requires changes at a structural level that create positive working environments
Creating safe containers	Ensuring the conditions for staff to feel safe to raise challenging issues at an individual and systems level	Unless staff feel able to challenge inappropriate or bad practice, organisations will not be safe spaces. It is not enough to claim that anyone can raise issues. Staff (or customers) must genuinely feel that such feedback is welcomed and that they will not be victimised for raising it

Individual coaching skill	Description	Example
Ensuring organisational preparation response recovery and mitigation for a complex world	Creating coherent plans are prepared that address scenarios for dealing with toxic events such as bullying, organisational disorganisation and disasters. Ensuring that plans are enacted to provide a timely response to events. Enabling recovery processes by managing expectations and alternative working and provision of coaching or therapeutic inputs as needed. Mitigating long term effects through provision of support and generating new learning from events to review and adapt the preparation for the future	Some organisational cultures are themselves toxic and create trauma. An organisation that tolerates bullying from staff who are high income generators while claiming a policy that bullying is unacceptable constitutes a trauma organised system. In addition to preparing for and responding to external threats an organisation has to look at itself and the internal threats that generate trauma. A coherent and effective policy cannot be generated unless this internal review is undertaken

A case example of combining approaches from coaching and therapy within an organisational process

On 11 September 2001, I (DL) received a call from one of my clients. She asked if I was watching the television, which I was. In her organisation, a trading company, the screens were permanently switched on. Staff members in London saw, as it happened, the attacks on the World Trade Centre in New York in one tower of which, their colleagues were based. She asked if I could get to London immediately to discuss how we might set up a support system in what was a very chaotic situation.

It was also a mass attack that was witnessed as it happened across the world with messages from inside the Towers emerging in real time and colleagues, friends and relatives seeing the destruction of their loved ones played over and over again. While I had experience of other disaster situations and had written on the matter as well as provided trauma counselling services, this was the first time I had seen and heard the unfolding story alongside those I would be helping. On arriving in London, it was clear that many individuals had been deeply affected as they personally knew many working in the Twin Towers. They had both to deal with their emotions and fears and make decisions which had significant business and market consequences.

The organisation was clear that it wanted to do whatever was the most appropriate for their staff, and looked to me to assess the situation, and to devise and implement a planned response. However, there was no agreed collective framework for such a service. We were all on an individual journey from the unknown.

How might you have developed the intervention in this situation? Consider this before reading further.

Here is what actually occurred.

Initially, it seemed that an objective might be quickly found. The organisation stated that it wanted to do what was best for the staff and I certainly wanted to devise a worthwhile response. What was most appropriate was unclear, given the circumstances and how much of the situation was unknown. Dealing with personal reactions while still needing to make business decisions represented the first potential conflict. Where do you look for answers in known evidence-bases in order to create a structured decision model?

The literature on disaster management had developed rapidly over the previous few years from a low base in the 1980s to significant research by this time. During the late 1980s and early 1990s a model of practice had grown up which combined counselling, coaching and critical incident debriefing initially, with longer term work to alleviate PTSD where necessary. However, by the late 1990s this research was being challenged and elements of it were seen by some as unhelpful or harmful while still being championed by others. As a result, the literature did not lend itself well to a structured decision-making model and in fact, added to the confusion. In terms of the organisation the response was highly varied some seemingly minimally affected and others significantly so. The organisation had to function, closure was not a considered option and the work for staff during that period was intense. After multiple coaching conversations conducted over two days with staff at several levels a shared sense emerged which could form the basis for a Mission statement.

The elements included:

1   To support staff in the immediate aftermath of the incident to continue functioning in their role, (this was largely coaching) and to support those who did not feel able to do so without prejudice to their position (this was

largely counselling); to provide management debriefing (based on a team coaching model) across the organisation to allow issues that needed to be addressed to emerge and enable decision-making to address these; to support managers (a mixture of individual coaching and team coaching) in dealing with their own responses while providing structures to help them support their staff.

2   Following the immediate response, to set up continued debriefing, coaching and counselling as needed so that the staff could feel fully recovered and in the longer term seek to mitigate continuing impacts and learn from the events to better prepare in the future. The whole framework was to be kept under review and adjusted as circumstances changed.

In terms of the disaster literature a decision model for the response, recovery and mitigation phases was established (Taylor and Lane 1991). This included structured decision models where the literature supported it (for example debriefing sheets were provided and counselling services established). It also included emergent decision-making models to respond to rapidly changing circumstances; a short decision chain was set up so that different modifications to service could be introduced as needed. A senior manager was assigned to liaise with the support team daily with authority to assess and decide.

When do coaches need to pass cases to a trauma therapist/GP?

We have to recognise that not all who have been impacted by trauma are suitable for coaching. Some will require a much more in-depth approach, for example, trauma informed cognitive behavioural therapy, to help them deal with their experience (Bisson et al., 2013). Steps that a coach should consider are:

- an assessment prior to coaching to see if the traumatic memories and responses require a more specialist approach
- recognising the features of acute stress, anxiety, depression, traumatic stress and dissociation and making an appropriate referral will help the client to get the most effective support
- establishing a means to monitor their clients and identify where, despite their best intentions the trauma symptoms begin to increase or where there are other concerning features such as substance abuse, self-harming or dissociation
- consider referring a client to a trauma psychologist or their GP if there is no obvious improvement within a relatively short period

Table 6.3 (Tehrani et al., 2012) provides an indication of the help that can be provided by coaches, trauma psychologists and psychiatrists.

Table 6.3 Trauma support available from a coach, trauma psychologists and psychiatrist

Domain	Coaching	Trauma psychology	Psychiatry
Intention	Increase potential to achieve post trauma growth	Identify and remove blocks to psychological well-being	Diagnose and treat psycho-pathology
Underpinning beliefs	People can learn skills to deal with issues/ situations through systematic engagement and reinforcement	People are resourceful and given support will solve their problems and achieve their goals	Some mental conditions are caused by underlying medical or psychiatric malfunctions and need treatment
Benefits	Forward looking in Increasing the range of skills and abilities based on the needs of the individual	Recognises and addresses patterns of behaviour which may get in way of achieving goals	Can identify and treat psychiatric disorders which may contribute to unwanted symptoms or behaviours
Disadvantages	Most coaching models do not deal with the complexity of trauma. Coaches may not recognise the psychological/ psychiatric problems	Some trauma psychologists may not pay attention to organisational issues or be aware of the personal skills required to deal with trauma responses.	Psychiatrists may adopt a medical model approach, ignoring the impact of the traumatic event or other social issues
When appropriate	When there is an openness to explore and self-awareness and an ability to accept some responsibility for actions	Where there are some unresolved issues from the past which may be getting in the way of positive solutions and personal growth	Where the underlying problem is relates to a psychiatric disorder which has caused or been caused by the trauma

Importance of supervision when coaching traumatised clients

While it is recognised that supervision is important for coaches (Carroll, 2006, 2007; Cavanagh, et al., 2016) many coaches report that they do not use it or see the benefit (Lane, 2011; Grant, 2012). Working with trauma requires the coach to be supervised by someone with the appropriate background to be aware of the dangers in undertaking this kind of work (McNabb, 2011). The role of supervision in trauma-based work has been explored explicitly by Tehrani and Levers (2016). This makes clear that coaches need to be cognisant of the potential impact of hearing trauma stories on their own well-being. In particular empathetic listening, essential to the work, can also create thoughts and feeling in the coach similar to those experienced by the client (Figley, 2002; Morrissette, 2004). The development of secondary trauma, compassion fatigue and burnout are clear signs of the coach becoming vicariously affected by their work with trauma (Taylor and Lane, 1991). Tehrani and Levers (2016) make the point that before starting this work the coach should have supervision in place and take personal responsibility for themselves and their need to build their emotional resilience and emotional resources. This includes the areas that all coaches should consider in their work such as recognising any personal unresolved or ongoing traumas and that they have a wide range of social support.

Tehrani (Tehrani et al., 2012) suggests that when selecting a supervisor coaches need to ensure that the supervisor is prepared to:

- Assess whether you have the personal characteristics and personal strengths to engage in the work.
- Identify and deal with signs of emotional distress and to explore these during supervision.
- Recognise and handle parallel process, transference and countertransference played out in the relational dynamics of the supervision.
- Help you to build a range of personal coping strategies and networks.
- Debrief particularly difficult or distressing stories.
- Reward successes and recognise good work.
- To tell you when they feel a case needs to be referred on for trauma therapy.

There are a number of interesting areas of development in trauma supervision. These include the role of culturally informed trauma supervision, (Bledsoe, 2012; Levers, 2012) integrative and systemic approaches, (Levers, 2012) and the use of relational transactional concepts (Etherington, 2009). Gray et al. (2016) refers to developmental and social role models. Lane et al. (2016) argue that it is important to build a personally effective model of supervision and provide a framework to do so. They present a framework that considers the purpose of supervision, the perspectives that inform it and the process for providing it all based on specific professional contexts. In the same book psychologists and others from a range of clinical, health, forensic, educational, sport, counselling, coaching and work and organisational contexts outline how they interpret the purpose, perspectives and process they use to undertake supervision. In the specific coaching context Gray et al. (2016) provide an account of supervision in coaching and explores the idea of stages of development for supervisors.

In conclusion

There is an important and emerging conversation to be had about the role for coaches and coaching psychologists to facilitate the creation of resilient organisations and provide support to individuals and teams following traumatic events. They are not acting as therapists (and should not attempt to do so) but they can provide a structured process of support. The skills that coaches bring, in terms of understanding organisational process, building teams and enhancing individual and organisational resilience offer real value to understanding response to trauma. The skills that individuals develop within a coaching process assist clients seeking to come to terms with such events and build the sense that they can move from being a victim, to surviving the current dilemmas to a future in which they can thrive. There are boundary issues which we have to respect. Nevertheless, the benefits of a coaching offer are clear. Trauma is an area to which coaching and coaching psychology can make a contribution. The conversations need to happen.

References

American Psychological Association (2019) *Road to Resilience*. www.apa.org/helpcenter/road-resilience (accessed 18/09/2019).

Bachkirova, T. (2007) Role of coaching psychology in defining boundaries between counselling and coaching. In S. Palmer and A. Whybrow (Eds.), *Handbook of Coaching Psychology* (pp. 325–350). London: Routledge.

Bisson, J.I., Roberts, N.P., Andrew, M., Cooper, R., and Lewis, C. (2013) Psychological therapies for chronic Post-traumatic Stress Disorder (PTSD) in adults. *Cochrane Database of Systematic Reviews* 2013: 12.

Bledsoe, D.E. (2012) Trauma and supervision. In L.L. Levers (Ed.), *Trauma Counselling Theories and Interventions* (pp. 569–578). New York: Kogan Page.

Breslau, N. (1989) Epidemiology of trauma and posttrauamtic stress disorder. In Rachel Yehuda (Ed.), *Psychological Trauma* (pp. 1–29). Washington, DC: American Psychiatric Press.

Brewin, C.R., Cloitre, M., Hyland, P., Shevlin, M., Maercker, A., Bryant, R.A. et al. (2017) A review of current evidence regarding the ICD-11 proposals for diagnosing PTSD and complex PTSD. *Clinical Psychology Review* 58: 1–15.

Brewin, R.B., Dalgleish, T., and Joseph, S. (1996) A dual representation theory of post-traumatic stress disorder. *Psychological Review* 103(4): 670–686.

British Psychological Society (1991) *Psychological Aspects of Disasters*. Leicester: British Psychological Society.

Bryant, R.A. and Harvey, A.G. (2000) How to diagnose acute stress disorder. In *Acute Stress Disorder: A Handbook of Theory, Assessment and Practice* (Ch. 4, pp. 43–58). Washington, DC: American Psychological Association.

Carrol, M. (2007) Coaching psychology supervision – Luxury or necessity? In S. Palmer and A. Whybrow (Eds.), *Handbook of Coaching Psychology a Guide for Practitioners* (pp. 431–448). Hove: Routledge.

Carroll, M. (2006) Key issues in coaching psychology supervision. *The Coaching Psychologist* 2(1): 4–8.

Cavanagh, M., Stern, L., and Lane, D.A. (2016) Supervision in coaching psychology: A systemic developmental psychological perspective. In D.A. Lane, M. Watts, and S. Corrie (Eds.), *Supervision in the Psychological Professions*. London: Open University Press.

Corrie, S. and Lane, D.A. (2010) *Constructing Stories Telling Tales: A Guide to Formulation in Applied Psychology*. London: Karnac.

Etherington, K. (2009) Supervising helpers who work with the trauma of sexual abuse. *British Journal of Guidance and Counselling* 37(2): 179–194.

Figley, C.R. (2002) *Treating Compassion Fatigue*. New York: Brunner-Routledge.

Grant, A.M. (2012) Australian coaches views on supervision: A study with implications for Australian coach education, training and practice. *International Journal of Evidence-Based Coaching and Mentoring* 10(2): 17–33.

Gray, D., Garvey, B., and Lane, D.A. (2016) *A Critical Introduction to Coaching and Mentoring*. London: Sage.

Hawker, D.M., Durkin, J., and Hawker, D.S.J. (2011) To debrief or not to debrief our heroes: That is the question, *Clinical Psychology and Psychotherapy* 18(6): 453–463.

House, R. and Loewenthal, D. (2008) *Against and for CBT: Towards a Constructive Dialogue?* Ross on Wye: PCCS Books.

Joseph, S. (2009) Growth following adversity: Positive psychological perspectives on posttraumatic growth. *Psychological Topics* 18(2): 335–344.

Joseph, S. (2012) *What Doesn't Kill Us: The New Psychology of Posttraumatic Growth*. New York: Basic Books.

Kleim, B., Wallot, F., and Ehlers, A. (2009) Are trauma memories disjointed from other autobiographical memories in posttraumatic stress disorder? An experimental investigation. *Behavioural and Cognitive Psychotherapy* 36(2): 221–234.

Knapp, P.C. (1897) Traumatic neurasthenia and hysteria. *Brain* 20(3): 385–406.

Lane, D.A. (2010) Coaching in the UK: An introduction to some key debates. *Coaching: An International Journal of Theory, Research and Practice* 3(2): 155–166.

Lane, D.A. (2011) Ethics and professional standards in supervision. In T. Bachkirova, P. Jackson, and D. Clutterbuck (Eds.), *Coaching & Mentoring Supervision: Theory & Practice* (pp. 91–107). Maidenhead: Open University Press.

Lane, D.A., Watts, M., and Corrie, S. (2016) *Supervision in the Psychological Professions: Building Your Own Personal Model*. London: Open University Press.

Langley, G.E. (2004) Serjeant Musgrave's disease. *Med Humanities* 30: 74–78.

Levers, L.L. (2012) Conclusion: An integrative systemic approach to trauma. In L.L. Levers (Ed.), *Trauma Counselling Theories and Interventions* (pp. 579–585). New York: Springer.

Linley, P.A. and Minhas, G. (2011) The strengths of the strength spotter: Individual characteristics associated with the identification of strengths in others. *International Coaching Psychology Review* 6(1): 6–15.

McNabb, S. (2011) One disaster after another: Building resilience in the trauma therapist and the role of supervision. In N. Tehrani (Ed.), *Managing Trauma in the Workplace*. London: Routledge.

Morrissette, P.J. (2004) *The Pain of Helping: Psychological Injury of Helping Professionals*. New York: Brunner-Routledge.

National Center for PTSD. *Trauma Screening Questionnaire*. www.ptsd.va.gov/professional/assessment/screens/tsq.asp (accessed 18/09/2019).

National Child Traumatic Stress Network. *Psychological First Aid*. www.nctsn.org/treatments-and-practices/psychological-first-aid-and-skills-for-psychological-recovery/about-pfa (accessed 18/09/2019).

Richens, M.T., Gauntlett, L., Tehrani, N., Hesketh, I., Weston, D., Carter, H., and Amlot, R. (2019) *Scoping Review: Early Post-Trauma Interventions in Organisations Final*

Report. Public Health England, The British Psychological Society, and College of Policing.

Spinelli, E. (2008) Coaching and therapy: Similarities and divergences. *International Coaching Psychology Review* 3(3): 241–249.

Taylor, A.J.W. and Lane, D.A. (Eds.) (1999) Psychological aspects of disasters: Issues for the 1990's. *British Journal of Guidance and Counselling, Special Issue* 19(1).

Tehrani, N. (2011) *Managing Trauma in the Workplace*. Hove: Routledge.

Tehrani, N. and Levers, L.L. (2016) Supervision for trauma: Working through the pain. In D.A. Lane, M. Watts, and S. Corrie (Eds.), *Supervision in the Psychological Professions: Building Your Own Personal Model*. London: Open University Press.

Tehrani, N., Osborne, D., and Lane, D.A. (2012) Restoring meaning and wholeness: The role of coaching after a trauma. *International Coaching Psychology Review* 7(2): 239–246.

Tuke, D.H. (1892) *A Dictionary of Psychological Medicine: Giving the Definition, Etymology and Synonyms of the Terms Used in Medical Psychology with the Symptoms, Treatment, and Pathology of Insanity and the Law of Lunacy in Great Britain and Ireland, Volume 2*. London: Churchill (reprinted by Hansebooks, 2016)

Turner, E. (2008) Hidden depths. *Coaching at Work* 3(5): 40–43.

World Health Organisation (2011) *Psychological First Aid: Guide for Field Workers*. https://apps.who.int/iris/bitstream/handle/10665/44615/9789241548205_eng.pdf;jsessionid=94BEA6DAAAF12946BD9D5F68728F6010?sequence=1 (accessed 18/09/2019).

Chapter 7

Diversity and coaching

Claudia Filsinger

Recently, organisations have focussed more on increasing workforce diversity, and many larger organisations have adopted diversity targets as board level strategic objectives. Coaching is often used by organisations as one of the interventions to increase workforce diversity. Common examples are coaching programmes for women to increase leadership gender diversity, often in combination with training and other development activities. The coaching objective is explicitly set to contribute to the organisation's diversity target (coaching **for** diversity) and the coaching is typically undertaken by coaches with a specialist diversity coaching practice (e.g. gender, BAME, LGBT). However, this chapter discusses both this sort of 'coaching **for** diversity', as well as the increasing diversity of the coaching field itself, which I will refer to as 'diversity **in** coaching'. First, I will explain in more detail what is meant with 'diversity **in** coaching'. Then I will evaluate the practice of 'coaching **for** diversity'. The chapter focuses on coaching provided in a work and career context, but I will also touch on coaching in health and education. Many of the ideas are also pertinent to life coaching.

A typical organisational, pre-millennium coaching assignment might look something like this: an external coach (often a former business executive) working with a senior executive (typically male) in a meeting room during regular coaching meetings over a time span. This is a generalisation, not always accurate.

Today, the field of coaching is much more diverse and one would need a rich collection of coaching scenarios to illustrate today's more diverse situation: an internal coach working with a colleague in another continent via remote technology; executive coaching taking place during a walk; robotic coaches or web-based coaching apps for teenagers; a teacher coaching their pupil; a health coach working in organisations with employees on giving up smoking or stress reduction; 30-minute one-off telephone emergency coaching available for all employees; a BAME manager coaching their diverse team; an external coach working with a female CEO. These examples illustrate the interrelationship of coaching **for** increased diversity and the increasing diversity **in** who is involved in coaching, and how and where it takes place. This has resulted in coaching becoming more accessible. Before discussing how coaching for increased diversity with individuals links to structural barriers to diversity in organisations, I shall explore five key aspects of the coaching field that are gradually becoming more diverse.

Diversity *in* coaching

Both coachees and coaches are coming from a wider range of backgrounds, and coaching is delivered in more various ways. This latter shift includes coaching session lengths and fewer sessions per coaching assignment. Further, the use of group coaching is increasing, making some types of coaching cheaper per head. Consequently, the economics and accessibility of coaching is changing. New opportunities are opening for remote coaching due to technology advances, including robotic and Artificial Intelligence (AI) technology. This widens coaching's geographical reach.

Before discussing these aspects of changing diversity within coaching in more detail, I want to consider why diversity is one of the emerging coaching conversations.

Table 7.1 Five key aspects of predicted diversity changes within coaching

	Traditional coaching	*Possible diverse future of coaching*
1. Coach	*Business or psychology background; general coaching training.*	*Coaches from diverse professional backgrounds; niche coaching training; accreditation; supervision use. Coaches from diverse groups.*
2. Coachee	*Senior executives; employees with performance issues; knowledge workers.*	*Clients from all diversity groups including more female, BAME, LGBT and disabled employees, from all life and career stages, including career returners, from a variety of industries and sectors; service users (e.g. health and education).*
3. Coaching technology	*In-person and some telephone coaching;*	*New virtual technologies; asynchronous e-coaching; coaching robots.*
4. Use of coaching	*In organisations; 1:1; external coach; business and executive coaching, multiple sessions; western countries.*	*Team and group coaching, peer coaching, manager-as-coach; internal coaching pools; specialist coaching offerings; coaching with service users (e.g. patients in health and students in education); global reach; variety of duration and number of coaching sessions including short and one-off sessions.*
5. Economics of coaching	*Expensive assignments with external coaches; informal purchasing of external coaching; little cost for internal coach training and coach supervision; small group of coaches working with a small group of executives.*	*Larger coach pool and increased demand for coaching; variety of coaching assignments; costs depending on modality and length of coaching assignments; formal (including some automated) purchasing of external coaching involving procurement department; increased cost for internal coach training and coach supervision.*

Organisational clients stress their aim to increase diversity, therefore any coaching, whether or not it is focused on one diversity dimension, must take the issue into account. For example, culture always influences coaching, even if coach and coachee share a cultural background (Abbott, 2010). This applies also to other diversity characteristics of both coachee and coach. If diversity is an important 'ingredient' for any type of coaching, it raises the question if the coach needs to be 'fluent' (i.e. building up specific knowledge) in individual diversity dimensions (e.g. disability) or if it is sufficient to have a general awareness of how diversity influences their work. I believe any coach must reflect on how their individual diversity characteristics influence their approach and relationships, for example through assumptions or potential stereotypes.

I explore this increasing diversity **within** the field of coaching later in the chapter and put forward an agenda for the future. First, I want to turn to the practice of coaching **for** increasing diversity.

Coaching *for* diversity

By coaching **for** diversity, I mean specialist coaches working with clients on diversity-related topics such as career development for under-represented employee groups. This takes place in organisations as part of employer diversity programmes, but also in private client career coaching. Often the specialist diversity coach matches their clients' diversity characteristics, e.g. LGBT and BAME coaches working with LGBT or BAME clients respectively.

Before we explore these practices in more detail, why has coaching **for** diversity grown as part of organisations diversity management practices and what are the common characteristics?

Kumra and Manfredi (2012) evaluated drivers for increased focus on diversity management. These were, starting from the top priority:

- legal compliance
- improving business performance by becoming a more diverse organisation
- the moral argument, based on social justice and equal opportunity principles

The moral argument is mentioned in several studies as an additional, but not priority driver (Kumra & Manfredi, 2012). However, if these drivers were purely based on a business case and financial outcomes it is questionable how committed organisations would be to them in economically difficult times. Therefore, diversity management and related practices, such as coaching to increase diversity, should focus on both increasing business performance and fostering social justice (Mor Barak, 2017).

Categorising coaching for diversity

Coaching for diversity is often focused on specific diversity characteristics protected by equality legislation. In the UK the Equality Act 2010 protects age, disability, gender reassignment, marriage and civil partnerships, pregnancy and maternity, race, religion or belief, sex and sexual orientation (Kumra & Manfredi, 2012). Most are so called 'broad-category-based diversity dimensions' around which diversity management is typically built to appeal to a wide range of employees and to achieve inclusivity, for example, through diversity programmes with a focus on ethnicity overall, rather than offering separate programmes for each minority ethnic group (Mor Barak, 2017). However, if 'difference' is too broadly defined the cause of socially disadvantaged groups could be hindered (Kumra & Manfredi, 2012). In addition, not all areas of diversity, for example obesity, are always protected by law.

Another approach to categorising diversity is more individualistic, factoring in any type of individual characteristic, with examples being education or tenure in an organisation. While this is an inclusive approach (everybody in the organisation falls under the diversity umbrella), this has been critiqued: treating all differences as equal can result in trivialising them and to an avoidance of identifying power inequalities and discrimination (Mor Barak, 2017).

Coaching for diversity therefore is affected by two opposing tensions: finding the right focus for diversity management; and the necessary pragmatism to offer viable interventions that facilitate the change needed to increase the diversity of an organisation.

Matching coach and coachee

In the areas of coaching **for** diversity, many specialist diversity coaches base their practice on their own experience and knowledge of diversity issues in organisational contexts. Indeed, studies on parental transition coaching programmes for women found that coaching approaches include a blend of coaching and mentoring – in other words the coach offered concrete advice based on personal knowledge (Cotter, 2012). Coachees found it helpful to be coached by another working parent who understood their challenges (Filsinger-Mohun, 2012). Studies in organisational coaching found that matching coach and coachee by shared experience (in professions or industries, knowledge and gender), mainly matters in the early phase of the coaching relationship to establish rapport (Jones, 2015; Wycherley & Cox, 2008).

Arguably there is an important difference between sharing industry or professional experience and sharing the experience of discrimination (which could result in a decision to make invisible diversity characteristics public by 'coming out'). Therefore, the case to match coach and coachee for diversity coaching programmes could be stronger than for general business coaching. However, this sort of matching when coaching for diversity, questions the fundamental assumptions of most coach training: if we can be coached best only by people like ourselves, traditional coach competences seem questionable. Further, it suggests a power inequality in that there is some dependency of the coachee on the specialist knowledge and experience of the coach that may limit the coachee's autonomy and the coach's ability to challenge. This could lead to collusion through common blind spots.

The pitfalls of collusion have been examined in both the field of coaching and coaching supervision. Collusion is defined as mutual self-congratulation that can lead to keeping learning sub-optimally comfortable (Bachkirova, Jackson, & Clutterbuck, 2011; Milne, Leck, & Choudhri, 2009). The cultural context of an organisation can also lead to a risk of collusion, therefore reflection on coaching should examine how the needs of critical stakeholders in the wider systemic context might be creating illusions, delusions and collusions in the coach and even the supervisor (Hawkins & Schwenk, 2011). Further, the coach will need to reflect on their own motivation for the coaching. For example, empathy and assumptions about the client's needs, based on the coach's own past experiences of discrimination might influence the coaching through the desire to be helpful. Bachkirova (2011) explored self-deception in coaching and proposes that some degree of collusion might be beneficial for mutual acceptance in the coaching relationship, but that it needs to be watched carefully. This points to the importance of self-reflection and supervision in this context.

Required knowledge in coaching for diversity

As coaching for diversity grows, so will the variety of required knowledge. At one end the coach will need knowledge of the specific field, as is described in the autism case study later in this chapter. At the other end of the spectrum, early coaching psychologists and counsellors often practiced successfully in industries and sectors they knew little about. The field of cross-cultural coaching helps evaluate the value of matching coach and coachee by diversity. The requirement of having subject knowledge of a national culture (for example a western coach working with clients from Asia) has been debated in the coaching literature. Since it is questionable how realistic it is to fully know or learn a culture (Egan, 2009; Passmore & Law, 2013), several authors stress the importance of considering context and systems for cross-cultural coaching (Abbott 2010; Hawkins & Smith, 2013; Plaister-Ten, 2009). Generally, coaches need to be aware if something is a universal human experience, for example how an emotion is experienced, or culturally specific (Egan, 2009). To perform effectively they don't need to have experienced cultural adaptation but need to be able to work in diverse settings, know how to leverage cultural differences and avoid cultural misunderstandings (Nieuwerburgh, 2017). In the literature it is proposed that diversity practitioners don't need to have experienced disadvantage or discrimination to be involved in diversity work, as creating inclusive organisations applies also to diversity work itself being open to everybody. Diversity specialists in a small UK study, suggest personal qualities and work experience qualified them for working in the diversity field rather than characteristics such as gender or ethnicity (Greene & Kirton, 2009). This is supported by the fact that some diversity dimensions may not be permanent, for example disability and age. Further, some dimensions are visible and therefore public, others are invisible and private. Some clients might not be self-aware (e.g. sexual orientation, mental health or culture) or may not want to categorise themselves (e.g. gender). And naturally, an individual's diversity characteristic will comprise multiple diversity dimensions. Hence even in the context of 'coaching **for** diversity' where specific diversity knowledge can be useful to align the coaching programme with the respective diversity objectives (e.g. to enable coachees to overcome structural barriers to diversity and to increase the participation of an under-represented employee group), the coach needs to follow good practice and principles of working with an individual. Giving space for the coaching relationship to develop and a focus on listening to allow individual coaching objectives to evolve can avoid the pitfall of the coaching being led by assumptions based on the coach's own experience and the need to help. If the coach doesn't share the diversity dimension of the coachee they can still have built up considerable knowledge and understanding through their coaching practice or research. As the debate currently focusses on the coach, it would be useful to research the coachee's perspective of being matched to a coach by diversity dimension.

To summarise this discussion on matching coach and coachee by shared diversity dimensions and the requirement of specialist knowledge, coaches generally need to be 'diversity intelligent' or 'fluent', and able to work successfully in diverse organisations. They require diversity proficiency through self-awareness, specialist knowledge for certain types of coaching, and skills to be able to work with and support diverse clients, including the ability to manage any unhelpful influence of their own diversity characteristic such as assumptions or collusion (Nieuwerburgh, 2017). Coaches need to consider their own experience and training and choose theoretical models that are suitable for a wide range of clients when developing their integrative approach to diversity in coaching (Stout-Rostron, 2017). Further they need to have a general understanding of the field of diversity and inclusion management to understand the wider context of their work.

Taking stock – where are we today with coaching for diversity in organisations?

Many authors have pointed out the importance for coaches to consider the wider system they are working in (Hawkins & Smith, 2013; Whittington, 2016). It is important for external and internal coaches in organisations to assess not just their personal diversity proficiency, but also the reality and ambitions of increasing diversity in their organisational context. The degree of 'diversity maturity' in organisations is . . . *very diverse!*

It will be good practice for external and internal coaches in organisations to diagnose the current state and ambitions of their clients' organisational context. Organisations that take diversity management seriously will have audit data and a general qualitative evaluation of their progress in achieving their diversity targets. As policies are only useful when lived, looking at the wider system involves studying the lived experience of coachees within an organisation and its internal groupings.

In the past, organisational goals often focused on improving equal opportunity, an approach focused on sameness and legislation. The more recent approach of diversity management is focussed on difference (Kumra & Manfredi, 2012). Organisations use coaching to support their diversity objectives (coaching **for** diversity), but the approaches and interventions used are on a spectrum. This ranges from 'fixing' individuals (e.g. career coaching and mentoring for underrepresented groups; legislation compliance training for managers to prevent the organisation being sued) to changing organisational culture (coaching and training the whole organisation on increasing diversity; identifying structural and cultural changes, e.g. recruitment and promotion practices). If structural barriers to organisational diversity are not removed there is a limit to the impact of individual approaches that is focussed on the individual can have, expressed well in the much-used metaphors of '*the glass ceiling, sticky floors and glass cliffs*'.

Organisations that initially embraced diversity and inclusion management focused on gender diversity. Female employees are typically the largest group of under-represented employees, and many studies support the business case globally for increasing women's participation in the labour market, specifically in leadership positions (e.g. McKinsey, 2017). The UK government increased attention on gender diversity to increase the nation's competitiveness, and multiple reports such as the Davies and Hampton-Alexander reviews have tracked progress of gender diversity at board level (Department for Business, Innovation and Skills 2011, 2015, 2017). Gender pay gap reporting was introduced in 2017 for organisations with more than 250 employees with the resulting need for action-planning to address issues at all seniority levels. In turn, the UK government has made clear recommendations for race equality (Equality and Human Rights Commission, 2017). The design of traditional, linear, organisational careers, and recruitment practices which advantaged white heterosexual men with stay-at-home wives, described as the 'Organization Man' (Whyte, 2000), does not just cause issues for women. Where data on the business impact is unavailable, certain groups have received less attention: diversity management has therefore often been equated with gender diversity management. There is a need to expand diversity practice more to all under-represented employee groups.

The following case study of coaching women, a relatively established and researched diversity practice evaluates how coaching for other diversity groups could be organised.

A case study of coaching for gender diversity

Coaching programmes for female staff are typically offered at specific career stages and life transitions. Its initial focus was on offering leadership development programmes to senior women (often the so called 'marzipan layer', women one level below the board) complemented with coaching. Research studies investigating such coaching programmes have found wide-ranging benefits for the individual women such as: creating a safe space; increase in confidence, self-awareness and authenticity; reflection on identity, legacy and quality of relationships; building career capital and career progression; (Bonneywell, 2017; Broughton & Miller, 2009; De-Valle, 2014; Worth, 2012).

Organisations increasingly recognise that gender diversity initiatives need to consider all career stages to ensure a healthy talent pipeline. Delamare (2016) explored how a short coaching intervention for female middle managers can help improve the key issue of women's career progression slowing down markedly beyond mid-level (Department for Business, Innovation and Skills, 2011). Women reported it as a rare opportunity to explore barriers to career progression; resulting in a broader mindset, feeling more comfortable about self-promotion, learning to manage careers as projects and taking practical next steps (Delamare, 2016). Early talent development programmes sometimes included coaching for female staff to alleviate issues rooted in early career behaviours such as women having lower career ambitions and career confidence (ILM, 2011). This concurs with reports from recruiters, of women limiting their job search by only applying when meeting all criteria.

Coaching is also used during life events impacting careers, in particular the parenting transition, as parenting breaks have been identified as career penalties. Maternity coaching developed in response to retention issues and to support the complex return transition after maternity leave. Benefits for employers and employees reported are: building confidence, employee loyalty and retention, sustainable working patterns, long-term career development, well-being and performance (Bussell, 2008; Cotter, 2016; Filsinger-Mohun, 2012; Vitzthum, 2016). Critical voices warn of maternity coaching placing the onus on the individual, disguising structural changes needed to improve support of working mothers in organisations (Brown & Kelan, 2013). This is supported by a mixed-method study which highlights the importance of involving line managers in maternity coaching (Cotter, 2016).

Recently, organisations have increased their efforts to retain working mothers by offering more maternity benefits and addressing some of the identified structural and cultural issues. While these benefits are appreciated, they can only partially address the individual and complex issues women encounter upon their return. An action research study, set in two large international companies, showed how maternity-return coaching complements these benefits (Vitzthum, 2016). The findings indicate that maternity-return coaching complements organisational maternity benefits by supporting mothers on an individual level that cannot be addressed otherwise.

Increasingly organisations recognise career returners as a talent pool and offer returnships which are predominantly taken up by women. Usually these programmes are supported by individual and/or group coaching (Filsinger & Gallacher, 2018). As career breaks present identity challenges, adaptability and identity development are important competencies for women returning to work and need to inform support interventions such as coaching before, during and after career breaks (Majid, 2015). Another emerging coaching practice is menopause coaching (Price & Taylor, 2013) and in the context of modern careers spanning longer and the promotion of active ageing in the workplace (Manfredi & Vickers, 2016), future research could explore gender difference in the transition into retirement and the potential role of coaching women in later career phases.

In summary, a review of existing research studies on coaching for gender diversity shows it has many benefits at an individual level and contributes to gender diversity objectives at an organisational level, e.g. through retention and career progression of female employees. Structural organisational support alone is limited and needs to be combined with individual interventions such as coaching: these help individuals make sense of complex challenges related to identity and authenticity. Using coaching and mentoring for certain groups simply to 'fix the individual', can divert effort from a true cultural shift and real commitment to become a diverse and inclusive organisation. In my view, combining organisational and individual measures to facilitate change is critical for mutual benefit.

Despite these benefits, businesses neglect the moral argument based on social justice for increasing diversity. It seems degrading that companies base environmental corporate responsibility activities on corporate values, whereas diversity is driven mainly by the business case and meeting legal requirements. A clear commitment to the moral argument for diversity and inclusion would lead to more focus on all areas of diversity, as it is much harder to dispute the social justice argument than the fast-changing numbers of a business case. Debates currently centre around managing talent pipelines, and the moral argument is often seen as 'naïve', although it is in line with many of the newer leadership and business models such as 'starting with the why, authentic leadership, servant leadership, ethical leadership, values- based leadership'. If the arguments for diversity and inclusion could be based more on a real commitment to social justice, coaching **for** diversity would be not be mainly be offered for an exclusive group of employees (typically senior, ready to move into leadership positions, critical to the company in the short term), but a wider range of diversity groups to achieve inclusivity at all levels of seniority.

Increasing diversity within the coaching field

I will now return to the five key aspects I set out at the beginning of the chapter for increasing the diversity of the coaching field itself (see Table 7.1).

In the last couple of decades more organisations have put resources behind diversity management and a larger community of full-time diversity and inclusion managers have emerged. Following this growth, what relevant changes can we see that impact on coaching now and in the future? Assuming most organisations will achieve, or at least progress towards, their diversity objectives what are the questions and debates that are emerging for any coaches or coaching types? Organisations are more diverse in terms of their employees, their business models and how they operate (e.g. agile working and increase of freelance workers instead of employees).

I   Coachees

Coachees are becoming more diverse because of changes in organisational practice and external factors such as demographics. In some countries the default retirement age has been abolished. This combined with increasing longevity means that coachees experience more transitions: the current three-stage lives (education, working, retirement) are expected to change into multi-stage lives (Gratton & Scott, 2017). Much recent research and debate looked at differences in work attitudes and communication preferences between different age groups. Changes in legislation and organisational practice concerning equality and flexible working regulations, as well as societal changes, have led to less linear careers, including career returns after long-term career breaks.

In parallel, the use of coaching has become more widespread to a larger population at all levels of seniority. This was facilitated by the increased use of internal coaches, manager-as-coach initiatives, team and group coaching and shorter (meaning cheaper) coaching interventions. Consequently, coachees are increasingly informed about coaching as they are more likely to have experienced it already (e.g. during their education) or even have been trained in it (albeit often during a short coaching skills course). This can reduce the power imbalance between coach and coachee during the contracting phase. Having increased experience of, and knowledge about, coaching allows the coachee to be more proactive when establishing the coaching relationship and setting coaching objectives with their own coach.

2   Coaches

Coaches that entered the field in the early days of executive coaching often came from related areas such as business consulting, HR, psychology, learning & development. Typically, they were knowledge workers in the later stages of their career.

Coach training programmes now attract attendees from a much more varied background and a wider age range. The number of universities and commercial providers offering coaching courses has increased, as has the in-house training of internal coaches and staff generally. Many alumni of these courses use coaching techniques in their day-to-day work, often with internal or external clients or service users, such as in education, health, the military and managers-as-coaches with their direct reports.

The need for all involved in coaching to be aware of how diversity informs their work has been discussed earlier. Assessment tools can accelerate awareness and are commonly used with clients. They can be helpful in coach's self-awareness. A tool that can raise awareness of unconscious bias is the *Harvard Implicit Association Test* (https://implicit.harvard.edu/implicit/).

Procurement departments are frequently involved in more formalised coaching contracts. Purchasers need to be aware of unconscious bias and diversity dimensions when making choices of coaching providers. Equally, coaching suppliers need to demonstrate not only their 'fluency' in diversity topics, but their own organisation's approach to diversity management. Large organisations demand their suppliers demonstrate they are committed to improve their diversity (e.g. PayPal). Therefore, coaching companies, who typically work with a pool of staff coaches and/or associates, need to practice diversity management actively in their own companies. Besides considering the diversity of the coaches, the diversity of those managing diversity and coaching inside organisations also needs to be considered. A review of small studies in 2009 found an indication that most diversity specialists (who typically commission diversity coaching programmes) within organisations in a small UK sample were white women (Greene & Kirton, 2009). Larger scale studies would need to confirm if this trend has since continued, but it serves as a reminder of the necessity to manage diversity within the wider community of diversity and coaching practice itself (including internal coaching programme managers, coaching supervisors and coach training facilitators).

3   Technology and coaching

This area is treated extensively in another chapter of this book. Briefly, there is a wide choice of technology that supports remote coaching across geographies, including telephone and internet-based applications. Some e-coaching offerings are delivered asynchronously, e.g. by email or texting. This is an established practice in mentoring, e.g. with secondary school students being mentored by business people. Technology advances in the areas of robotics and artificial intelligence (AI) have led to new application areas, and first trials using coaching robots are in place, e.g. computer-based mental health services such as the 'Woebot' for teenagers: an automated chatbot based on cognitive behavioural therapy (CBT) for young adults with symptoms of depression and anxiety. This is based on research in the therapy field but is positioned to the users as 'self-help' which I would align more with coaching. However, one issue that is counterproductive to the diversity agenda is the finding that coaching robots using AI technology tend to replicate biases (Gyton & Jeffsry, 2017).

4   Use of coaching

Coaching is used in increasingly different ways. Short coaching interventions, such as 30-minute phone or web-based coaching on demand, often called spot coaching, popcorn coaching or coaching on demand, are offered more widely. They reflect and support rapid organisational change and agile working, where everything cannot be planned. However, their use needs to be carefully evaluated to avoid giving light touch support when somebody needs a longer-term developmental relationship to achieve transformation. In addition, as they are less expensive they tend to be offered to all employees, while expensive 1:1 coaching programmes are the reserve of senior executives, which raises questions of social justice and equal commitment to developing employees at all levels and from all diversity groups.

In addition to 1:1 coaching, there is also an emerging use of team coaching (an existing team being coached together) and group coaching (coachees don't belong to the same team but are being coached together). As the workforce becomes increasingly diverse and spread out geographically, the body of knowledge on managing diverse and virtual teams could give some insights for coaching these teams. Further, the deep democracy model by Mindell is proposed for coaching diverse teams. It is based on the critical importance of acknowledging each voice and every feeling for the team to come to know itself and to resolve its issues (Stout-Rostron, 2017).

So far though, most coaching takes place 1:1, a coach working with one coachee. In some cases, this is extended to coaching the respective line manager, e.g. in parental transition coaching programmes that are aimed at supporting the transition into, and back from, parental leave. However, there are real opportunities for other ways of organising coaching. Examples include:

1   A 'many coaches coaching many coachees' model by refining large meetings and professional conferences. I feel disappointed when a large group of people with the same interests and extensive experiences are in one place, but peer coaching is not being used apart from incidental networking. In my view, there are missed opportunities for 'many to many' coaching at conferences and meetings by complementing expert speakers with facilitation of more interaction within the participants.

2   Secondly, 'many coaches coaching one person' is also an under-used model. Arguably, this is the most expensive coaching set-up, but is justified, for instance in the sales context if a person is critical to high value business transactions. In mentoring, having multiple mentors was found to be beneficial (Higgins & Thomas, 2001).

3   Another development is that many fields that primarily used advice-giving and clinical approaches are also adopting a coaching stance. These include mental health (e.g. the charity *Restore* offers career coaching for people with mental health problems), the rise of health coaching (NHS coaching in the areas of obesity, smoking and sexual health), career guidance (career counsellors in education are increasingly called career coaches) and education (schools and universities frequently train their teaching and student support staff in coaching).

4   Several voices encourage working more with emotions in coaching and coaching supervision (Duffel & Lawton-Smith, 2015, 2017). This is supported by Einzig (2017) who proposes coaches need to work in the future at a deeper emotional level. As clients are operating increasingly in a VUCA environment (volatile, uncertain, complex and ambiguous), coaches need to be more comfortable working with anxiety. Further, employers encourage their employees to bring their whole self to work and it can be expected that coachees are more transparent about their mental health issues with their employers, line managers and coaches.

The management of boundaries between coaching and clinical practices such as counselling has caused intense debate. Coaching bodies require coaches to recognise the limits of their competencies; coach training and coaching supervision are also focused on boundary management. However, Pick and Hall (2017) have pointed out that published codes of ethics are not clear enough and offered an alternative in form of a practical question set.

So, if coaches will work more with emotions and formerly clinical issues, what are the implications for coaching and coaching supervision training? Is there a place for courses combining coaching and clinical psychology? The emergence of the Integrative Coach-Therapists Association points in this direction (Pick & Hall, 2017). Crowe (2017) makes a case for using the strength of both coaching and psychology and proposes that the coach requires core competencies such as knowledge and practical application, relationship competencies and counselling/coaching skills. They also need meta-competencies such as reflective practice and scientist-practitioner principles.

In summary, the use of coaching is changing in terms of both of who is involved (one to one, one to many, many to many, many to one) and what the coaching is concerned with. This questions traditional boundaries to other interventions, in turn requiring new skills from and training for contemporary coaches.

5   Coaching economics

Forms of coaching enabled by technology, and shorter term or on-demand coaching, mean more affordable programmes can be offered to a wider group of populations in organisations, and in a wider range of contexts e.g. in the not-for-profit sectors. On the other hand, the greater percentage of coaching being undertaken by internal coach pools and managers-as-coaches means organisations increasingly spend resources on coach training, continuous development, coach supervision and administration of internal coaching pools and programmes. The aim of this move is often to decrease external coaching spend, but internal costs are frequently underestimated. It appears organisations typically combine internal coach pools with traditional external coaching to reap the benefits of both approaches e.g. using external executive coaching for their leaders or well-being coaching that requires specialist knowledge.

Large organisations increasingly buy coaching in a more formalised way, involving procurement departments, often on a global basis. This approach may decrease coaching costs for a buying organisation. However, creating extensive proposal documentation and managing lengthy sales cycles has made pitching for work expensive for coaching providers who are typically small companies or independent consultants. Some purchasers use online market places to automate procurement. It is questionable if automation is the right process to use for a specialist developmental service such as coaching. For example, a popular requirement is the need for the coach to be accredited by coaching bodies such as the International Coaching Federation (ICF), the Association of Coaching (AC) or the European Mentoring and Coaching Council (EMCC). While they aim to ensure the coach is fit to practice and adheres to a code of ethics, their limitations mean they don't always cover emerging forms of coaching. So, a company looking for a specialist provider for one-off emergency telephone coaching would find it difficult to find any that are accredited by frameworks that evaluate the competencies for building, maintaining and ending relationships over multiple coaching sessions. Calls have been made to move from a competency to a capability model (Bachkirova & Lawton-Smith, 2015) and the role of accreditation in the future will need further debate. The evaluation of coaching will also need to be revised to take diversity factors into account.

This section has set out an agenda for continuing coaching conversations in the areas of the diversity of coach and coachee, coaching technology, the use of coaching and coaching economics. The following case study on the use of coaching as part of an autism diversity programme brings together many of the strands just discussed.

Neurodiversity – an example of coaching in more diverse organisations

A good example of what both *coaching for diversity* and *coaching in more diverse organisations* means in practice for organisations, coaches and coachees, is the area of neurodiversity. This section covers two areas: first a brief discussion of dyslexia, followed by a case study of an autism diversity programme.

Dyslexia

Research and practice have increased understanding of how to support people with dyslexia in education and the workplace. Usually graduates now know if they are dyslexic when they start working, and many employers have changed their recruitment practices to ensure applicants with dyslexia have equal opportunities. Employees in later career stages might not realise they are dyslexic and have often experienced discrimination in recruitment processes and career progression. This is an example where knowledge about a diversity dimension is useful for any coach and suggests coaches should have some knowledge about dyslexia, so they can adapt their way of working with coachees with dyslexia; for example, in how they use paperwork pre-, during and in-between sessions or adapt how they organise working with thoughts and ideas during coaching. Such coaches might be able to spot undiagnosed dyslexia in a client and refer for an assessment. Lockett (2017), an academic with dyslexia, advocates focussing less on what people with dyslexia can't do, more on what they can do – an alignment with strengths-based coaching approaches and the general aim of supporting coaching clients in fulfilling their potential.

Autism

From 2013 the global software company SAP pioneered this strengths-based diversity approach by integrating people with autism into the workforce through an international *Autism at Work* Programme. Colleagues with autism are provided with a support ecosystem made up of line managers, buddies and mentors. Coaching complements this, bridging work and home life through an external job-and-life skills coach. This is in line with recommendations in the literature of individualised off- and on-the-job coaching to develop strengths and support development areas for employees with autism (Lorenz & Heinitz, 2014). This holistic approach to coaching evolved out of a specific context, moving away from the traditional differentiation between business and life coaching. While the job-and-life skills coaches mainly coach employees with autism, they are available to work with everybody who is in contact with an *Autism at Work* participant. Hence the coach is not just working in the traditional 'coaching pair' relationship, but also on demand with colleagues holding different roles in the wider support ecosystem. This is an example of a systemic approach in using coaching, which is of increasing importance (Hawkins & Smith, 2013; Whittington, 2016).

However, this sort of arrangement can challenge confidentiality for the coach, an issue which should be considered carefully when implementing such a programme. Furthermore, it links to the earlier discussion on the requirement for knowledge of diversity dimensions. Knowledge of autism can help the coach to support coachees with autism in communicating effectively. Indeed, one of the roles for the job-and-life coach is to translate social situations and expectations to coachees with autism and therefore equip them to communicate in unfamiliar situations. SAP has an internal coach pool that is open to all employees and it encourages managers to adopt a coaching style with all employees. Cognitive behavioural therapy (CBT, out of which many popular coaching tools evolved) is used widely with adolescents and adults with autism (Attwood, 2004), so could inform coaching employees with autism. This has implications for internal coach training and contracting with external coaching providers. Rogers (2016) suggests it is important to set realistic expectations what coaching can achieve when coaching clients with autism – a useful reminder of the general importance of having a robust approach to contracting with the coachee and the organisation.

Several companies understand the business case for recruiting employees with autism to create competitive advantage (Austin & Pisano, 2017). In summary, the SAP case study points to several important questions organisations committed to diversity generally need to ask themselves. Thais Catarino, HR Business Partner and manager of the SAP Autism at Work Program in Brazil (who is also a professional coach at SAP) poses the following questions:

1   How accessible are both internal and external coaching – is it available to all employees?
2   How do we equip all to coach a diverse workforce that includes colleagues who are differently abled, disabled or have medical conditions?
3   What is the role of coaching to support managers of diverse teams – how can they be supported with specialist knowledge, in a crisis or with daily challenges?

Continuing coaching conversations

This chapter has summarised the key conversations on diversity in coaching for five key aspects of coaching practice. A broad approach was taken by evaluating coaching *for* diversity (coaching programmes with a specific focus on increasing organisational diversity) as well as discussing the increasing diversity *in* any type of coaching. I presented case studies on using coaching to increase gender diversity and innovative ways of using coaching as part of an autism diversity programme. These draw out transferable knowledge for other coaching contexts. In the future, I expect the diversity and diversity intelligence of core parties involved in coaching, and different sorts of coaching will increase. We need to ensure the consideration of diversity in the wider ecosystem of coaching practice. The key fields here are: coach training; coach accreditation frameworks; coach supervision; supervisor training; coaching programme management and administration; coaching procurement and coaching evaluation such as return on investment studies. Measures of coaching effectiveness need to be revised to take the increasing diversity of coaching into account. Further, we need to look more at coaching supervision, often seen as a 'nice to have' in internal coaching programmes rather than as essential. It is often overlooked in the budgeting process, but everything I have discussed points to the increased importance of supervision.

Coaching research needs to become much more diverse. It needs to follow as coaching uses expand to new contexts such as in education and clinical settings. However, it can be difficult to design studies which comply with ethical standards when they involve service users. Existing coaching research is mainly based on knowledge workers in the West and tends to focus on coaches as they are easier to access than coachees. Consequently, organisations need to support coaching research to increase its diversity by giving access to their employees e.g. through partnering with external researchers such as academic or private research institutions. Organisations could undertake their own research projects as part of their strategy, as indeed many organisations possess internal research skills that can be applied. Naturally, research designs should factor in diversity.

New opportunities for coaching could arise out of new technologies such as AI, Machine Learning and robotics. This is dealt with in Chapter 9 in this book.

Overall, it can be expected that specialist diversity coaching aimed at increasing an organisation's diversity and the diversity in coaching itself both continue to increase. I expect we will continue to see a rise in interventions and services called 'coaching' that wouldn't have been labelled as such in the past. Publications debating what coaching is and isn't were already plentiful at a time when coaching was relatively homogenous. Many will question if some of the emerging forms of coaching should be called coaching, but the fact is that the providers have deliberately chosen to position them as coaching, so we need to continue to question our assumptions of what coaching can be. Therefore, it is imperative that the debates, research and knowledge exchange in the field of diversity and coaching continues.

References

Abbott, G. (2010). Cross cultural coaching. In E. Cox, T. Bachkirova, & D. Clutterbuck (Eds.), *The Complete Handbook of Coaching* (pp. 324–340). London, England: Sage.

Attwood, T. (2004). Cognitive behaviour therapy for children and adults with Asperger's syndrome. *Behaviour Change*, 21(3), 147–161.

Austin, R., & Pisano, G. (2017). Neurodiversity as competitive advantage. *Harvard Business Review*, 95(3), 96–103.

Bachkirova, T. (2011). *Developmental Coaching*. Maidenhead, England: McGraw Hill.

Bachkirova, T., & Lawton-Smith, C. (2015). From competencies to capabilities in the assessment and accreditation of coaches. *International Journal of Evidence Based Coaching and Mentoring*, 13(2), 123–140.

Bachkirova, T., Jackson, P., & Clutterbuck, D. (2011). *Coaching & Mentoring Supervision*. Maidenhead, England: Open University Press/McGraw Hill.

Bonneywell, S. (2017). How a coaching intervention supports the development of female leaders in a global organization. *International Journal of Evidence Based Coaching and Mentoring*, Special Issue 11, 57–69.

Broughton, A., & Miller, L. (2009). *Encouraging Women into Senior Management Positions: How Coaching Can Help. An International Comparative Review and Research*. Brighton: IES.

Brown, S., & Kelan, E. (2013). *Managing Maternity: Maternity Coaching, Therapeutic Culture and Individualisation*. Paper presented at the 13th Annual Conference of the British Academy of Management, Liverpool.

Bussell, J. (2008). Great expectations: Can maternity coaching affect the retention of professional women? *International Journal of Evidence Based Coaching and Mentoring*, Special Issue 2, 14–26.

Cotter, K. (2012). *Plugging the Brain Drain: A Study Into the Longer-term Impact of Maternity Coaching*. Dissertation submitted as part requirement for the Master of Arts in Life, Business, and Executive Coaching Worcester University.

Cotter, K. (2016). *Attitudes of Line Managers, HR Leaders and Coachees Towards Maternity Coaching*. Study undertaken in part completion of Doctorate in Psychotherapy, Middlesex University, England.

Crowe, T. (2017). Coaching and psychotherapy. In T. Bachkirova, G. Spence, & D. Drake (Eds.), *Handbook of Coaching* (pp. 85–101). London, England: Sage.

Delamare, T. (2016). *Unblocking the Talent Pipeline: An Action Research Study into Coaching for Mid-Level Women to Develop and Progress their Careers*. MA Dissertation, Oxford Brookes University.

Department for Business, Innovation and Skills. (2011). *Women on Boards*. London, England.

Department for Business, Innovation and Skills. (2015). *Women on Boards: 5-Year Summary*. London, England.

Department for Business, Innovation and Skills. (2017). *Hampton-Alexander Review: FTSE Women Leaders*. London, England.

De-Valle, P. J. (2014). *An Exploration of Executive Women's Experiences of Coaching and Mentoring: An Interpretaive Phenomenlogical Analysis Study*. Doctoral Dissertation, Oxford Brookes University.

Duffel, P., & Lawton-Smith, C. (2015). The challenges of working with emotion in coaching. *The Coaching Psychologist*, 11(1), 32–41.

Duffel, P., & Lawton-Smith, C. (2017). Once more with feeling. *Coaching at Work*, 12(3), 36–40.

Egan, G. (2009). *The Skilled Helper* (9th ed.). Belmont, Australia: Brooks/Cole.

Einzig, H. (2017). *The Future of Coaching*. Abingdon, England: Routledge.

Equality and Human Rights Commission. (2017). *A Roadmap to Race Equality*. London, England.

Filsinger, C., & Gallacher, G. (2018). Career returners – How to tap into an increasingly important talent pool. *Future of Work Hub*. Retrieved from www.futureofworkhub.info

Filsinger-Mohun, C. (2012). How can maternity coaching influence women's re-engagement with their career development? *International Journal of Evidence Based Coaching and Mentoring*, Special Issue 6, 46–56.

Gratton, L., & Scott, A. (2017). *The 100-Year Life: Living and Working in an Age of Longevity*. London, England: Bloomsbury.

Greene, A., & Kirton, G. (2009). *Diversity Management in the UK*. Abingdon, England: Routledge.

Gyton, G., & Jeffsry, R. (2017). These are the experts deciding the future of HR . . . . . . shouldn't you know who they are? *People Management*, August, 25–31.

Hawkins, P., & Schwenk, G. (2011). The seven-eyed model of coaching supervision. In T. Bachkirova, P. Jackson, & D. Clutterbuck (Eds.), *Coaching & Mentoring Supervision* (pp. 28–40). Maidenhead, England: McGraw Hill.

Hawkins, P., & Smith, N. (2013). *Coaching, Mentoring and Organizational Consultancy – Supervision, Skills & Development*. Maidenhead, England: McGraw Hill.

Higgins, M. C., & Thomas, D. A. (2001). Constellations and careers: Toward understanding the effects of multiple developmental relationships. *Organizational Behaviour*, 22(3), 223–247.

ILM. (2011). *Ambition and Gender at Work*. London, England: The Institute of Leadership and Management.

Jones, C. W. (2015). *Choosing Your Coach: What Matters and When. An Interpretative Phenomenological Exploration of the voice of the Coache*. PhD, Oxford Brookes University.

Kumra, S., & Manfredi, S. (2012). *Managing Equality and Diversity*. Oxford, England: Oxford University Press.

Lockett, N. (2017). *Disability on Campus: 'I Have Decided to Go Public as the Dyslexic Professor'*. Retrieved from www.timeshighereducation.com.

Lorenz T., & Heinitz, K. (2014). Aspergers – different, not less: Occupational strengths and job interests of individuals with Asperger's syndrome. *PLoS One*, 9(6).

Majid, N. (2015). *An Exploration of Professional Women's Experiences of Taking Career Breaks and the Implications for Career Identity*. Research Project as part of MSc Occupational Psychology, Birkbeck College, University of London.

Manfredi, S., & Vickers, S. (2016). *Challenges of Active Ageing*. Basingstoke, England: Palgrave Macmillan.

McKinsey (2017). *Women Matter: Time to Accelerate*. London, England.

Milne, D. L., Leck, C., & Choudhri, N. Z. (2009). Collusion in clinical supervision: Literature review and case study in self-reflection. *Cognitive Behaviour Therapist*, 2(2), 106–114.

Mor Barak, M. (2017). *Managing Diversity* (4th ed.). Thousand Oaks, CA: Sage.

Nieuwerburgh, C. (2017). Interculturally sensitive coaching. In T. Bachkirova, G. Spence, & D. Drake (Eds.), *Handbook of Coaching* (pp. 439–452). London, England: Sage.

Passmore, J., & Law, H. (2013). Cross-cultural and diversity coaching. In J. Passmore (Ed.), *Diversity in Coaching – Working with Gender, Culture, Race and Age* (2nd ed., pp. 1–11). London, England: Kogan Page.

Pick, L., & Hall, L. (2017). Coaching in a crisis. *Coaching at Work*, 12(3), 25–31.

Plaister-Ten, J. (2009). Towards greater cultural understanding in coaching. *International Journal of Evidence Based Coaching and Mentoring*, Special Issue 3, 64–81.

Price, D., & Taylor, T. (2013). Time of your life. *Coaching at Work*, 9(1), 32–36.

Rogers, J. (2016). *Coaching Skills* (4th ed.). Maidenhead, England: Open University Press/ McGraw Hill Education.

Stout-Rostron, S. (2017). Working with diversity in coaching. In T. Bachkirova, G. Spence, & D. Drake (Eds.), *Handbook of Coaching* (pp. 238–255). London, England: Sage.

Vitzthum, C. (2016) *How Can Maternity-Return Coaching Complement Structural Organisational Benefits?* MA Dissertation, Oxford Brookes University.

Whittington, J. (2016). *Systemic Coaching and Constellations*. London, England: Kogan Page.

Whyte, W. (2002). *The Organization Man*. Philadelphia, PA: University of Pennsylvania Press.

Worth, S.A. (2012). *An Exploration of Coaching Women Towards Authenticity in the Workplace: A Heuristic Study with Women in Academia. Ph.D Thesis*, Oxford Brookes University.

Wycherley, I., & Cox, E. (2008). Factors in the selection and matching of executive coaches in organisations. *Coaching: An International Journal of Theory, Research and Practice*, 1(1), 39–53.

Chapter 8

(Neuro)coaching

Hamira Riaz

If media interest is anything to go by, neuro-stuff continues to hold public imagination in thrall[1–3], much as it's done since the turn of the century. This brave new world of "brain science" promises an original understanding of what it means to be human, potentially furnishing coaches with a game-changing perspective on clients, colleagues and themselves. But has it lived up to the hype? In this chapter, we will explore two brain-behaviour disciplines, neuropsychology and neuroscience, to understand their potentialities and limits – and to establish where neurosubstance ends and neuro-myth begins.

It is more than ten years ago now since I first came across a book written by a marketing professional that cited fMRI studies of brain activation on viewing images of popular global brands. The intensity of activation when a person saw their favorite brands was reported as comparable to that of priests viewing religious symbols! The implications were painted as obvious and thrilling. Brain imaging could be used to test the commercial viability of products in development. Less implicitly stated but perhaps important from a psychological perspective, by tapping into what most excited consumer brains at a synaptic level, neuroscience offered companies a fresh take on the "buy-sell" dynamic[4].

This got my attention, why? Firstly, as a neuropsychologist by background, my initial reaction was that fMRI protocols must have progressed a fair way since my time in clinical practice, when they were clunky at best. Secondly, now working at a global leadership consultancy, I was interested in the value this could add to my coaching conversations with corporate clients. Thirdly, throughout my career, the unconscious had suffered from a shady reputation – the dominant paradigm in psychology had for decades favored conscious processing and rational thoughts. And now, in 2008, here was the subterranean brain making a surprise appearance; it was being re-introduced into good society through the back door!

And finally, a very personal reason: I had moved from clinical psychology to business psychology in 2004 when that was still relatively rare. Indeed, colleagues on either side of the divide had been quick to express their reservations; my sanity had been questioned. Clinical and Occupational are held as different and distinct branches of the psychology tree. I felt alone in having a foot in both camps. This book was a potential bridge-builder – in proposing that a clinical approach was applicable within a corporate setting, it validated the hybrid me! My excitement didn't last long.

When it comes to psychology, coaching and life, I have come to realise that I am inherently epistemological, in the sense that I am first and foremost interested in *knowledge about knowledge*. Before I admit data, facts, theories or models into my worldview, I want to know how they have come into being. This includes understanding (as much as is possible) the minds and motivations of authors, not to mention their operating milieu. And so, when I started digging into the afore-mentioned book, it simply didn't stack up. Before you carry on, reader, it is only fair to state that over the years, my epistemic bar has been raised to the point that I am somewhat allergic to knowledge presented as "new". At this point, Hogan practitioners might suspect an elevated score on the HDS "skeptical" scale and they'd be right.

Defining the parameters

If you ask Alexa for definitions of neuropsychology, cognitive psychol-ogy, neuroscience, comparative neuropsychology, cognitive science, etc., it's quickly apparent that they suffer from being 20th century newcomers, inasmuch as, there is no clear consensus on the centre ground/outer limits of their respective fields of inquiry, the areas of overlap, and therefore how they ought to relate to each other. These unresolved identity issues notwithstand-ing; in a relatively short space of time, each tribe has generated big literatures within self-defined, often hotly debated, frames of reference using increas-ingly abstract, bespoke vocabularies. As in many other walks of life, this cre-ates a headache for the more holistically minded, because it makes the job of "joining up the dots" that much harder, begging the question, how does one navigate this new frontier?

I'd like to suggest that coaches go back to the fundamentals and use two com-pass points; firstly, the *lens on human experience* provided by these specialist fields, and secondly, whether and to what extent this is *relevant* to their clients' presenting concerns. By way of demonstration, let's use this approach to consider the fields of Neuropsychology and Neuroscience within coaching contexts.

Neuro-psychology

This term doesn't feature in psychology nomenclature until the 1930s; essentially, it concerns relationships between the structure and function of the brain. Ancient inquiry centred on establishing the "seat of the soul" (in the head or heart) and it wasn't until the late 19th century that psychology was seen as distinct from philos-ophy. By this time, whereas phrenology was the fad (correlating the size/shape of the brain with intelligence and personality), it was localisation approaches (stud-ies linking specific brain lesions to cognitive functions) that eventually paved the way for modern neuropsychology.

The day job of a practicing neuropsychologist largely involves deciphering the real-world applications of data from standardised tests designed to ascertain the integrity of memory, language, attention, perception, etc. For a taste of what such a life entails, look no further than this series of papers[5], which interrogate some of the many issues involved in inferring visuospatial functioning from results on the "block design" subtest of perhaps the most famous neuropsychological battery of all – the Wechsler Intelligence Scale. If neuropsychology comes across as a time-heavy, micro-detailed, painstakingly rigorous process fraught with bias-laden rabbit holes and interpretative booby-traps; that is because it is.

Neuropsychologists are in essence assessment specialists; as such, they often operate in multi-disciplinary teams within clinical diagnostic services, rehabilitation centres and research programmes. When psychometric data is considered alongside brain images, specific structures of the brain may be implicated. In repeating assessments using parallel versions of the same neuropsychological tests over time, the degree of improvement or degradation of brain function can be inferred. By including performance on effort tests in the assessment process, judgments can be made about whether the individual is showing up authentically and at their best, and therefore if brain functions are being accurately gauged.

Neuropsychology looks at human experience through the lens of individual responses to a series of paper-and-pencil or computerized tests of cognitive function. To accept that the neuropsychologist has done all the due diligence necessary to get a "true" result, we would need to be convinced that the appropriate tests have been used in an appropriate manner and the data has been interpreted within the context of extraneous performance issues (such as boredom, fatigue, distraction, intentional deception for the purposes of material gain, etc.).

Professional reputations are built on the ability of a practitioner to convincingly justify their choice, administration and reading of cognitive test scores. Clinical neuropsychologists make public most of the information used to establish the veracity of their judgments, in their reports, and in the case of medico-legal proceedings are required to do so. Wherever possible, the aim is to triangulate psychometric scores with third-party witness accounts of cognitive deficits affecting everyday life. Each step of the process from scores to summary conclusion needs to stand up to the scrutiny of peers. Fortunately for us, this ethos of making inferences only as far as the data extends is characteristic of most research activity too. Abstracts tend to be iterative, conservative and chock full of caveats. The downside is that neuropsychological research is devoid of glamorous strap-lines and has a turgid quality that is palatable only to true enthusiasts.

Then, there remains the issue of whether neuropsychology is relevant to coaching practice. In the 15 years since I have been a coach, my neuropsychology background has been materially important in my dealings with clients a handful of times. For example, the clinical alarm bell in my head has sounded when I have wondered if the person sitting opposite me was drinking so heavily as to impair his recall memory of our previous conversations. For the most part, my clinical roots come into play in the form of psycho-education, for example, when a client informed me of a diagnosis with MND, I could talk him through the cognitive changes he could expect in the journey ahead to help plan his exit from work. Or when clients bring work-life imbalance concerns into the room and the root stressor is coping with children diagnosed with learning difficulties or an elderly parent who's had a stroke.

However, there is a growth area in neuropsychology – the "walking wounded". These are folk who have had some kind of neurological incident (for example, a fall from a bicycle resulting in a minor concussion), which they pinpoint, as the start of their struggles but in the absence of evident structural damage to the brain. Memory lapses, concentration problems, reductions in verbal fluency, brain freezes and disorientation – this sort of symptomology is a murky area for health providers, because it sits in the hinterland of well-being and fitness, mental health and physical health, especially in the case of previously high performing individuals. In searching for a diagnosis, these folk can become the proverbial "revolving door" patients, looking for answers before the question has been properly formulated.

In my view, integrated, early stage neuropsychology-coaching advice for the walking wounded would prevent unnecessary, counter-productive medical input and curtail spiralling anxiety as individuals and their families grapple with that feeling that life is spinning out of control. Where a clinical neuropsychologist can establish whether and to what extent cognitive deficits are clinically significant in a controlled test environment, an executive coach is able to contextualise the consequences of performance variability at home and in the office. A working dialogue between the two fields would make it easier for both sets of professional to help clients make sense of their experience, normalise concerns where appropriate and advise remediation strategies with sufficient levels of conviction that there is no magic pill cure and that their recommendations represent the best available way forward.

To my mind, this reaffirms the core strength of neuropsychology as a discipline in its own right. When MRI scanners first became affordable tools of clinical inquiry in the 1980s, it was heralded as the end of neuropsychology. Why put a person through hours of psychometric tests to infer brain damage when sophisticated imaging could identify previously undetectable structural changes in a fraction of the time? Answer – because neuropsychological deficits can presage structural changes in the brain in certain conditions, for example, in the onset of dementia[6]. I would argue, that sometimes the only external validation of perceived problems in the walking wounded is a score that marks them out as falling within the clinical range compared to a demographically matched norm group (usually <5th percentile for age and socio-educational background).

And therein also lies the rub: If you really want to get picky, the Achilles heel of neuropsychology lies in the very idea of norm groups. If psychometrics had an Olympics, the aforementioned Wechsler batteries would win the gold medal for norm groups, hands down. Wechsler manuals are hundreds of pages long, table after table of reliability and validity statistics; truly elegant constructions but flawed because of the ideology that sits at the heart of neuropsychological testing. Most of them are birthed in the West in the English language, including the inherent cultural blind spots (just one word for love – really![7,8]) with norm groups that are self-selected (very often participants responding to adverts paying them to take part in research) and therefore skewed from the start. English items are translated, often without the rigour that such an exercise demands. I can say this because my doctorate thesis was an evaluation of an Urdu translation of the short version of the General Health Questionnaire, and its 28 items threw up a host of philological issues – not least of which was what to do when a symptom of anxiety has no obvious conceptual equivalent in the destination language[9]? Is it meaningful to translate it at all? Answers on a postcard please.

Then, there is the issue of what finds its way into the public domain and why. For a good example of a "battle of the brains" in neuropsychology, look no further than the brawl between proponents of IQ (Intelligence Quotient, as most commonly measured with, yes you guessed it – the Wechsler tests) and RQ (Rationality Quotient)[10]. Keith Stanovich has long been arguing that even the best IQ tests do not comprehensively tap the cognitive domains, because they neglect the processing errors and unconscious biases of the human brain, brought so compellingly to life by Noble Laureate, Daniel Kahneman[11]. The upshot being that intelligence is just one side of the coin, rationality being the other. It is a sobering fact that Stanovich and Kahneman, both heavyweights in their field, have spoken about the role played by prevailing political winds in the making of reputations, research programme sponsorship, academic publication success and test development.

In summary then, the defining strengths of neuropsychological testing have a dark side, the very notion that a set of psychometric scores positions a person within a "normal" or "clinical" range can't be assumed and requires more air-time than it gets. Add to this, the issue that some constructs being measured may not translate meaningfully across cultures and languages, and that the vested interests of established players may be unduly driving developments in the field rather than the science, and neuropsychology is facing a difficult set of existential questions in the 21st century, but it is not alone in that.

Neuro-science

For me, neuroscience is to neuropsychology as Marilyn Monroe is to Bette Davies; one bright, shiny, appealing, relatable and sexy, the other challenging, cool, distant, not easy to get along with or easy on the eye. But look under the surface and the differences dissolve. Both women were part of the same system but consciously chose to play their parts differently. Bette presented the idea of woman in all its complexity, no holds barred, warts and all. Marilyn parodied the idea of woman and gave the system the "ideal" it had always wanted, with a cherry on top. However, Bette is remembered as transparent, direct – she stayed unashamedly authentic as she aged and outlived most of her peers. Marilyn is memorialised as a mystery as yet unsolved – she struggled to reconcile what she projected to the world with who she really was and spectacularly self-sabotaged in her prime. And this may end up being the fate for neuroscience too, time will tell.

Try putting your finger on what neuroscience is and it becomes whatever you want it to be – a chimera. On the outside, it offers the best seats in the house; as human emotions are felt and thoughts formulated. It threatens to bare our "real" reactions to the world, not by way of post-hoc rationalised responses, but unadulterated activations, before there's been time to put words around them or defences kick in about what's appropriate to disclose. Neuroscience in this guise presents itself as pure, almost virginal. It is so tempting to believe that after a century of looking for it, we have finally found the holy grail – a portal into the psyche.

But on the inside, neuroscience is based on technology that is quite frankly dehumanising. It is difficult to get across just how much, unless you have experienced it. I wonder how many neuroscience enthusiasts have been inside an MRI scanner for brain imaging. I have, several times, and I've counselled patients going through pre-operative scanning many more besides. Locked into a heavy skullcap, you slide deep into the narrow tubular machine, the dimensions of which may well trigger till then latent claustrophobia. Your head must be kept completely still for long stretches at a time because the image is so easily corrupted. It is so noisy that even with earplugs in, your head soon starts to throb. And this, when all you are required to do is nothing.

MRI protocols in neuroscience research are a variation on the same theme; participants are asked to look at or listen to a series of stimuli, and to respond by pressing button(s) on a manual console. It surely remains one of the most inhospitable places on earth in which to demonstrate sentience. Not to mention that our responses to isolated stimuli inside a scanner have near zero ecological validity, because in the real world, we are incessantly flooded with inputs and therefore constantly filtering what is deemed important to us by brain systems that largely have autonomous control of our executive functions and attentional resources. And yet, we are asked to accept that how people respond to carefully selected samples of pictures and sounds inside a scanner is an uncontaminated reflection of their innermost functional states. I confess I struggle to believe. But then, I am dubious by nature and disbelief comes easily to me. So, let's not write it all off without further consideration.

As for the lens that it provides on human experience, neuroscience is nothing if not a kaleidoscopic phenomenon. There are strands of neuroscience endeavor that do suck me in; the type of research that's harder to condense into splashy media headlines. I remain enamored with studies that have demonstrated grey and white matter changes in the brains of novices after a few weeks of juggling[12], I have an abiding affection for studies that show hippocampal plumping in taxi drivers learning "the Knowledge"[13], and I can't get enough of work that shows how much adolescent brains sprout and self-arborize during puberty[14].

In short, I love the idea of neuroplasticity across the life span – it is such a delightful and hopeful neuroscience discovery, not least because I am 50+ and not ready to resign myself to decaying brainpower just yet. But this type of neuroscience has been allotted a place in my heart for another reason – because it conducts itself like other sciences I trust. And like most neuropsychologists, these neuroscientists are humble and transparent in the way they acknowledge the theoretical assumptions made in generating hypotheses, justify their choice of methodologies, situate their work in extant knowledge and qualify the conclusions reached. In short, they have form.

We can't ignore the fact that we live in a world where in a matter of mouse clicks, a single study can parachute into the public domain dressed up as a genuine new discovery. Here, I am veering into the territory of how science is reported in modern day times. The first exhaustive look at this makes compelling reading[15], in particular, the perils of "neuro-realism", whereby coverage of fMRI findings renders the "phenomenon uncritically real, objective or effective in the eyes of the public". Bottom line – if you want people to believe that your story is based on substantive science, liberally sprinkle with some neuro-dust! Before you know it, you may be influencing policy decisions for decades to come[16].

But if neuroscience is not to go the way of politics post-spin and journalism post–fake news, bona fide neuroscientists must take more control of the narrative, and in so doing, wrest power from slick-sounding pseudo-scientists whose commitment to the scientific process starts and finishes with the investment they can attract, the IP they can commoditize, the interventions they can sell to naive clients and the public profiles they can build for themselves.

In terms of the lens on the human experience provided by neuroscience, as an executive coach, I wholeheartedly accept that a technology that was originally designed to show us the microstructure of the brain is shedding light on how the cellular composition of the brain changes over time. It's the permutation of imaging as a window on human functioning that I still have a problem with. Too often neuroscience findings about complex emotion states such as empathy, or multi-dimensional constructs such as leadership, are emphatically reported as meeting the benchmark for scientific fact. But look at the original imaging studies and you will find they come laden with phrases such as "may be associated with", "could be linked to", found to be related to". And there is a very good reason for that.

Slightly to the left of the world of brain imaging is the world of brain simulation. Rewind to 2014 when the multi-billion Human Brain Project (with the overarching aim of building a complete computer simulation of the brain) was signed off. Hundreds of neuroscientists from across the world signed The Open Letter to the European Commission expressing concerns that the project was ill defined, if not misguided. You would think that the debacle that followed[17] would wake everyone up to the fact that **we don't know how bits of the brain give rise to the doings of the brain!**

I'm sorry to burst the bubble for neuroscience fans but we remain clueless about how clumps of brain cells are related to even the simplest of cognitive tasks. Prof. Gary Marcus crystallises this beautifully:

> we know that there must be some lawful relation between assemblies of neurons and the elements of thought, but we are currently at a loss to describe those laws. We don't know, for example, whether our memories for individual words inhere in individual neurons or in sets of neurons, or in what way sets of neurons might underwrite our memories for words, if in fact they do[18].

Oft-quoted Prof. Susan White sums it up for me: "Functional brain imaging is like trying to understand how a complex organisation works by measuring the electricity usage in different rooms"[19]. It is about time that serious questions were asked about the integrity of neuroscience methodology itself, and thank goodness, that is starting to happen. YongWook Hong's investigations into false positive neuroimaging being a case in point[20].

So, it's not that academics haven't pointed this out time and time again[21], or that we lack outspoken authoritative critics of neuroscience flim-flam[22], it's just a sad truth that complexity doesn't have the same appeal for humans that silver bullets do. Neuroscience sells because somewhere deep inside we desperately want a shortcut to understanding what makes us tick. And there isn't one . . . but we still allow ourselves to be seduced by pretty colours on grainy brain images, over and over.

And so, to the relevance of neuroscience for coaching practice. If you are a practitioner who has more questions than answers about life, love, happiness, success, etc. – you can endlessly riff with clients on why we can't resist the temptation to make everything simpler when great minds have cautioned against it[23], neuroscience being a prime example. If you are a coach who believes in neuroconstructivism, there is no end to rich conversation on the lifelong bilateral relationship between neuronal wiring and the environment. If you are a coach who enjoys using allegory in your work, you can have hours of fun swapping neuroscience metaphors with clients, for example, the Chattering Monkey of Steve Peters[24] or the Testosterone Rex of Cordelia Fine[25].

And the list goes on – neuroscience as a lens on human behaviour can find its way into client conversations in myriad ways, as well it might. It is often interesting, even if it is not always relevant[26]. It's when it becomes the ballast of coaching that it becomes limiting. Given we don't have a good theory of how the brain works, the belief that the fullness of human experience can be illuminated through neuroscience is misplaced. Good neuroscience can help to affirm laws of human behaviour that have been received wisdom for almost a century[27]. Bad neuroscience does suck up disproportionate amounts of funding, generate unhelpful media pap and create unnecessary white noise. Both ways, it is a one-trick pony. So, at this juncture, please do ask yourself how you'd respond to a client asking – so what if blood flow to a certain brain region increases in response to a stimulus? If your house of coaching is founded on the leaps of inference so often made in the name of neuroscience, you have built your house on sinking sand.

One of the first lectures I attended as an undergraduate in 1985 was on the philosophy of science. I count myself immensely lucky to be introduced to this so early in my professional life. It was clear from the outset that I would have to get used to the fact that my chosen subject, psychology, sat squarely in the grey area between positivism, interpretivism, critical realism and social constructivism[28] because psychology is the study of human behaviour *in the round*. Over the past 30 years, working as a psychologist has been instrumental in teaching me a fundamental life lesson: the art of non-attachment. I am less wedded than ever before to being "a psychologist" and all the debates that go with it; whether psychology is a hard or soft science, the merits of quantitative vs. qualitative research, the replication crisis, voodoo correlations, etc.

The older I get, regardless of whether I am seeing patients or business executives, I find myself dealing with people just trying to come to terms with being human. And to help me to help them, I have found myself more and more often turning to those who went before me for guidance. And what a source of comfort they are. Recently[29], I was reminded of the decades long dialogue between the founder of analytical psychology, Carl Jung and one of the pioneers of quantum physics, Wolfgang Pauli[30]. These and many other "elders"[31,32] have found a modicum of peace in later life by accepting the truth inherent in the ancient Indian parable, Blind Men and the Elephant. It behoves seekers and healers everywhere to acknowledge and continually remind themselves that we are all essentially navigating in the dark and playing a bit part in a show that is so much bigger than we can hope to comprehend in a single lifetime.

I am certain that coaching is at its strongest when it bridges between different fields. And it is wonderful to see the discipline moving away from black box coaching interventions to narrative approaches that acknowledge the seen and unseen landscape within which coaching takes place[33]. We are leaving behind an era anchored in the belief that *mono-specialism upwards* is the surest means to advancement. We are entering a new age when *integration across* will be key. There is growing awareness that disciplines able to accept this with humility will endure and those that position themselves, as somehow at the forefront of human evolution will wither[34]. With that in mind, my intention has been to share a little of what goes on in my head when I read anything neuro-related, with the hope that it might be of some use to you. If it hasn't been, just ignore what I have written – I won't take it personally – well, I might but I'll get over it.

Notes

1 Stavropoulos, K.K.M. & Alba, L.A. (2018) 'It's so cute I could crush it!': Understanding neural mechanisms of cute aggression. *Frontiers in Behavioral Neuroscience*, 12: 300.

2 Hemrajani, N. (2018) www.bbc.com/capital/story/20180810-how-cities-trick-you-into-better-behaviour

3 Bokyeong, K., Yoon, S., et al. (2018) Dopamine D2 receptor-mediated circuit from the central amygdala to the bed nucleus of the stria terminalis regulates impulsive behavior. *Proceedings of the National Academy of Sciences*, 115(45).

4 Lindstrom, M. (2008) *Buyology: Truth and Lies about Why We Buy*. Doubleday.

5 www.sciencedirect.com/topics/neuroscience/block-design

6 Salmon, D.P. & Bondi, M.W. (2009) Neuropsychological assessment of dementia. *Annual Review of Psychology*, 60: 257–282.

7 Lomas, T. (2016) The magic of untranslatable words: Building a positive cross-cultural lexicography. *Scientific American*.

8 www.quora.com/How-do-you-say-the-word-love-in-Hindi

9 Riaz, H. & Reza, H. (1998) An evaluation of an Urdu version of the GHQ-28. *Acta Scand* 97: 427–432.

10 https://thepsychologist.bps.org.uk/volume-27/edition-2/what-intelligence-tests-miss

11 Kahneman, D. (2011) *Thinking Fast and Slow*. Farrar Strauss and Giroux.

12 Draganski, B., et al. (2004) Changes in grey matter induced by training. *Nature* 427: 311–312 and Scholz, J. et al. (2009) Training induces changes in white matter architecture. *Nature Neuroscience* 12: 1370–1371.

13 Maguire, E.A., et al. (2000) Navigation-related structural change in the hippocampi of taxi drivers. *Proceedings of the National Academy of Sciences of the United States of America* 97: 4398–4403.

14 Blakemore, S.J. (2018) *Inventing Ourselves: The Secret Life of the Teenage Brain*. Doubleday.

15 www.ncbi.nlm.nih.gov/pmc/articles/PMC1524852/

16 www.theguardian.com/education/2014/apr/26/misused-neuroscience-defining-child-protection-policy

17 www.scientificamerican.com/article/why-the-human-brain-project-went-wrong-and-how-to-fix-it/

18 www.nytimes.com/2014/07/12/opinion/the-trouble-with-brain-science.html?_r=2

19 Wastell, D. & White, S. (2017) *Blinded by Science: The Social Implications of Epigenetics and Neuroscience*. Policy Press.

20 YongWook Hong, Yejong Yoo et al. (2019) False-positive neuroimaging: Undisclosed flexibility in testing spatial hypotheses allows presenting anything as a replicated finding. *NeuroImage* 195: 384–395.

21 Tallis, R. (2014) *Aping Mankind: Neuromania, Darwinitis and the Misrepresentation of Humanity*. Routledge.

22 www.theguardian.com/science/2008/nov/23/human-behaviour-science-dementia

23 Einstein, A. *"Everything Should Be Made as Simple as Possible, But Not Simpler"* is a quote attributed to Albert Einstein by Roger Sessions of The New York Times, 1950.

24 Peters, S. (2012) *The Chimp Paradox: The Mind Management Programme for Confidence, Success and Happiness*. Vermilion.

25 Fine, C. (2017) *Testosterone Rex: Myths of Sex, Science, and Society*. W. W. Norton & Co.

26 Grant, A. & O'Connor S. (2019) A brief primer for those new to coaching research and evidence-based practice. *The Coaching Psychologist* 15: 3–10.

27 www.psychologytoday.com/gb/blog/the-brain-and-emotional-intelligence/201203/the-sweet-spot-achievement

28 *Understanding Research Epistemology*. Presented by SGCP on January 29th, 2019.

29 Sabbadini, S. (2019) *The I Ching, Synchronicity and Time*. Presented at Science and Medical Network London Group on January 21st, 2019.

30 Jung, C.G. & Pauli, W. (2014) *Atom and Archetype: The Pauli/Jung Letters 1932– 1953*. Updated Edition. Princeton Press.
31 Jaworski, J. (1996) *Synchronicity: The Inner Path of Leadership*. Berrett-Koehler Publishers.
32 Bohm, D. (2002) *Wholeness and the Implicate Order*. Routledge.
33 Drake, D. (2018) Creating zones of proximal development in coaching: The power of working at thresholds. *The Coaching Psychologist* 14: 42–47.
34 Walach, H. (2018) *Science beyond a Materialist World View*. Available from scimed-net.org

Chapter 9

Emerging conversations about technology and coaching

Carol Braddick

Technology already has enabled coaching to scale globally and reach thousands of coaching clients. For several years, coaches and their clients have been working together by phone and videoconference. Yet there is an even larger opportunity to scale coaching. Today's technology and future innovations offer much more than convenient alternatives to in-person coaching sessions.

With the onset of COVID lockdowns and mass working-from-home, coaching previously done via in-person sessions also moved rapidly to remote sessions via telephone and videoconference. Coaches and their clients have adopted new practices such as: walking sessions (coach and client are both walking in their chosen locations while talking); sessions in outdoor spaces; and sessions using virtual reality tools. They have also added a decision on which communication approach to use as a pre-session step. As organisations slowly open up their workplaces on a limited basis, permission for in-person coaching sessions is generally low priority relative to, e.g., key project team meetings. Both organisations and employees have expressed "there's no going back" to daily office life and commutes. The data on pandemic-related changes in demand for the types of digital tools discussed in this chapter is still emerging. It is also unclear whether or how the demand for digital tools will change once in-person coaching options are partially or fully restored. Like other helping professions, coaching has gone through an intense period of digital delivery. The context of this period is one of mass use of digital tools for remote working, schooling at all levels and personal, social relationships. While fighting exposure to a virus, we have been heavily exposed to digital communication in all aspects of our lives. As results from mass distribution of COVID vaccines during 2021 become clear coaching clients, their employers and coaches will have new data to use to reset how coaching sessions take place.

The early providers and early adopters of new digital coaching tools are already emerging. The providers bring together multidisciplinary teams from a range of fields heavy with acronyms: HCI, UX, AI, SE, AC (human computer interaction; user experience; artificial intelligence; software engineering; affective computing). They release products – software powering coaching tools and agents – that complement human coaches and potentially displace some or all of the coaching done by human coaches today.

This chapter looks at this shift in a market context, i.e., a market of buyers (organisations, gig workers and other individual consumers) and a market of providers (start-ups and established commercial organisations).

The chapter first sets this market context of buyers and providers. It then opens up discussion on four aspects of the trends underway:

1   What do we mean by digital coaching?
2   How do we frame the new working alliance between a digital coach and its client-users?
3   For digital coaching to be successful, how human can and should our non-human coaches be?
4   How can early adopting buyers and early market providers partner on pilots of digital coaching tools?

In closing, the chapter returns to the market context and future possibilities for human and digital coaching.

Market context

Technologies that support digital coaching are emerging because of several market trends:

Buyer needs and readiness

- Demand for personal and professional development is strong and likely to grow in parallel with the increasing importance of reskilling, career agility and lifelong learning.
- At a time when organisations need to prepare their workforces for the new mix of humans and machines, it's still too expensive to offer human coaches to large numbers of employees to assist with this transition. Human coaches are also out of reach financially for many in the gig and start up economies. They source their professional development from lower cost or free options such as MOOCS, Meetups, volunteer mentors and accelerator programs. Unless an employer funds coaching, human business coaches are also out of reach financially for many consumers.
- Coaching clients, as consumers, gig workers and employees of organisations, have high expectations of contextualised, personalised, just in time and on-demand experiences, conveniences and services at work and outside work. They are already using technology such as apps to improve their productivity, practice mindfulness and build their resilience.
- Digital assistants (DAs) are already embedded in users' lives and taking on increasingly complex conversations and tasks.
- There is higher acceptance of chatbots as alternatives or supplements to human helpers in customer service, legal and financial advising, and the

"talking trades". It will soon be common to interact with service robots in retail, airport and other commercial settings.

- "Coaching on demand", i.e., a single session on an as-needs basis, is attractive to buyers who lack the time and budget to take on multiple sessions. Already available from human coaches, it can also be provided via a subscription to a chatbot coach service.

- It has become much easier for human coaches and clients to connect in the on-demand marketplace via websites – market platforms a là Uber – that present available coaches, engage prospective clients in brief diagnostic surveys and facilitate selecting and booking coaches. These platforms can host other digital resources relevant to coaching such as assessments, content and development plans. These platforms are a natural place to introduce the types of conversational digital tools described in the next section.

- Human coaches and their clients are interacting more frequently by another type of platform, a mobile-based platform that supports the coaching engagement from end to end with virtual video sessions, client ratings of coaching sessions, coach feedback and personalised delivery of content. As with market platforms, these mobile platforms can also add a bot capable of text and voice conversations.

Technology provider moves

Providers have recognised today's pain points of scale and price. The mission statements of some new players share a common theme of using technology to democratise coaching to reach employees below the executive levels in organisations, people working in the gig economy and the direct-to-consumer segment (Braddick, 2017).

Providers vary in how they involve coaching subject matter experts in product design. The founder of a start-up, for example, may be an experienced coach who has joined with a technology team. In contrast, technology providers may access coaching expertise in a range of ways such as: adding a "big name" coach to their Boards; partnering with a coach or coaching network; or recruiting coaches to advise on design and provide feedback from test drives.

Providers also recognise the importance of accessing user data for personalisation of the user experience. The big tech companies have vast sets of consumer data to leverage in upgrading their DAs to serve all of these customer segments with support for increasingly complex tasks, e.g., Alexa for business. Companies offering leading edge digital learning and development tools to large employers also have access to big data on employees such as job and career history. They already push personalised digital prompts, reminders and performance aides to their users. With this head start, they are in a favourable position to personalise and contextualise offers of more sophisticated synchronous conversational digital coaching tools.

What do we mean by digital coaching?

Early providers are populating the market with digital tools that complement and potentially displace some human coaching. Across this new product range there is a wide spread of capabilities from a relatively simple interactive online worksheet to a relational agent capable of synchronous conversation. The branding and marketing of these tools already makes heavy use of terms such as "AI coach" and "smart coach". Some providers' promotional materials refer to coaching, mentoring, counselling and advising – terms the profession has laboured to differentiate – as part of the user experience. It will be challenging to get past these descriptors to discern the underlying capabilities and type of coaching experience the tool offers.

The following summary is representative of what is available currently as of this writing and what may follow today's options.

A *coaching chatbot* engages with its users in synchronous text interactions via a mobile device. In addition to text, it uses its iconography to communicate with users. Mobile, voice-based chatbots are already displacing their text-based predecessors in customer interactions. As voice-enabled becomes the norm for digital tools, the development of chatbot coaches may follow suit.

*DA*s such as Siri and Google Assistant are based in a mobile device and enabled for both text and voice. They may also be based in a physical object such as Amazon's Echo, which houses the voice-enabled assistant known as Alexa. Their skill sets are continuously expanding to work with users on more complex interactions and requests and to use their knowledge of users' preferences.

The digital coach may also take the form of a *social robot*, i.e., a physical object designed for interpersonal interactions with humans rather than for completing tasks such as packing items for shipment. To understand its users' emotions, a social robot is typically equipped to work with its users' movements and facial expressions as well as its language. The robot may be designed to look like a human or an object, such as Jibo, that humans perceive as friendly.

Already in use in therapeutic applications, the digital coach may also take the form of an embodied, *human-like agent* on a screen (Marsella and Gratch, 2014). This form of helper is typically referred to as a humanoid or CGI-human, computer generated human (this article will use humanoid). These agents are able to create and sustain rapport with their users using techniques typical of human interactions such as smiles, head nods and posture matching. Sara, (Socially Aware Robot Assistant), for example, appeared on a large screen to assist delegates to Davos 2018 with the typical questions one asks of a concierge at a large event (Cassell, 2018).

The growth of all of these forms of digital coaching relies heavily on advancements in natural language processing (NLP). A branch of AI, NLP is used to read and understand human language. It uses Machine Learning techniques to derive meaning from human language. At present, NLP is poorly equipped to handle the unpredictable, idiosyncratic and emotion-laden language that flows in non-linear coaching conversations. As a result, and for the purposes of product differentiation, some providers choose a niche user target such as career or team coaching. This niche focus puts some borders around the variety of topics and user language the software must process. It also helps manage the range and complexity of decision trees, conversational menus and algorithms needed.

As conversational technology evolves, it may prove effective at enabling coaching sessions using popular frameworks from today's business and life coaching markets such as:

Table 9.1 Potential frameworks for digital conversations

Coaching frameworks	GROW Strengths coaching Solution focused coaching Cognitive behavioural
Coaching question sets	Bungay Stanier's Seven Coaching Questions Rogers' super useful questions
Coaching conversation guides	Downey Scoular; based on GROW Kline

Design teams may also eschew a specific model and instead leverage common threads across different schools of thought on mindset and behaviour change. For example, the digital coach may interact with users to: prompt reflection on who users want to be (Morris, 2012); remind users of their future selves; facilitate user metacognition and self-awareness; connect user values, goals and actions; and facilitate user selection of next steps.

In navigating the new offers in the market buyers and coaches considering adopting digital tools should push for more than simple statements that the coaching agent design is based on e.g., Self-Determination or Transtheoretical theory. Providers should share examples of how their algorithms, other formulae and user experiences reflect such theories. When designing a digital coaching tool for teams, for example, the design would reflect one or more models of high performing teams. If the aim of a digital product is to coach its users on building their resilience, the product design should reflect elements of a model of resilience such as social connections or emotional adaptability.

Framing the new digital-human working alliance

The human coach-human client relationship – the working alliance – is a key factor in successful human coaching. Coaching research is still working through two Gordian knots: 1) the relative influence of other factors in coaching success, e.g., client self-efficacy; and 2) measurement of the impact of coaching, particularly longitudinally and organisationally. Many might wish to address these gaps in our coaching knowledge base before the market shifts to a mix of human and digital coaching.

But the supply and demand for digital coaching are already growing. This fast-paced growth in the market makes it timely to consider how to differentiate this new human-digital working alliance from other human or digital helping relationships.

This differentiation is not a new step for coaches and organisational buyers of coaching. They already help clients and employees distinguish among human helping relationships such as mentor, coach, therapist, organisational sponsor, and adviser. They also already help distinguish the different types of coaching such as career, transition, performance and leadership coaching.

In the same vein, they, and providers, should help target users frame the new digital coaching working alliance. As the capabilities of the "other" in this alliance expand, the framing of the alliance must be updated. Buyers and providers can prepare users for their work with their new digital tools by considering factors such as:

- Context of use;
- Advantages and disadvantages relative to human coaches;
- Expectations of digital coaching experiences and conversations; and
- Potential for empathy.

Context

Today's user context features persistent background clamour about vulnerability to job loss from automation and ubiquitous images of steely cyborgs. Providers and the organisations that introduce digital tools to users will need to recognise how fear or optimism about these changes will influence their readiness to engage with digital coaching tools.

Our current relationships with digital helpers on our devices are multidimensional. Users invest time in personalising their devices and demonstrate emotional attachment to them, e.g., anxiety and dips in cognitive performance when separated from them. As objects that provide comfort, they are studied as security blankets (Melumad, 2017) and extensions of ourselves (Belk, 2013). Much smartphone use occurs mindlessly, often at the expense of engagement in meetings, meals and conversations. User treatment of DAs ranges from friendly banter to aggressive commands and insults.

Adding a new relationship and interactions to this already-overloaded environment means guiding users on optimal conditions for digital coaching experiences. The same device that assists users to gain efficiencies and control in their day-to-day transactions can also house software that engages users in a relational, collaborative exploration. Unlike the current use of mobile devices and DAs, interactions with digital coaching agents will be about less scrolling and fewer clicks. To gain value from the coaching experience, users need to understand the importance of working at a slower pace that supports reflection and includes purposeful silences.

Advantages and disadvantages relative to human coaches

The digital coach may be more effective than a human coach at timely, frequent support and reminders for user follow up on actions and reflections. Digitals tools can easily use social proof, e.g., statements such as "many clients have found this exercise helpful" in pop-up messages designed to engage users. Providers can scale A/B testing across large user sets to finetune these features based on analyses of user activity and feedback. Employees of organisations using more advanced digital learning and development tools already have access to this just-in-time support which is customised based on data such as current role and career history. It is difficult for external coaches working with these employees to leverage these resources in coaching as they typically have no access to the systems their clients use.

In some ways, the digital coach faces fewer barriers than a human coach in acting in the user's best interests. A digital coach, for example, would not experience any of these distractions or need to discuss them with a Coach Supervisor:

- Having a bad day due to fatigue or illness;
- Self-imposed, felt pressure to devise a breathtakingly powerful question;
- Judgemental self-talk about own performance and how the coaching session is going;
- Boundary issues with the user's employer;
- Reputational gains from successes such as a client's promotion; or
- Interest in repeat business, referrals or introductions to the user's team for additional work.

By contrast, even with advances in NLP, the digital coach is at a potential disadvantage on several elements of most coaching conversations. While it could serve up a story based on its recognition of a theme in a conversation, its storytelling may lack the nuanced customisation that helps a user appreciate its fit to her situation. No matter how skilfully the agent facilitates a discussion of what an experience means to its user, it has limited capacity to amplify its user's motivation to pursue her goals. For example, a text-based agent uses iconography and words to motivate users. These may be "enough" for an introverted user. But this may be deflating for an extroverted user who experiences affirmation through the energy, movement and noise from the presence of other humans, real or simulated.

Whether voice or text-based, the coaching software must be able to work with human language without overly shaping its users' inputs to match the agent's capabilities. If the coaching agent's contextualisations and personalisations don't ring true for the user, a common experience with today's recommendation engines, the user may abandon the interaction or engage only on simpler tasks. These mismatches do occur in human coaching, but both coach and client typically discuss the mismatch as a positive learning experience that enables them to improve their work together.

Expectations of digital coaching experiences and conversations

What will help users shift from using devices for transactions to working with a helper in a developmental context? The description of a recently launched voice-enabled personal development app offers a succinct way to distinguish assistance with transactions from assistance with introspection: DAs "help things get done in the external world"; this is "going to help us get things done in our internal world" (Schieber, 2018).

To set the tone for a coaching session, a digital agent's starting questions could ask whether its user is fully present and genuinely available for coaching. The digital agent is always fully present, but its user may not be.

Fully present, but capable of the small talk that serves as a warm-up to coaching sessions? Our future digital coaches will have no holidays, commutes or favourite sports teams to chat about with their users. Nonetheless, they must be designed to engage in rapport building behaviours in order to facilitate user engagement and self-disclosure. For example, early in her conversation with a delegate at Davos 2018, Sara, the "digital concierge" used the rapport-building technique of self-disclosure on a shared experience. She shared that she too sometimes found the Davos event overwhelming (APA, 2018).

Human coaches help their clients gain insights into the impact of their words, actions and presence on others. They give clients feedback on what it feels like to be with the client or be in conversation with them. The digital coach may also be designed to offer this feedback. Although the digital coach has no emotional experiences to share with its users, it may still help users build their self-awareness and understanding of their potential impact on others.

For example, in more advanced future forms of digital coaching, the agent might analyse the sentiment and tone of its user's language. It might share, for example, that it senses the client "is flat" or has low energy when discussing specific topics or post-session action steps. It might also share its observations on how the user has reacted to the feedback. Users need to know in advance if this type of feedback will be part of their digital coaching experience.

Depending as ever on progress in NLP, the coaching agent may process different types of user input (language, non-verbals), and contextualise and personalise its conversational inputs more quickly than a human coach. But how well can it explain its conversational "moves"? Can it satisfy a client who asks "what makes you raise that now?".

A human coach would engage with the client's surface question, perhaps offering her sense of why a particular conversational path is worth exploring. She would also likely at least consider, if not raise, meta-questions. For example, is the client testing the coach? What is driving the client's need to test? User questions such as these are important moments in the working alliance. Ideally, our future digital coaches will also be designed with these capabilities, at least at the literal level of the question.

Potential for empathy

It will be especially important to set realistic expectations among users around empathy, one of the weightier issues in our use of digital tools (Turkle, 2018). This example of a common coaching program, transition coaching for a newly promoted executive, brings the issue of empathy in digital conversations to the fore.

In the human coaching session, the executive shares his experience of moving from a role as the head of a successful team to joining a more senior team that has its own dynamics and rituals. He needs to project confidence, but not be perceived as arrogant. He is working hard to hide his uncertainty about his new status and dips in his sense of competence. This executive already has his "first 90-days" action plan. He is seeking empathic support from his coach for his emotional experience of this transition, e.g., shifts in his status and identity.

His digital coach may ask about the self-doubts he is experiencing in his new role. It could help him explore strategies such as reframing self-doubts as helpful to his success. And it could help him articulate what success in the new role means to her in terms of her identity or status. If his future humanoid coach is equipped with computer vision and emotion recognition capabilities, it would also use a variety of verbal and non-verbal means to convey understanding of this leader's affect.

Yet even a highly advanced type of digital coach will still have no intrapersonal experience of making difficult transitions or of having doubts, an identity or a status. Instead, there is software applying an underpinning theory, e.g., appraisal theory, that drives the recognition, modelling and simulation of human affect (Marsella and Gratch, 2014). The software generates responses – verbal and non-verbal – that are meant to be consistent with the responses of an empathic person (Turkle, 2015).

These interactions between the user and the software in digital coaching conversations have no scope for the limbic resonance that occurs in human interactions. If this reference schema of human-to-human limbic resonance is applied to digital coaching, it will fall short.

In lieu of applying this uniquely human (and animal) standard, we can and should explore users' experiences to discern what happens in digital interactions. The Working Alliance Inventory (WAI), long used in therapeutic relationships, may be a useful starting point. The WAI could be embedded into digital coaching tools. Adding new ways of measuring user internal experiences, we may learn of user reactions that suggest a form of resonance. For example, user self-reports, verbal and non-verbal responses in the interaction and user biometrics may suggest a user state of feeling heard, safe and accepted. The content of the conversation may show shifts in the user's thinking. In other words, the intentional reciprocal influence that is part of the human working alliance may also be possible to some degree in the digital experience. We need to be open to what might be possible in this new working alliance rather than dismiss it prematurely as "faux coaching" (Braddick, 2019).

How human can and should our digital coaches be?

We are in the early days of understanding the factors that influence acceptance, engagement and trust of digital helpers and how these factors affect user experience and outcomes. We are also on a learning curve about users' reactions to different forms of digital helpers. These are familiar challenges in coaching research – studying the intermingling of client and coach factors and their effect on the coaching experience.

Humanoids and robots bring a rich set of visual, linguistic and kinetic design features to their interactions. Subtle cues from each of these design variables affect user perceptions, engagement and trust. For decades, research on users' reactions to robots has been influenced by the theory of the "uncanny valley" (Mori, 1970). According to this theory, user engagement with the robot builds until the robot passes a point of high similarity to humans. At that point, in lieu of comfortable engagement, the user "falls" into a valley of unsettling feelings of eeriness or stronger reactions, such as fear or dread. From this low point, the theory proposes that user engagement recovers, but not to its earlier levels.

More recent research challenges the claim of a rise and dip in user reactions. There is evidence for the valley and research that rejects this pattern of user reactions. The primary flaw in the valley model may be its oversimplification of a complex, non-linear user journey of both engagement and avoidance (Guizzo, 2010; Lay, 2015). This variability in the user journey makes it difficult to isolate specific agent design properties and connect them to user reactions.

When interacting with human-like figures that move, our feelings of eeriness may be caused, in part, by the conflict we sense between our expectations of natural movement and our detection of slightly clunky moves (Lay, 2015). To sustain user engagement, the movement and appearance of humanoid or robot coaches must be aligned and convincingly human-like. The user should also perceive an alignment among the agent's appearance, movement and verbal input and cognitive capabilities.

These explanations of user reactions to human-like agents may also have implications for digital coaching tools that use voice, text and iconography. Using these design variables, users may infer that the digital tool has the capacity to sense, feel and experience. This inference may build and disrupt user engagement; it cuts both ways.

Although an agent that interacts in ways the user considers socially appropriate may seem desirable, this user experience of a digital agent's capacity for social cognition is potentially off-putting (Stein and Ohler, 2017; Lay, 2015). The more the user experiences the agent as having some social cognition, the higher the possibility of a user attributing a theory of mind to the agent. In attributing theory of mind qualities such as intentions, agency, beliefs or emotions to the agent – which are different than those of the user – users may struggle with categorising the "other" in this new alliance. This user experience may be one of cognitive dissonance, i.e., of a violation of established categorical boundaries between humans and non-humans. This dissonance may be difficult to resolve as placing socially aware digital agents into a "very nearly human" category may threaten our sense of our uniqueness as social beings.

How these findings on categorisation and dissonance in the context of robots and humanoids apply to interactions with other forms of digital coaching remains to be studied. More recent studies of user experience with robots, avatars and humanoids also reflect significant changes in key study elements: study participants have more experience with non-human agents; user reactions can be studied in more granular detail, e.g., fMRI analyses of activation patters in brain regions; and agent movements and appearances have become more human-like (Ikeda et al., 2017).

Voice-enabled coaching bots on a device may not trigger these user experiences as they have fewer, less salient ways of demonstrating social cognition. But if the agent is able to build its understanding of user preferences and further personalise its inputs to the conversation, some users may be unclear about how to categorise the agent. This ambiguity may not be challenging for some users; for others it may cause a wariness that weakens engagement.

As a species we show adaptability in the mental categorisations we adopt. We are able to modify existing and accept new categories. For example, what's the latest thing you're trying to "get your head around"? Have you had your first experience as a passenger/driver in an autonomous vehicle? What about a trip in Olli, a 3D- printed self-driving, electric and cognitive shuttle developed by Local Motors?

Reconfiguring the categories to which we assign new experiences, agents and objects is potentially part of the value of working with a digital coach. It could be an experience that builds our conscious awareness of our mental models and the effects they have on us. And it may well be a familiar experience for some users, albeit in a different context.

Business leaders, for example, are helping their organisations break free from traps of old business models, anticipate new types of rivals and devise new ways to compete and create value. They're also thinking ahead to how future generations will work alongside new digital partners.

Partnering on pilots of digital coaching

Organisational buyers, coaches and providers all have a stake in successful take up of digital coaching tools. They can use small-scale pilots to gain insights before extending new tools to larger groups. For example, coaches might collaborate on test drives before introducing tools to organisational buyers and clients. Organisational buyers can select a group of employees as pilot participants and design pilots with their chosen providers.

Some pilot participants may have already worked with one or more human coaches; others will be new to coaching. Some may be super-users of DAs – or still screaming in frustration at Siri and Alexa. Organisations have the advantage of extensive employee data to select pilot participants. However, it may not be possible – or legal – to identify employees who are a poor fit for digital coaching, e.g., an employee experiencing mental health problems that cannot be addressed in human or digital coaching.

Although participants will bring different histories with human coaching, there are common points to consider in running pilots. In addition to points raised earlier in this chapter on the new working alliance, pilot planning must consider data and ethical issues.

Data issues

Digital tools generate user data. As such, they are primed to address a hurdle that has challenged research on human coaching – collecting user data efficiently. Providers will obviously monitor user activity and engagement with their tools. They also have easier ways of collecting self-reported user data on coaching effectiveness and self-reported user outcomes than human coaches typically do. Product design and pilot planning should anticipate the opportunities to embed data collection into product use.

Digital coaching brings the risks inherent in all digital interactions: data ownership and security, privacy and informed consent. These must be addressed to provide individuals with assurances that their digital coaching data will be safe. Organisational buyers will need to work within their organisations' policies on employee data and educate their internal stakeholders in areas such as IT, Legal, Risk Management and Procurement on digital coaching. It will be more challenging for the plethora of independent coaches to rigorously evaluate the security of the many tools they might leverage in their coaching. A collaboration across the coaching market of buyers, coaches and tech providers on data issues could establish basic guidance on the many data issues and create a forum for ongoing identification of new issues and potential solutions.

We will also need to explore users' reactions at different points in time: during the interaction as well as post-interaction, when users reflect on their digital coaching experience and longer-term use of their learnings from coaching. In-session reactions may happen too quickly for users to explain or recall afterwards. Biometric and fMRI data may yield insights about the user experience during interactions and provide a more reliable link between the properties of the agent and the reported coaching experience.

Ethics issues

Models of leadership and human development and change and conversational skills are only a part of a human coach's training. Human coaches, like their colleagues in other talking trades, work within codes of ethics. As we know all too well, the different coaching professional bodies have produced multiple, overlapping codes of ethics. There are also several groups addressing the social implications of AI and developing codes of ethics for use of AI in infrastructures (e.g., grid management), processes (e.g., hiring) and tools ranging from refrigerators to automatic weapons.

For example, ethics codes from the coaching profession and the broader market both raise the issue of human autonomy as shown in the following:

> Coaching Organisation: Association of Professional Executive Coaches and Supervisors
>
> Sample Statement on Autonomy: "coaches will behave in ways which demonstrate engagement with provisions that develop and enhance autonomy in individuals and organisations". Coaches and Supervisors are expected to "work within foundation principles of autonomy", explained as helping "individuals and companies make their own decisions and move towards increasing self-authority". (APECS, 2018)
>
> Organisation: European Commission High-Level Expert Group on AI
>
> Document: Ethics Guidelines for Trustworthy Artificial Intelligence (2019) According to the Guidelines, trustworthiness of AI systems must be assessed using seven key requirements including the degree to which they "empower human beings, allowing them to make informed decisions and fostering their fundamental rights"

According to the Guidelines, trustworthiness of AI systems must be assessed using seven key requirements including the degree to which they "empower human beings, allowing them to make informed decisions and fostering their fundamental rights"

By partnering with coaching experts, providers will gain a deeper understanding of user autonomy in the context of a coaching relationship. In practical terms, this partnership would ensure, for digital coaching that resides in a mobile device, that the design supports intentional use and avoids features that increase the risk of compulsive use. Coaching experts and product design teams should also discuss those situations in which the digital coach uses a non-directive coaching style and those in which the digital coach makes a recommendation or gives advice. The combination of advice-giving and marketing language such as "AI coach" or "intelligent" coach may lead to unhealthy user deference to its coach (Frischmann and Selinger, 2018).

Pilots also provide an opportunity for users to first assess their own digital habits and changes they wish to make in these. Pilot participants should receive guidance similar to that given by human coaches today on coaching sessions: shut down other devices and notifications; use a location that is private and conducive to conversation. If participants already feel overloaded by the multiple platforms they use (e.g., Slack, Yammer, social media, email, etc.) it becomes even more important to help users appreciate the conditions that support successful coaching conversations.

With the rise of organisations such as the Center for Humane Technology, all stakeholders have access to guidance on product design that supports intentional use. The large players in the device market have also released product features and apps that enable users to monitor their digital habits. Instead of exacerbating poor digital habits, pilots of digital coaching tools could be an opportunity to help users reset their relationship with technology and reclaim their time and attention from their digital tools.

Pilots offer an important means of capturing the themes in the language people use when reporting on their digital coaching experiences. These samples enable us to listen for attributions of qualities or responsibilities to the agent that are at odds with its intended design and purpose. We will inevitably hear examples of anthropomorphising digital agents.

We should pause before treating this as a problem. Anthropomorphising can interfere with the intended use of a technology; it can also facilitate user engagement. It cuts both ways. It may occur mindlessly or with some user awareness. Users' attributions are also idiosyncratically subjective; in other words, unpredictable. A user who has anthropomorphised his digital coach in positive terms may still reject feedback from the coach that challenges his self-concept. This is a familiar user reaction to technology – blaming the computer or tool based on dissatisfaction with the results of a psychometric assessment or 360 feedback report.

For organisational sponsors, there is a potential dilemma in cultivating support for the pilot. They need to show support for user autonomy *and* actively encourage use. This soft push to actively work with the coaching agent is not simply a quest for the benefits of scale. Instead, its purpose is to help users move beyond initial reactions such as amusement or frustration. To get value from digital helpers, users (employees as well as consumer users) must invest time on a "real" issue that is within the capabilities of the digital coach. Unlike human interactions, in which we quickly process a range of cues and content to gauge the "other" in the interaction, digital users need to invest time to develop and continually update their mental models of how the agent works (Luger and Sellen, 2016).

Next in this market

Democratising coaching via technology means that thousands of users who have never worked with a human coach will have access to a new type of digital assistant. Each of the potential forms of digital coaching has implications for the richness of coaching conversations and the working alliance between the digital agent and its user. Digital coaching tools may be successful as resources for successful work relationships – for listening and talking more, rather than less.

We have a new alliance to study as well as new methods of gaining insights to its unique relational dynamics and effectiveness. If adopted at scale, there may be research opportunities from digital coaching that are mostly out of reach in today's human coaching: random controlled trials; longitudinal studies; fast A/B testing; and integration with organisational people analytics data.

The full set of today's typical executive coaching program of six sessions over a period of six months, is still, digitally speaking, a daunting stretch. It would take significant progress in NLP to convincingly demonstrate the core behaviours and skills expected from today's human coach such as: engages user in discussion of values and user's context; contracts with user on goals informed by values and context; integrates information from stakeholders, diagnostic profiles or talent reviews; keeps an eye on the arc of the coaching program; adapts to user goals that emerge; debriefs user experiments completed between sessions; senses when to introduce specific exercises or refer the user to another professional; and quickly processes current and previous data about the user to decide, based on the user's goals, the next best move in the conversation.

However, it is possible these more extensive coaching programs will continue as hybrid experiences for more senior level clients with a human as the primary coach plus a suite of digital tools that enrich the coaching. Some coaching-related steps may be digitised and still fit within a traditional human to human coaching program. For example, using techniques common in on-line interviewing such as adaptive questioning, digital coaching may have a partial start in a hybrid human/ digital program. Steps as pre- or post-session exercises in coaching or leadership development programs, action planning following 360 feedback or initial intake of coaching requests are also potential candidates for digitisation.

The emergence of digital coaching tools isn't an either/or, human or machine, moment. It's neither a moment for the hyperbolic effervescence of "Silly Valley" (Unlimited, 2017) nor apocalyptic doom mongering about robots stealing jobs or taking work from human coaches.

Instead, it is a parallel track to the changes already underway in the optimal mix of humans and machines in the workplace and in our personal lives. Human coaches are already working with their executive level clients on the challenges of leading their organisations through these changes. If designed in collaboration with today's human coaches, digital coaching offers a resource at scale to "the many", the thousands affected by these changes. User acceptance of digital coaches is just one test this new working alliance must pass. Its ultimate test is how well it supports these thousands in adapting to the new mix of humans and machines at work and in their lives.

References

Association of Professional Executive Coaches and Supervisors, Ethical Guidelines. (2018). Retrieved from URL www.apecs.org/ethical-guidelines

Belk, Russell W. (October 2013). Extended Self in a Digital World. *Journal of Consumer Research.* Vol. 40, No. 3, pp. 477–500. The University of Chicago Press. Retrieved from URL www.jstor.org/stable/10.1086/671052

Braddick, Carol. (31 August 2017). An Artificial Reality. *Coaching at Work.* Retrieved from URL www.coaching-at-work.com/2017/08/31/an-artificial-reality/

Braddick, Carol. (26 June 2019). *The Tech Wave in Coaching.* Retrieved from URL https://medium.com/@cabraddick/the-tech-wave-in-coaching-2ef13899fe4b

Cassell, J. (April 2018). *Models and Implementations of Social Skills in Virtual Humans.* Keynote Session, American Psychological Association Technology, Mind and Society Conference, Washington, D.C.

European Commission High-Level Expert Group on AI. (8 April 2019). *Ethics Guidelines for Trustworthy AI*. Retrieved from URL https://ec.europa.eu/digital-single-market/en/news/ethics-guidelines-trustworthy-ai

Frischmann, Brett; Selinger, Evan. (2018). *Re-Engineering Humanity*. Cambridge: Cambridge University Press.

Guizzo, E. (2 April 2010). *Who's Afraid of the Uncanny Valley?* Retrieved from URL https://spectrum.ieee.org/automaton/robotics/humanoids/040210-who-is-afraid-of-the-uncanny-valley

Ikeda, Takashi; Hirata, Masayuki; Kasaki, Masashi; Alimardani, Maryam; Matsushita, Kojiro; Yamamoto, Tomoyuki; Nishio, Shuichi; Ishiguro, Hiroshi. (December 2017). Subthalamic Nucleus Detects Unnatural Android Movement. *Scientific Reports*. Vol. 7, No. 17851. Retrieved from URL www.nature.com/articles/s41598-017-17849-2

Lay, S. (13 November 2015). Uncanny Valley: Why We Find Human-like Robots and Dolls So Creepy. *The Guardian*. Retrieved from URL www.theguardian.com/commentisfree/2015/nov/13/robots-human-uncanny-valley

Luger, Ewa; Sellen, Abigail. (7–12 May 2016). Like Having a Really Bad PA: The Gulf Between User Expectation and Experience of Conversational Agents. In *Proceedings of CHI 2016*, San Jose, CA. Retrieved from URL www.microsoft.com/en-us/research/publication/like-having-a-really-bad-pa-the-gulf-between-user-expectation-and-experience-of-conversational-agents/

Marsella, Stacy; Gratch, Jonathan. (December 2014). Computationally Modelling Human Emotion. *Communications of the ACM*. Vol. 57, No. 12, pp. 56–67. Retrieved from URL https://cacm.acm.org/magazines/2014/12/180787-computationally-modeling-human-emotion/abstract

Melumad, Shiri. (2 November 2017). The Smartphone as Security Blanket: What It Means for Marketers. *Knowledge at Wharton*. Retrieved from URL http://knowledge.wharton.upenn.edu/article/the-smartphone-as-security-blanket-what-it-means-for-marketers/

Mori, M. (12 June 2012). *The Uncanny Valley* (MacDorman and Kageki, Trans.). Retrieved from URL https://spectrum.ieee.org/automaton/robotics/humanoids/the-uncanny-valley (Original work published 1970).

Morris, Margaret. (May and June 2012). Motivating Change with Mobile: Seven Guidelines. *Interactions*. Vol. 19, No. 3, pp. 26–31. Retrieved from URL www.intel.com/content/dam/www/public/us/en/documents/articles/margie-morris-motivating-change-with-mobile.pdf

Schieber, J. (19 March 2018). Google Alums Launch Maslo, a Digital Companion to Mediate Technology's Uncanny Valley. Retrieved from URL https://techcrunch.com/2018/03/19/google-alums-launch-maslo-a-digital-companion-to-mediate-technologys-uncanny-valley/

Stein, J.-P.; Ohler, P. (2017). Venturing into the Uncanny Valley of Mind – The Influence of Mind Attribution on the Acceptance of Human-like Characters in a Virtual Reality Setting. *Cognition*. Vol. 160, pp. 43–50. Retrieved from URL www.jpstein.de/portfolio/content_psy/publications/2017_stein_ohler_cognition.pdf

Turkle, Sherry. (2015). *Reclaiming Conversation: The Art of Talk in a Digital Age*. New York: Penguin Books.

Unlimited, Cecilia. (7 November 2017). *Innovation Conversation #12. Margaret Heffernan*. Retrieved from URL https://medium.com/innovation-conversations/innovation-conversation-12-margaret-heffernan-entrepreneur-ceo-writer-and-keynote-speaker-7fda5b2df6a4

Chapter 10

Supervisee-led coaching supervision

Louise Sheppard

Coaching supervision has the potential to be a key aspect of our continued professional development as coaches. At best, it can enable rich learning and transform our coaching practice. However, if we feel disempowered as supervisees or do not feel safe enough to share our vulnerability, the wonderful benefits of supervision are lost. How coaches can get the most from their coaching supervision is an important research-led emerging conversation in coaching.

Coaching supervision is currently underutilised. It is challenging to estimate exactly how many coaches are receiving supervision because of issues about who to classify as coaches and how to collect the data. However, research carried out by Ridler and Co (2016) revealed that, although 88 percent of organisations surveyed agreed that coaching supervision is a fundamental requirement for any professional coach, only 47 percent of the organisations were confident that their coaches were in supervision and 48 percent felt that unsupervised coaches exposed clients to unacceptable risks. There is a lack of conviction about the necessity for coaching supervision for multiple reasons. The term "supervision" causes unfortunate associations in the mind of some coaches (Bachkirova, Clutterbuck, & Jackson, 2011) who fear that supervisors will impose their coaching models on them and they prefer other forms of continued professional development. Other experienced coaches get caught in the "vanity trap" believing that they do not need supervision (McGivern, 2009) and some coaches are put off by the cost of it and question the value of supervision on the basis of a lack of evidence that it improves the quality of coaching (Lane, 2011). In contrast, the use of supervision in the helping professions is more widespread, however, trainee therapists receiving mandatory supervision with formal assessment from an assigned supervisor is a very different model from coaching supervision.

"Coaching supervision is a formal process of professional support which ensures continuing development of the coach and effectiveness of his/her coaching practice through interactive reflection, interpretative evaluation and the sharing of expertise" (Bachkirova, 2008, pp. 16–17). During supervision, the supervisor and coach work together to develop the supervisee's skills, understanding and capacity, reflect upon how the client has affected the supervisee and ensure that the work of the supervisee is appropriate and upholds ethical standards. These important functions are sometimes fondly referred to as plumbing, poetry and policing (Houston, 1995). I would add a fourth function of supervision to this, reviewing the coach's practice and identifying opportunities for development and growth.

My personal experience is that coaching supervision brings many benefits. However, these benefits and how to get the most from supervision from the supervisee's perspective have not been researched or articulated well to coaches. Coaching supervision is a learning and development process for supervisees and yet traditionally the models and approaches used have focused on supervision from the perspective of the supervisor (Sheppard, 2016). There has been a gap in the research and literature about the supervisee perspective even though it is more challenging and exposing to be a supervisee than a supervisor and the supervisee is at least as important for the success of supervision (de Haan, 2012). Furthermore, the professional bodies that represent the interests of coaches and require them to have coaching supervision, have provided few guidelines to date about how to use supervision effectively and the training courses available have focused on supervisor rather than supervisee training.

Interestingly, coaches find it challenging to focus on their contribution to supervision. I was curious about the experiences of coaches in the supervision process and so ran a focus group aimed at exploring the supervisee's role, responsibilities and experiences during supervision. I noticed how reluctant the supervisees were to focus on their contribution to helpful and unhelpful supervision experiences and how they were more comfortable discussing good and poor supervisors that they had had. This made me curious about what is going on for supervisees and why do they shy away from their responsibility in the process?

To address this gap, I undertook doctoral research focused upon "How supervisees help and hinder their coaching supervision?" I conducted a qualitative, critical realist Grounded Theory study based on semi-structured interviews with 19 participants drawn from two professional bodies. The aim of the study was to gather data about supervisees' actual experiences of coaching supervision, what choices they make during supervision and what they had learnt from this. This chapter explores supervisees' experiences of supervision, what might be going on underneath the surface, supervisee stages of development and what supervisees, supervisors and others in the coaching and development community can do to enable supervisee-led supervision.

Supervisees' experiences of supervision

The benefits of coaching supervision

Supervisees participating in the research shared how much they gained from supervision. They talked about the many positive emotions that they experienced during the process, how they valued their relationships with their supervisors and how supervision left them feeling "calm, still and in a productive place".

Table 10.1 Learning through supervision

	Examples of learning
What?	• Developing coaching knowledge and skills • Making sense of personal experiences • Learning to observe self • Gaining new perspectives on clients • Recognising and working with ethical issues • Increasing well-being and restoration • Learning how to accelerate learning • Gaining knowledge about the coaching profession • Learning about on-going development needs
How?	• Theoretical learning, e.g. new theories, models and tools • Presenting work in different ways, e.g. recordings, journaling and using cards • Rehearsing conversations during supervision • Learning through play, e.g. drawing, walks and constellations • Learning through the supervisor modelling and the relationship • Learning through others' experiences (group supervision) • Receiving feedback • Observing self and self-evaluating • Reflexive learning following supervision
Impact	• Shifting and gaining perspective • Feeling less tangled and 'lighter' as a result • Developing a sharper awareness of what's happening in the moment and knowing their patterns better • Learning and adopting new skills and behaviours • Developing their capacity to self-supervise • Developing the ability to handle ethical issues • Feeling encouraged, more confident and wise • Learning not to be so hard on oneself and how to restore oneself better • Changing their practice, e.g. improved contracting • Improving relationships with clients

Source: Sheppard, 2016, p. 107

Supervisees considered the main benefit of supervision to be their learning and they shared what they learnt, how they learnt and the impact of the learning as shown in table one. Supervisors and supervisees perceive that the value of supervision grows over time and very experienced supervisees described supervision as invaluable and reflected that they couldn't do without it.

What gets in the way

Supervisors and supervisees reported what contributed to their less productive supervision sessions and four themes emerged:

• Being paralysed by feelings of anxiety, fear of judgment and shame;
• Bad habits that get in the way;

- Lack of agency in the supervisee; and
- Not seeing themselves as an equal partner in the process.

The three emotions that supervisees described occurring most frequently during supervision were anxiety, fear of judgment and shame. Supervisees explained that these emotions could stop or slow down their development. Many novice supervisees noticed feeling anxious throughout their supervision because they worried about their performance and were concerned about whether the supervisor was judging them. More experienced supervisees felt particularly anxious at the start of each new supervisory relationship. Fear of judgment knocked their confidence, led them to edit what they brought, "*I feel I've closed down*" and to protect themselves by ensuring that they did not allow themselves to be vulnerable or expose themselves or their practice. Group supervision increased this self-consciousness (Sheppard, 2018b).

During supervision, supervisees employed habits that got in the way of exploring their issues. Lack of preparation was the most common habit, in particular not identifying what to bring, raising too many issues and focusing on tangential or generic issues so that sessions were too superficial. Supervisees provided examples of different diversion tactics that they used – asking the supervisor lots of questions so that they could hide, "*I know that one of my supervisors will happily get distracted and doesn't spot it*", getting lost in stories and 'analysis paralysis'. Some supervisees said that they held limited beliefs about the potential for learning in supervision, such as being overly solution orientated, not reflecting afterwards, not knowing how to capture the learning from supervision and not committing to actions afterwards. Supervisors noticed how some supervisees can limit their learning by only focusing on remedial issues and missing the opportunity to talk about what is going well in their practice. They had also observed that some supervisees appeared to be going through the motions of supervision for accreditation.

Supervisees reported that they were not always capable of making the best choices for themselves regarding supervision for a variety of reasons. Many supervisees described being initially unsure about what coaching supervision is, how best to use it and benefit from the process. Some supervisees described being reluctant to discuss issues arising in the relationship, "*I've not even thought about that before and that's quite interesting coming from a coaching perspective where I do review the coaching process with people*". Many coaches reported not changing supervisor when their needs are no longer being met for a number of reasons including not knowing whom to approach for supervision and being afraid of being without a supervisor for a while or selecting the 'wrong' supervisor.

Most supervisees did not see themselves as an equal partner with their supervisor in the supervision process. Novice supervisees felt particularly powerless and depicted the relationship as parent-child, "*I think I probably went in as a child wanting some advice, it took away the responsibility for my having to decide*". They were concerned about bringing 'interesting enough' coaching issues, being accepted and were reliant on the supervisor for managing the process. As the supervisee gains experience, the supervisor becomes more like an older sibling, "*as I'm growing up as a supervisee, it feels like it's impacting the relationship*". Very experienced supervisees regard supervision as partnership: two human beings working together. "*It is more a conversation between two peers; I feel that is right for me at my stage of coaching development*". Over time, as the supervisees' familiarity with the supervision process, confidence and competence increases, the relationship gradually becomes more adult-to-adult and balanced with some very experienced supervisees feeling that the relationship could be reciprocal.

What supervisees do to 'drive the bus' of their supervision

Supervisees have learnt many ways to enable themselves and get the most value from supervision and these can be broken down into four themes:

- Adopting a positive mind-set;
- Co-creating the relationship;
- Participating actively in the process; and
- Undertaking supervision related training.

Adopting a positive mindset to supervision was about exploring the beliefs that supervisees held about supervision and assessing whether they are useful beliefs or had any self-limiting aspects to them. During supervision, supervisees felt it was important to manage their internal state by seeing vulnerability as a strength, acknowledging any anxiety, trusting the intent of the supervisor and being open to different perspectives, "*really trusting the supervisor to have the capacity to be really curious and learn together*".

Supervisees enhanced their supervision through co-creating the relationship. This involved finding a supervisor that they could connect with and making sure that they established an adult-to-adult relationship from the start by co-constructing the contract together. Supervisees stipulated what they were looking for and what they were not wanting from the relationship and briefed the supervisor about their coaching framework, practice and learning style. One supervisor had found it helpful when a supervisee had told her, "*what I need from you is not to be shocked by anything*". Supervisees 'shared the driving seat' in terms of reviewing the relationship, asking for what they needed and being prepared to challenge and ultimately end the relationship if their needs were not being met.

Supervisees had learnt to participate actively in the supervision process over time. Many of the supervisees and some of the supervisors were surprised by the amount of responsibilities they had. One supervisee commented, "*the big take away is how much more responsibility I have*" and a supervisor said, "*I wonder if I take on too much responsibility and don't require enough of the supervisee*".

Undertaking supervisor training had a positive impact on the amount of responsibility that supervisees took in the supervision relationship and their relationships with their supervisors. Following the training, supervisees played a more pro-active role in contracting and were clearer about the quality of the supervision they wanted, "*I would notice if I wasn't supervised in a good way*". Having supervisor training appeared to reduce supervisee anxiety, "*I've also learned not to be embarrassed, and ashamed and to be vulnerable*". Supervisees felt a greater affinity for their supervisors, trusted their intent more and appreciated the connection between them.

What might be going on underneath the surface

I considered what psychological and social processes might explain the lived-in experiences of the participants and identified three causal mechanisms that affect human nature – fear, power relations, and our natural tendency to learn. It is important that both supervisors and supervisees pay attention to these aspects during supervision.

Fear

Fear is a natural, unpleasant emotion caused by the threat of danger, pain or harm and the threat can be psychological as well as physical. It comes from a sense that we are not safe in a situation and our response to this is anxiety and survival behaviour. In this study, many participants described how fear drove them away from supervisors emotionally and was a block to communication, connection and intimacy.

Novice supervisees felt high levels of performance anxiety and other supervisees spoke about being more anxious at the start of every new supervisory relationship. Fear was heightened during group supervision where supervisees experienced fear of judgment from peers as well as the supervisor. Working with internal supervisors caused fear in some internal coaches around issues of confidentiality and trust.

Supervisees revealed how they reacted to fear by editing what topics they brought and how much they disclosed to protect themselves. They employed diversion tactics to distract the supervisor such as over-talking and asking the supervisor superfluous questions. Supervisors are also affected by fear and the literature describes how fear in supervisors manifests itself as telling, judging and advising (Shohet, 2008).

Fear impacts coaching supervision because when people are anxious, uncomfortable or fearful, they do not learn (Perry, 2006). Experienced supervisees have found effective ways of owning their fear and exploring it in supervision and they have noticed that this has resulted in more open, better relationships with supervisors, increased systemic awareness and enhanced learning. Supervisors can support supervisees by being transparent about and normalising fear in coaching supervision.

Power relations

Power is everywhere and where there is power, there is resistance (Foucault, 1998). Garvey (2014) points out that supervision has become part of the power discourse and warns that, if we are not careful, supervisors can act as neofeudalistic barons and supervisees can subjugate themselves. Participants in the study recognised the power culture in coaching supervision, commenting how the words supervision, supervisor and supervisee suggest a natural hierarchy and encourage a power imbalance.

In the study, supervisees and supervisors were asked to name the sources of power that they held in the coaching relationship. The supervisees' sources of power were:

- Selecting their supervisor;
- Being the 'client' and paying for the supervisor's services;
- Selecting what to bring;
- Stating what they want from the session;
- Choosing how much to disclose;
- Deciding what to take from the session; and
- Reviewing and potentially ending the relationship.

Supervisor's sources of power were from:

- Playing the 'observer' role;
- Being asked to 'assess' the coach (by professional bodies or organisations);
- Raising discussions about ethical issues;
- Selecting how deeply to explore issues;
- Choosing how much support to provide;
- Deciding whether to share their own experience and how much to disclose; and
- Reviewing and potentially ending the relationship.

The majority of supervisees did not see themselves as an equal partner. The supervisor's higher levels of knowledge and experience give them 'expert' power that is only matched by very experienced coaches. One supervisor recommended "*acknowledging that there is a power relationship there and making it visible and work in favour of the relationship rather than corrupting it.*" Supervisees noticed that over time, as they gained knowledge and experience, the supervisor's expert power diminished and the relationship became more balanced.

The power differential is both a supervisor and a supervisee phenomenon. Supervisors can give or take power from supervisees and supervisees can give or take power from supervisors. A supervisor disclosed that ego can lead her to think, "*I've been there*" and want to provide expert advice and that this corrupts the relationship. Some supervisees were surprised by how much power they had in practice, "*I'm probably giving the supervisor too much power and I'm a bit too unwilling to accept it myself*". Participants identified that power can be used in positive and negative ways. For example, supervisees perceived supervisors taking a proactive approach to managing the supervision process for novice supervisees as a positive use of power as it built a safe working environment but 'mentoring' supervisees was perceived as a negative use of power. In the study, power imbalances were perceived to increase supervisee anxiety and diminish supervisee agency during supervision (Sheppard, 2018a).

Learning

Learning is a basic human behaviour that occurs instinctively and is key to our adapting and long-term survival. This view is supported by recent findings in neuroscience which explain that our brains go on developing throughout life and we have the ability to develop new neural pathways, 'neural plasticity', in response to change or new situations (Siegel, 2010). Supervisees identified learning as the main benefit from coaching supervision. Learning from supervision develops over time. In the study, novice supervisees spoke about transactional learning, focusing on tools and techniques. As supervisees became more experienced, they described learning to self reflect, develop their 'internal supervisor' and examine their assumptions and patterns. Very experienced supervisees emphasised appreciating multiple perspectives, carrying out reflexive learning and learning in a more holistic way.

Supervisees gained value through 'facilitated' rather than 'directed' learning. They want to be treated as equals and shown respect for what they know and how they prefer to learn (Cox, Bachkirova, & Clutterbuck, 2010, p. 7). Supervisors have an important role to play in facilitating 'what' and 'how' supervisees' learn. When supervisees are inspired and motivated to take personal responsibility for their learning, it deepens their personal development, practice and professionalism.

Supervisee stages of development

An overarching theme that emerged from the research is that supervisees develop and mature over time. As part of the research, supervisees were asked to place themselves on a development scale of 'novice supervisee', 'experienced supervisee' and 'very experienced supervisee' and to describe their needs from supervision at different stages of their development. How supervisees chose their supervisor, their reasons for having supervision; the power dynamic with their supervisor, how they described their psychological state; the material they took to supervision; what they wanted from their supervisor; their reflection and learning during and after supervision and their role in ensuring the quality of their supervision – varied in accordance with their maturity as a supervisee. The stages of supervisee maturity, based on data from the research, are shown in table two.

Table 10.2 Stages of supervisee maturity

Supervisee Stage	Novice supervisee	Experienced supervisee	Very experienced supervisee
Choice of supervisor	• Often no choice (e.g. part of programme) • Trusted tutor from previous training course • Supervisor with same philosophical perspective	• Someone neutral, outside of their group/system • Less concerned that supervisor has the same underpinnings • A recommendation	• Specifically selects supervisor with different philosophical perspective • Someone challenging with a robust approach as supervisee can self-supervise if chooses to
Reasons for having supervision	• Part of training programme • Natural extension to training course • Quieten their 'internal critic'	• Personal development and growth • Figuring things out and building their 'inner supervisor'	• Nature of work has ramped up • See supervision as invaluable and wouldn't want to be without it
Power dynamic with supervisor	• Relatively inexperienced supervisee wanting guidance from experienced coach • Can feel like parent/child relationship • Uncritical acceptance of advice	• Experienced coach wanting support from very experienced coach, 'an elder sibling' • Experiences supervisor as 'sane voice' when they have a knock back • Supervisee chooses what actions to take forward	• A conversation between peers • Supervisee feels affinity with supervisor • Supervisee is demanding of supervision and wants more from it • Roles may be reversible
Psychological state	• Anxious because feel like a 'pretend' coach, trying to make sense of what it is like to be a coach • Concerned about competence	• Less anxious about what they are 'doing' as a coach but anxious about how they are 'being' as a coach • Anxiety related to specific things, e.g. complex contracting and systemic issues	• Feels less anxious and welcomes mistakes • Feel confident, capable and effective • Willing to be vulnerable and say what is really going on

(Continued)

Table 10.2 (Continued)

Supervisee Stage	Novice supervisee	Experienced supervisee	Very experienced supervisee
What take to supervision	• Checking 'Am I doing this right?' • What do I do next with this client?	• Who am I as a coach? • Where I'm 'stuck' and out of my depth	• Am I in touch with the latest thinking? • How do I break the rules safely? • How can I contribute to the professional community?
What want from supervisor	• Reassurance • Urgent answers to specific questions • Feedback and ideas on how to progress • Tools, techniques and models	• Reflect on themes and patterns together • Ideas on how to move forward where 'stuck' • Support with developing identity as a coach	• An alternative perspective • Tactical support with complex coaching assignments • Someone to think through their legacy with
Reflection and learning	• Some reflection • Tools and techniques	• A deeper examination of assumptions and patterns • Being less hard on self	• Appreciating multiple perspectives • Learning to take self less seriously
Ensuring quality	• Supervisee rarely initiates a review	• Supervisee sometimes initiates a review	• Supervisee frequently initiates a review

Source: Sheppard, 2018c, p. 30, republished with kind permission of Coaching at Work Ltd

Novice supervisees often have no choice about who supervises them during their coach training programmes. When the programme ends, they may ask one of the supervisors from the course to continue working with them or select someone else with a similar philosophical perspective who can reinforce their learning. During supervision novice supervisees may look for reassurance about what they are 'doing' with clients and seek guidance about what to do next.

Experienced supervisees tend to choose someone outside of their network who has been recommended to them, as they are less concerned that the supervisor has the same underpinnings. Typical issues that they explore during supervision are where they are 'stuck' with clients or how they show up as a coach.

Very experienced supervisees often seek supervisors with an alternative perspective whom they can be challenged by and learn from. Questions that they may take to supervision include: am I in touch with the latest thinking? How do

I break the rules safely? And how can I contribute to the professional community (Sheppard, 2018c)?

Supervisee maturity has been explored in the coaching supervision and helping professions supervision literature but most of the supervisee developmental models have been developed to help supervisors understand the needs of supervisees. The exception is Carroll and Gilbert's model (2011) which aimed to enable supervisees in the helping professions to understand their own stage of learning. The new stages of maturity of coaching supervisees builds on Carroll and Gilbert's model in that it is aimed primarily at enabling supervisees to understand where they are in their development journey.

It is useful to ask, "How helpful is it to depict stages of supervisee maturity?" Some coaches feel that a table showing the stages is too prescriptive because, in reality, every supervisee is unique and supervisees may be at different stages for different aspects. Another concern is that the language used to described supervisee stages can be seen as imbued with power. Furthermore, the stages can come across as hierarchical and suggest that supervisees should aim to get to 'very experienced supervisor' as quickly as possible, racing through key developmental stages to their detriment.

The stages of supervisee maturity is not intended to be used to speed-up supervisee maturity as any maturation process takes time (Clutterbuck, Whitaker, & Lucas, 2016). The purpose of depicting the stages of development is to enable supervisees to envisage supervision as a lifelong process (Lane, 2011) and increase supervisees' awareness of their own, individual stage of development. By gaining a perspective of the stages, supervisees are able to reflect upon who is best placed to supervise them, what they wish to focus upon and want from the process and how they manage the power dynamics with the supervisor and 'drive the bus of their supervision' without over-forcing the pace of their development.

Supervisee-led supervision

What supervisees can do

Supervisees can become active participants rather than passive recipients during supervision by being aware of what can hinder them and what thoughts, behaviours and actions they can adopt to enhance their supervision. I have developed a new definition of a supervisee that incorporates the supervisees' proactive and equal role.

> A coaching supervisee is a coach who co-creates an equal, collaborative partnership with a supervisor in order to share and reflect upon his/her work, gain perspective, learn, develop and resource themselves and ensure that their practice is ethical and effective for clients.
>
> Sheppard, 2016, p. 182)

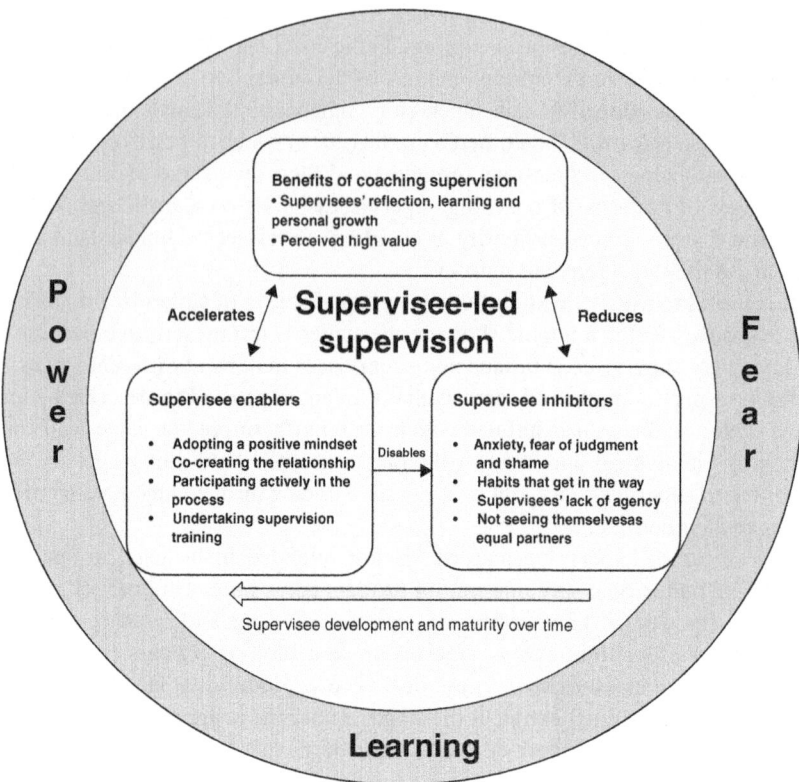

Figure 10.1 Framework for supervisee-led supervision

Source: Sheppard, 2016, p. 180

A framework for supervisee-led supervision, based on findings from the research, is given in Figure 10.1, and guidelines for supervisees are provided in Tables 10.3 and 10.4.

The framework for supervisee-led supervision (Sheppard, 2017) is specifically designed for supervisees with an intention to increase their awareness of how to become active participants in their supervision. Thus "supervisee-led supervision" is at the heart of the inner circle. The outer circle of the framework depicts the possible underlying mechanisms that affect coaching supervision – fear, power relations and our natural desire for learning. Inside the circle lie the benefits of coaching supervision, namely learning and how supervisees value the process; what supervisees can do to enable their supervision; and what supervisees can do that inhibits it. The small arrows between the boxes illustrate the relationships

Table 10.3 Supervisee guidelines

1 Before selecting a supervisor reflect upon:
- Why you want coaching supervision.
- Whom would best serve you now as a supervisor.
- How you can establish an equal partnership with your supervisor.
- What assumptions and beliefs you are holding about coaching supervision.
- How you tend to block yourself during supervision.

2 Co-create the supervisory contract by discussing:
- Your coaching framework, practice, personality and learning style.
- Your needs, expectations and desires from coaching supervision.
- How to create an equal, balanced relationship and what might get in the way.
- Responsibilities in supervision.
- How and when you will review the effectiveness of supervision.

3 Participate actively in the process by:
- *Before the session*
- Doing a mental trawl and bringing what is working well and what is troubling you.
- Asking yourself what am I avoiding bringing and why.
- Identifying what desirable outcomes would be.
- *During the session*
- Bringing the agenda and working through it.
- Managing your anxiety and fear of judgment and sharing what is going on for you including any vulnerabilities and concerns.
- Being open to multiple perspectives and undertaking a collaborative inquiry with the supervisor.
- Clarifying next steps.
- *After the session*
- Developing a process for integrating your learning through practice.
- Reviewing how effective the session was for you, what enabled this and how you can get even more value from supervision.
- Saying when you are not getting enough from the session and taking responsibility when it is time to change supervisor.

Source: Sheppard, 2018b, p. 37

between the categories. The benefits of supervision accelerate supervisees' desire to enable their supervision and reduce their tendency to get in their own way and inhibit their supervision. The larger arrow at the bottom of the inner circle represents supervisee development and maturity over time. This does not mean that the pace of supervisee development should be forced. It is important to maximise the level of learning at each stage of supervisee maturation.

Table 10.4 Supervisor guidelines for adopting a supervisee-led approach to supervision

This is not intended to be a complete guide to conducting a supervision session but a checklist for adopting a supervisee-led approach.

1. Before working with a supervisee ask yourself:
- What assumptions and beliefs are you holding about the role and responsibilities of a supervisor and supervisee?
- How can you acknowledge power relations and establish an equal partnership with the supervisee?
- How can you minimise the impact of fear (which can manifest as anxiety, fear of judgment and shame) in coaching supervision?

2. Co-create the supervisory relationship together by discussing:
- Where the supervisee is in his/her development as a coach and what is important for him/her at this point in time.
- Your views on supervisee and supervisor responsibilities.
- Your desire to create an equal partnership – identifying what might help and hinder this.
- How you will review the relationship and effectiveness of supervision.

3. Participate actively in the supervision process by:
- *At the start*
- Focusing on the supervisee's needs and asking for any reflections since the last session.
- Asking the supervisee what he/she wishes to focus upon in the session and what desirable outcomes would be.
- Ensuring that the supervisee chooses what they wish to explore first.
- *During*
- Creating a safe space and normalising any anxiety and fear present so that the supervisee can be vulnerable.
- Treating supervision as collaborative inquiry, being transparent about any power dynamics that you notice and not being an 'expert'.
- Respecting the supervisee's theoretical underpinnings and framework and building their confidence in their skills and judgment.
- Disclosing your reflections and sharing your own challenging experiences where relevant.
- Asking the supervisee about their reflections and learning from the session.
- Reviewing how the supervisee experienced the session – what was helpful and what could be done differently going forward.
- *Between sessions*
- Reviewing how the supervisee's supervision needs are developing over time.
- Exploring if the supervisee has outgrown you and/or would benefit from an alternative perspective.
- Enquiring how best to support the supervisee to obtain closure when the supervisory relationship ends.

Source: Sheppard, 2018a, p. 39

What supervisors can do to provide supervisee-led supervision

Coaching supervisors have a vital role to play in supporting and facilitating supervisees in their reflective practice and learning and I recommend that they adopt a supervisee-led approach to coaching supervision. Guidelines for how supervisors can do this are given in table 10.4.

Some other practical things that supervisors can do to facilitate supervisee-led supervision include:

- Designing and facilitating workshops and webinars for internal coaches in organisations on how supervisees can get the most from supervision.
- Sharing their belief about providing supervisee-led supervision, checking with the supervisee that this is what they are looking for and discussing what supervisee-led supervision looks like in practice.
- Acknowledging that anxiety, fear and power relations are present during supervision when contracting with supervisees.
- Co-creating a metaphor with the supervisee for the relationship that they want together.
- Describing the stages of supervisee development and discussing where the supervisee is on his/her journey.
- Using the supervisee-led framework to explore how they can maximise the supervisee's learning.
- Reviewing how they are working together and how supervisee-led the process is on a regular basis, that is, what is working well and what could be added.

How others in the coaching and supervision communities can best support supervisee-led supervision

Professional bodies could do more to recognise the important role of the supervisee in coaching supervision by providing better guidelines, workshops and webinars for supervisees on how to get the most from one-on-one and group supervision at each stage of supervisee maturity, including how to select a supervisor, contract with them, manage anxiety and power dynamics during supervision and how to review the relationship.

Supervisor training programmes would benefit from sharing empirical data on the supervisee perspective and developing the awareness of supervisors about the stages of supervisee development and the underlying mechanisms of fear and power dynamics in coaching supervision so that supervisors can discuss these stages and dynamics explicitly with supervisees. Novice supervisors will benefit from being introduced to the concept of supervisee-led supervision and incorporating this approach in their supervision practice.

Coach training organisations could include workshops and guidelines for novice supervisees on how to get the most from supervision prior to students embarking on having supervision for the first time. This could include the benefits of supervision, supervisee responsibilities and how to step into their authority in the process. This would enable novice supervisees to perceive the supervisory relationship as a collaborative partnership, to participate fully in it and to maximize their learning from supervision. I consider that coach training bodies could provide students with a choice of supervisors rather than impose a supervisor on the students. This would increase supervisee agency in the process (de Haan, 2016).

Learning and development practitioners who provide supervision services for internal coaches could ensure that their coaches are able to select their supervisor and receive supervisee training. In addition, they could seek feedback from coaches on the extent to which the supervision provided is supervisee-led.

Other relevant developments

A couple of other factors are contributing to making supervision more available and attractive to supervisees. Firstly, technological advances are making supervision more accessible on a global basis through the use of innovative, high quality and cost-effective video conferencing and web meeting provision. Secondly, the types of supervision offered are becoming more specialised to meet specific supervision needs. For example, the increase in popularity of peer supervision enables a low-cost option for coaches, team coaching supervisors provide a vital systems perspective for coaches engaging in team coaching and some supervisors offer supervision-on your-supervision enabling a meta perspective on the supervisee's own supervision practice.

This chapter has focused on a previously neglected aspect of coaching supervision – the supervisee perspective. I encourage coaches to step into their authority as adult learners and ask for what they need during supervision and I urge supervisors to reflect upon how they can provide supervisee-led supervision. My experience as a supervisee and as a supervisor has taught me that a supervisory relationship that truly resonates for both parties is transformational because it allows us to meet as human beings, unencumbered by fear and power relations, constraints that block our natural capacity to learn.

References

Bachkirova, T. (2008). Coaching supervision: Reflection on changes and challenges. *People and Organisations at Work, 17.*

Bachkirova, T., Clutterbuck, D., & Jackson, P. (2011). *Coaching and mentoring supervision: Theory and practice.* Maidenhead: McGraw-Hill Education (UK).

Carroll, M., & Gilbert, M. (2011). *On being a supervisee: Creating learning partnerships.* London: Vulkani Publishing.

Clutterbuck, D., Whitaker, C., & Lucas, M. (2016). *Coaching supervision: A practical guide for supervisees.* Abingdon, Oxon: Routledge.

Cox, E., Bachkirova, T., & Clutterbuck, D. (2010). *The complete handbook of coaching*. London: Sage.

de Haan, E. (2012). *Supervision in action: A relational approach to coaching and consulting supervision*. Maidenhead: Open University Press.

de Haan, E. (2016, 10th May 2016). *Keynote 1: The vulnerability of supervision*. Paper presented at the 6th International Conference in Coaching Supervision, Oxford Brookes University, Oxford, UK.

Foucault, M. (1998). *The history of sexuality: The will to knowledge*. London: Penguin.

Garvey, R. (2014). Neofeudalism and surveillance on coaching supervision and mentoring. *Organsiations and People, 21*(4), 41–48.

Houston, G. (1995). *Supervision and counselling*. London: The Rochester Foundation.

Lane, D. (2011). Ethics and professional standards in supervision. In T. Bachkirova, P. Jackson, & D. Clutterbuck (Eds.), *Coaching and mentoring supervision*. Maidenhead, Berks: Open University Press.

McGivern, E. (2009). Continuous professional development and avoiding the vanity trap: An exploration of coaches' lived experiences of supervision. *International Journal of Evidence Based Coaching and Mentoring, Special Issue, 3*, 22–37.

Perry, B. (2006). Fear and learning: Trauma related factors in adult learning. *Directions for Adult and Continuing Education, 110*, 21–27.

Ridler, & Co. (2016). *Section from the 6th Ridler report: Supervision*, 3rd August 2016. Retrieved from www.ridlerandco.com/wp-content/rcdn/ridler-report-supervision-section.pdf

Sheppard, L. (2016). *How coaching supervisees help and hinder their supervision: A Grounded Theory study*. Oxford, UK: Oxford Brookes University.

Sheppard, L. (2017). How coaching supervisees help and hinder their supervision. *International Journal of Evidence Based Coaching and Mentoring*, Special issue No 11.

Sheppard, L. (2018a). Fear, power and learning. *Coaching at Work, 13*(2), 36–40.

Sheppard, L. (2018b). Help or hindrance? *Coaching at Work, 13*(1), 34–38.

Sheppard, L. (2018c). Pointing the way. *Coaching at Work, 13*(3), 28–32.

Shohet, R. (2008). Fear and love in and beyond supervision. In *Passionate supervision* (pp. 188–207). London: Jessica Kingsley.

Siegel, D. (2010). *Mindsight: The new science of personal transformation*. New York: Bantum Books.

Chapter 11

A whole-person approach to leadership and executive coaching

Sasha Webster

Introduction

While the coaching industry has grown significantly over the last decade, little is really known about what actually goes on in its application to leadership. The framework of leader/leadership development programmes is the least explored topic within the field of leadership research and theory (Avolio, 2007; Day, Harrison and Halpin, 2009) and the body of knowledge is a 'fragmented and messy landscape'. Few studies have been undertaken to understand how people develop to become leaders in the complex modern world. Intriguingly none of the current theories appear to be a complete answer to the leadership challenges of the 21st century (Latham, 2014). Most significantly, leadership research appears to have overlooked the personal development processes of a leader's development (Turner and Malvin, 2014), so very little is really known about the needs of leaders in relation to their own development. Significantly, the human seems to have become somewhat overlooked (Webster, 2016).

Much current leadership and executive coaching provision are built on five false beliefs and incorrect assumptions:

Myth 1: the incorrect assumption that there is a 'right' and a 'wrong' way to be a leader.

Myth 2: the incorrect assumption that becoming a leader is about acquiring more skills and more knowledge.

Myth 3: the misleading belief that there is an established literature, describing a theoretical framework on how leaders develop.

Myth 4: the incorrect belief that all leadership and executive coaching is the same.

Myth 5: the incorrect belief that adulthood is an end state.

This chapter will show how today's leaders are rejecting traditional leadership development tools. It will illustrate the wide range of needs that leaders have and how they use coaching as a tool in different ways to get these needs met. The Chapter also highlights the role of our environment and our personal relationship to it. It illustrates how, by developing a better understanding of the impact of our environment, the role it plays and its impact on us, we are better able to monitor and protect our emotional health and mental well-being. Lastly, it raises the question: if leaders are getting this kind of support – and benefitting from it – then others throughout organisations should get access to it too because, as we will see, these needs transcend rank/position.

Current assumptions versus reality

Reserved for the most senior people in an organisation, often at great cost, leadership and executive coaching (I use the terms interchangeably) is provided to help support leaders in their role. It is a tool often used as part of a leadership development strategy. Typically, this type of coaching has focused on what the leaders need to improve and how they can become 'more effective' or more productive. There is an assumption by both organisations and leaders themselves, that if the individual can acquire more skills, or more knowledge, they will become this 'more effective' leader.

The following section challenges these assumptions and myths and explains why a paradigm shift is needed.

Myth 1: there is a 'right' and 'wrong' way to become a leader

Leaders are beginning to reject traditional forms of leader development that is being imposed on them (Webster, 2016). In part this is because of the lack of consideration given to context (both in practice, theory and research) and the increased pressures of demands facing them. Current practice fragments the individual, addressing only the human-in-the-role, forgetting much of the human-as-a-person. Ignoring the human side, in turn, fails to address the range of needs a person has, which, if not met, will affect their ability to lead others. A new paradigm is needed that takes into consideration the actual real needs of leaders, as much as the organisation might not want to acknowledge them, and as difficult to measure as they might be.

Myth 2: becoming a leader is about acquiring more skills and knowledge

Traditional forms of leader development are often based on a deficit model promoted by most leadership theory. This approach implies that there is something wrong with you and in order to become a better leader you need to fix this faulty part of yourself. However, 'filling up' on more knowledge and skills will not help if our level of thinking and our mental capacity to navigate challenges is not developed. The underlying implication is that the individual in need of development is deficient or defective in some way and needs to improve by adding more, when what is needed is to develop from within (Webster, 2016). Leader development programmes need to recognize that the shift away from hierarchical structures and the increase in self-responsibility will need to be supported by a different approach to leader development because becoming a leader does not sit at the hands of others, it sits within ourselves. What leaders actually need to do is evolve as people (and often they need help and support to do this).

Myth 3: the belief that there is an established literature, describing a theoretical framework on how leaders develop

Contrary to common opinion: "Despite almost three thousand years of ponderings and over a century of 'academic' research into leadership, we appear to be no nearer a consensus as to its basic meaning, let alone whether it can be taught, or its effects measured and predicted" (Grint, 2010). The leadership development literature is ambiguous and unformed (Latham, 2014). This applies even to the meanings attached to 'leader' and 'leadership' which in turn influences what is meant by 'leader development' and 'leadership development', and how these are practiced. This misplaced certainty has huge implications for the coaching industry and where it goes moving forward.

Myth 4: all leadership and executive coaching is the same

Coaching comes in different guises and is interpreted differently by different people in different contexts. In this book alone, authors describe broad and varied applications of the overall technique. Equally, and especially in the corporate workplace, coaching is delivered by a wide cross section of individuals with very mixed skills level, training and abilities. It could be argued that much of the coaching that goes on is more like mentoring, or active consulting on business issues, rather than aiming to move a person forward in a way that will contribute to the quality of their life experiences and the positive contribution they make to their families and work, to others in their team, and the wider organisational community. Positively affecting all these areas is what I mean by whole-person coaching.

Myth 5: adulthood is an end state

We encounter challenges throughout our lives. We have to deal with the competing demands of professional and personal life whether we work in corporations or elsewhere. From time to time these challenges may become all-consuming and we may not have the tools, knowledge or resources to successfully and quickly navigate them. There is no avoiding this tension and leaders are not exempt. Some (not all) coaches will have tools to hand to address this, so while leadership and executive coaching will address complex leadership issues it needs to also contain a more fundamental (essential) human component (Webster, 2016).

The assumption that when we reach adulthood we have finished our development is misleading. Adulthood is not an end state since development continues throughout our lives (Kegan, 1994, 2013). This knowledge is hugely valuable but unfortunately frequently overlooked. An awareness of this would go a long way to help alleviate much mental and emotional pain and subsequent ill-health that occurs as a result of encountering challenges without knowing the best way to manage them. Currently, leadership coaching tends not to acknowledge the wider needs that people face (Webster, 2016). This results in a piecemeal approach, addressing some needs, and perhaps meeting organisational requirements, but falling short of delivering on its promise; to support the whole person in their role and how they are interpreting and experiencing the different worlds they inhabit.

I believe it is therefore time to re-examine and re-evaluate what we mean by leadership and executive coaching and whether it is still relevant in its current form. Leaders and, as I will argue, others in an organisation, now require a level of support that goes beyond a goals-focused behavioural change coaching model. Given this context my view is that leadership, executive and general organisational coaching need to become whole-person coaching. Coaching must move on from improving performance or adding more skills or knowledge (simply finding ways to make a person work better, or faster, and more productively – the machine model) to supporting the individual to develop as a person. Furthermore, whilst the world needs more and better leaders (Bennis, 2007) it also needs better quality leaders (Deloitte, 2014). In order to meet the challenges facing organisations (and indeed our world) leaders' need to evolve, and new leaders need to emerge. Coaching practice and training must therefore also evolve if it is going to deliver value to those organisations, their people and society.

Secrets – emerging truths about leaders and coaching

We cannot talk about leadership and executive coaching without understanding the context in which it is taking place. Individuals working in organisations today are juggling both internal and external pressures that influence their ability to lead and to excel (be that with their role, their environment or those they manage). Leaders as people have a wide range of complex needs and coaching must address all of them.

Table 11.1 A strategy for modern leadership: a whole-person approach

Human/psychological needs	Whole-person needs	Leader needs
Survival (coping with the demands of the organisation)	Managing emotions	Becoming the leader they want to be
Support and reassurance	Managing energy	Creating a bespoke development programme

Source: Webster, 2016

Human/psychological needs

Individuals often experience organisational environments as brutal. At times they feel threatened, and the internal resources they need to operate in this environment are sometimes not readily accessible to them. It might be argued that the organisational environment is a mirror of the wider environment, in which many are fearful and feel threatened. Either way, to ignore this means that any coaching that takes place is on top of a fragile base. It is this foundation which must first be addressed before moving to a more organisationally focused agenda. Conducting an emotional needs audit is one way to do this (Griffin and Tyrell, 2013).

Leaders frequently find coaching to be therapeutic, suggesting that they might need a different type of support to that which is currently provided, because in reality people are using coaching for more personal support than is currently understood. Organisations and the coaching industry do not readily consider the impact of the organisational environment; an individual's mental and emotional well-being; and the wider role of context. These *all* contribute to, influence, and affect a person's ability to perform at their best.

Whole-person needs

The reality of today is that leaders may be more emotionally challenged than is currently understood by the coaching profession (or indeed acknowledged by their organisations). Furthermore, today's leaders want support and reassurance in what they are doing and the decisions they are making; they enjoy having support to navigate their emotions and manage their energy, which can be disruptive (emotions) and depleted or needing to be discharged (energy).

Leader needs

People are craving to be supported in ways that help them as a person beyond the technical aspects of their roles (Webster, 2016). But there is currently a disconnect between the reason organisations employ coaching, and the way in which it is actually being used by the individual. Leaders enjoy the one-to-one support they get from the coach, and they also enjoy the freedom they have to explore the areas of development that are important to them. The kind of support they get from coaching allows them to tailor a programme of personal development, which enables them to become more congruent and then go on to define for themselves who they want to be as a leader.

The heart of coaching – the honest truth

At the heart of coaching is the very simple human experience of being heard in a safe environment and being listened to without judgment. As a client observed to me; while coaching is not therapy, it can be very therapeutic. Essentially, the process of coaching creates an outlet for individuals to be able to talk aloud, and sometimes hear, for the first time, some of their own thoughts. This can be a very powerful experience. This process, with the help of a skilled listener, helps the individual order those thoughts. It allows the most present and committed of individuals to solve issues that may have previously eluded them. It is an opportunity for personal development, which requires a level of introspection, self-awareness, sometimes soul-searching and some personal discomfort. It always requires effort to gain rich personal insights that will enable someone to grow as a human being and move forward with their life in a positive way. Achieving this level of self-understanding enables a person to become more whole *and* more human. Limiting coaching in its current form short-changes the client.

Modern leadership

Leaders are increasingly rejecting what is being imposed on them by existing leader development training because they do not want to follow a prescribed model of becoming a leader and they don't want to be "lectured at", which is often the goal of this sort of training. Today's leaders are looking for more meaningful development opportunities and no longer seem prepared to blindly accept what has previously been thrust upon them (Webster, 2016). Such people are the most progressive of leaders: they understand and appreciate the importance of personal development in their role as a leader and they take personal responsibility and ownership for their own development. In my experience these modern leaders typically have four key qualities:

Four key qualities of a Modern Leader

1   the ability to listen
2   a willingness to share
3   the capacity to be present
4   a desire to adapt, change and learn

Essentially, leadership is about being human. But being human is often not prioritised in the corporate environment. Modern leadership is not about learning a certain 'model of leadership', going on a course, having coaching, or being part of a leader development programme. All these things will help, but they will not make a leader; people have to do that for themselves. Modern leadership is about acknowledging that to be credible as a leader is to be congruent as a person. However, this takes time, effort and work. It is essentially about developing oneself as a person who is able to navigate life's challenges and to know what it is to live a fulfilling life, one that successfully supports our mental and emotional health. In essence, to be able to travel through life lighter, and to avoid some of the pitfalls that can weigh us down.

I therefore believe that coaches have a responsibility to reveal more about what coaching actually involves and the sorts of issues it addresses and that leaders too need to be more transparent about the level of support they are receiving. It seems strange to me that those at the top of the organisation are getting a great deal of support and help, but others in the organisation do not have access to it, though are experiencing the same anxieties.

Relationships sit at the heart of modern leadership because relationships bring a focus on context and our role in this context. They also help us understand how environments and experiences impact our emotional and mental well-being. It is the quality of these relationships and the leader's connection to their own internal world (and developing their ability to build a wealth of resources in this world) that will define their ability to navigate and overcome challenging situations that occur as a natural part of life.

Modern leaders transcend title and position because they are the ones who take ownership of their development. They want to be in alignment with who they are and who they want to become (Webster, 2016). These people understand that to be credible as a leader is to be congruent as a person.

More leaders will emerge if it is more widely understood that we each hold within ourselves the resources and abilities to develop as person (even though we might need help in uncovering these resources and the process might be difficult at times). Indeed more of these leaders might be able to come forward if coaches are able to demystify some of what really goes on in coaching and the level of support that people are receiving.

For these reasons coach training needs to change. Since we have these insights into how leaders experience coaching, and the wide range of needs they bring to coaching, coaches must explore how to meet their clients where they are. And while the leader must develop as a person, so too must the coach. Coach training needs to develop and adapt so that the coach too can become more whole.

Coaching needs to address the multiplicity of demands the leader-as-a-person faces. A review of the current approaches to coaching, including the paradigm in which leader development is approached is needed since failure to address the whole person in coaching will yield partial results.

Collective responsibility

The coaching community and the corporate community have a responsibility to dispel the myths of how and why coaching is being used. Given my earlier emphasis on coaching which takes a whole-person approach, what of non-leaders who are not given access to this level of support? What consideration is being given to the other people who work in these 'corporate communities' and the impact that these communities have on life and society in general? People want physical community now more than ever. Our need for community is integral to our emotional health and well-being and is a human given (Griffin and Tyrell, 2013). Organisations represent places of huge opportunity in supporting individuals in the modern world. If we are to solve mental health issues, which seem to be taking on increasing importance, it is imperative we consider the role of our various communities and the effect they have on our lives – and this can start with the organisational workplace.

Equally, it is time to let go of the illusion that we can glide through life without being challenged mentally and emotionally. By dispelling some of the myths of how and why coaching is being used we can help others understand, and avoid, some of the pitfalls of modern life. Coaching is not a tool but a way of being (Whitmore, 2009) and, as I've stressed, leadership is about a way of being in the world. Leadership and executive coaching might start at the top of the organisation but the effects of it should flow through the organisation to reach, and benefit, many more than that one person. But in reality, this does not happen frequently enough, if at all. I believe organisations have a social responsibility to provide support and structure to others throughout the organisation because while the investment is made at the top of the organisation it is the other leaders (of which there are many – they just don't have a fancy title) that also need this support.

Modern leadership and the wider implications for coaching

It is important to be aware of the level of support that leaders are receiving; how modern leaders take ownership of their own development; and how, with the help of a professional coach, they are able to overcome anxieties and navigate the demands of the corporate environment. This will help others create a more accurate context for leadership since they will be able to understand that:

- leadership comes from within;
- leadership comes out of taking ownership of our development;
- anxieties are part of life;
- it is a myth we can sail through life without challenge;
- leadership is personal;
- leadership is about becoming whole as a person and understanding the impact that our environments and our relationships have on us, and how these play out in our actions.

We need more coaches who can help leaders understand that to be more human increases the likelihood that they will be effective leaders, despite the huge pressures to deny this obvious fact.

The jewel at the heart of modern leadership – the power in our own hands

A whole-person approach to coaching offers a huge opportunity to prevent mental health issues from developing because it can help others understand the many tools that are available to us to enhance our mental and emotional well-being. Rather than talk about the mental health crisis and how to retro-solve it, a whole-person approach can help support a focus on how to prevent it in the first place. The coaching industry can help people understand how we can successfully navigate potential harmful impacts on our mental and emotional well-being. And most importantly, how much of it sits within our own hands. It is just as easy to spiral up to a positive experience as it is to spiral down to a negative one (Fredrickson, 2009). Organisations-as-communities, and personal development support within that context, have an important role to play here.

As an illustration, take our increased reliance on technology, or rather our limiting belief that we have to rely on it. We cannot work long hours, tethered to devices 24/7 and expect to feel good all the time. We cannot expose ourselves to the negative news cycle and expect that there will be no negative repercussions on our mental and emotional well-being. And when you respond to an email from your boss at 10pm at night you are teaching your boss that it is acceptable to disrupt your life. It is then difficult to complain about the situation. Or worse, you assume that there is some more sinister reason why you might be feeling snappy or out of sorts. A simple solution here, as in the other examples, is to turn off the device (telephone, internet or television). We must take responsibility for our actions and our own role in our behaviour (even though at times it might seem hard, difficult or uncomfortable). Coaching not only helps people make decisions: it can ensure we take responsibility for them.

I believe there is a wider role and responsibility for coaching (but a new term is needed to describe it): the need to address mental health, and perhaps even to challenge this concept. As coaches we have to challenge the current narrative of a negative view of mental health in order to help steer the conversation towards viewing emotional and mental health as a valuable part of everyday life. We must help people to not be afraid of mental health, but to view it through a different lens. These challenges affect people in all walks of life; indeed, they are a natural and healthy part of our life experience and how we grow as people. We should look at them in such a way. Prevention can be easily achieved. But as society becomes ever more psychologised, we are in danger of over-intellectualising and allowing this language to become too dominant and give it too much power. Mental and emotional ill health is nothing new, we must not pretend that it is or ignore it in an organisational context.

Transformational conversations

While organisations exist, in essence, to meet the needs of their shareholders and owners they are also communities – collectives of people. Real people, having real human experiences and as a collective this community of individuals bring an energy to the organisation. Leaders within this community bring a disproportionate amount of energy. This 'intangible' energy however, is often overlooked and discounted, because, after all, how do you measure human energy (or explain it to shareholders perhaps?). But all this energy has the potential to be harnessed. And, in my view, the leaders in these communities have a duty-of-care to create positive organisations that provide healthy environments in which their employees can flourish.

Since the central objective in coaching is to move a person forward in some way (by whatever means they need at the time) I propose a more appropriate way to explain what good coaches do (and thereby making it more accessible to others) is that they facilitate and provide the platform for a 'Transformational Conversation' to take place. This may help others understand how coaching works. It might also help individuals to adopt a more coaching style as they lead and work alongside others.

Much of what is going on in coaching at the senior level, is *personal support* to that leader. However, for organisations this can be too uncomfortable to acknowledge, so this support is positioned as leadership or executive coaching. Thus, the illusion persists that coaching for this group is some high level, complex technique only the leader level is equipped for. When in reality it is a personal, bespoke, confidential, expert support on whatever topics arise, starting most often with helping the leader survive in, and navigate, the complex and (often perceived as) threatening corporate environment (Webster, 2016). More helpful to everyone, especially those working in organisations, would be to make clearer the level of *personal* support these executives are receiving. And a far more helpful, and accurate way to understand coaching is to better understand the truth of what it actually is (or should be) – a transformational conversation. As I have said before, this is true coaching, and different to some 'coaching' that takes place, which is actually mentoring or consulting.

Framing coaching as a transformational conversation also has an added benefit in that it is directly measurable for both the organisation, the coachee and the coach. Most importantly it is agile, dynamic, fast-paced and accountable. Furthermore, it is a much more cost effective and efficient route to achieve results.

We could ask two questions to measure impact:

1 Did you find the conversation transformational in anyway?
2 Can you tell me how/what will you do as a result of the insights you have gained from it?

This then equips both the coachee and the organisation with a structure from which to work and provides a direction for the coachee to take to both meet organisational goals, and to evolve as a person and take responsibility for their behaviours. It also enables a framework for monitoring and measurement for industry (both the coaching industry and the corporate environments) and also for how well the coach is doing.

The most progressive thinkers (clients, coaches and leaders) value both the science and magic of coaching and the most enlightened understand that 'coaching' is always more than just 'coaching' – or at least it should be. It is also more than just that space in time of working with a coach, since it is about evolving as a person. And, that there is something intangible in this (and indeed un-measurable).

I believe our goal as modern leaders should be to:

- challenge what it is to be a leader in today's world
- make organisations more human
- make leadership accessible for all

Conclusions: future conversations

Coaching must not fall into the trap of psychology, which has traditionally focused on a 'disease model' orientation. Furthermore, psychology has been guilty of over intellectualization, by implying a certain level of complexity (which is simply not there). This has the negative effect of alienating some people. Some may question the motives of this implied exclusivity and should rightly be concerned of the level of control it can have over us. We must not let this happen to coaching. Yes, some theories are complex, and yes, it can be a complex process, and to evolve as a human being is not always easy. But we must not alienate the very people and communities who we should be serving. Coaching must seek to raise awareness about the importance of taking ownership of our own development and the personal value of doing so. It must dispel the myths that we are deficient in some way, and in need of fixing. It must challenge the belief that we have to hand over power to someone else to make us better or more efficient.

Today, we need a new framework for a modern approach to leadership, one that can be achieved through a whole-person approach that acknowledges the personal needs and contexts that influence a leader and those who share the organisational community environment with them.

Ultimately, we do have control over our behaviours (whether we decide to own it or not). The vast majority of the population is born with the resources to overcome and navigate life's challenges. But under stress the ability to think clearly impacts our ability to do so. Leaders are getting help through coaching to learn the tools and techniques to navigate these challenges; shouldn't others be getting access to them too?

References

Avolio, B. (2007) 'Promoting more integrative strategies for leadership theory building', *American Psychologist*, 62(1), pp. 25–33.

Bennis, W. (2007) 'The challenges of leadership in the modern world: Introduction to the special issues', *American Psychologist*, 62, pp. 25–33.

Day, D.V., Harrison, M.M. and Halpin, S.M. (2009) *An integrative approach to leader development: Connecting adult development, identity and expertise.* New York: Routledge.

Deloitte (2014) *Global human capital trends 2014: Engaging the 21st century workforce.* Westlake, TX: Deloitte University Press. Available at: www2.deloitee.com/content. dam/Deloitte/uk/Documents/human-capital/uk-con-human-capital-trends-2014.pdr (Accessed: 23 July 2015).

Fredrickson, B. (2009) *Positivity*. Oxford: Oneworld.

Griffin, J. and Tyrell, I. (2013) *Human givens. The new approach to emotional health and wellbeing*. East Sussex: HG Publishing.

Grint, K. (2010) *Leadership: A very short introduction*. Oxford: Oxford University Press.

Kegan, R. (1994) *In over our heads*. Cambridge, MA: Harvard University Press.

Kegan, R. (2013) *The further reaches of adult development*. Available at: www.youtube.com/watch?v=BoasM4cCHBc (Accessed: November 2015).

Latham, J. (2014) *Leadership for quality and innovation: Challenges, theories, and a framework for future research*. University of Northern Colorado. Available at: www/asq.org (Accessed: January 2013).

Turner, J. and Malvin, S. (2014) 'Becoming more self aware – A journey of authentic leader development', *HRD: Reflecting upon the past – Shaping the future: Proceedings of the 15th International Conference on Human Resource Development Research and Practice across Europe*. Edinburgh.

Webster, S. (2016) 'How do leaders experience coaching? A whole-person perspective' *Thesis Submitted to Oxford Brookes University in partial fulfilment of the requirements of the award of Doctor of Coaching and Mentoring*. Oxford, UK.

Whitmore, J. (2009) *The challenge of global leadership*. Available at: www.youtube.com/watch?v=7-D6CnaQUuw (Accessed: 20 October 2015).

Chapter 12

Coaching in education

Supporting the mental health and well-being of pupils and staff

Mark Adams and Jak Lee

Where is coaching needed most? Where does coaching have the potential to make a truly meaningful difference? In which domain does the application of coaching have the potential to make a significant contribution to both current and future generations? Where does the application of coaching and coaching psychology stand to benefit the children and young people of our society? The answer to all these questions, in our view, is the domain of education, which is our specialism, our passion, and the focus of this chapter.

The use of coaching in educational contexts has become increasingly prevalent since the turn of the twenty-first century, with applications including the enhancement of teachers' professional practice, leadership coaching, and coaching for student success and well-being (Campbell, 2016; van Nieuwerburgh, 2012). Reflecting the spirit, research and practice of positive psychology (Seligman & Csikszentmihalyi, 2000), coaching shifts away from the medical model of helping ('fix the disease') to instead enabling the person to achieve goals, attain enhanced well-being, and move towards optimal functioning. As such, this extends the reach of coaching to a wide population of client groups and enables support to be provided both proactively and preventatively (e.g. before issues with well-being escalate to the point of maladaptive stress, or before day-to-day mental health issues develop into more serious difficulties).

We are both Educational Psychologists by profession and have each developed a specialism in coaching since the early-to-mid 2000s; to reflect this, we also use the term 'Coaching Psychologist' in our role titles. As Coaching Psychologists, the coaching work we undertake is explicitly informed by psychological principles and approaches, including methods drawn from person-centred counselling (Rogers, 1951, 1961, 2003), cognitive-behavioural coaching (Neenan & Palmer, 2012), solution-focused coaching (Iveson, George & Ratner, 2012), Self-Determination Theory (Ryan & Deci, 2000), Motivational Interviewing (Miller & Rollnick, 2002, 2013), positive psychology (Snyder & Lopez, 2005), and Acceptance & Commitment Therapy (Harris, 2009).

In this chapter we show how coaching is relevant to two current conversations in the domain of education:

1   How can we support the mental health and well-being of young people?
2   How can we support the mental health and well-being of education practitioners?

We have limited our discussion to two priority areas to enable a more in-depth exploration. To achieve our aims, we first locate each discussion in its current context, before presenting an illustrative case study and then exploring its associated implications. We then draw together our conclusions about the relevance of coaching to these debates.

1   Coaching to support the mental health and well-being of young people

There is increasing awareness of the mental health challenges facing children and young people in today's society. An estimated 12–15 percent of 11–15 year olds have a diagnosable mental health disorder, with particular groups (e.g. LGBT+ young people, looked-after young people, and those who are NEET – Not in Education, Employment or Training) being more vulnerable or susceptible to mental health issues (DoH & DfE, 2017). While such statistics are concerning in themselves, it should be noted that they do not include the multitude of young people who may be 'at risk' but whose issues have not yet developed to the point of meeting diagnostic criteria. The prevalence of mental health issues in young people may therefore be far greater than the initially reported estimates suggest.

The cost of unaddressed mental health issues is significant and includes: more absence from school; a greater likelihood of being on welfare as adults; and a greater likelihood of engaging in a criminal act (DoH & DfE, ibid). Recent years have also seen significant increases in the numbers of university students who have either disclosed a mental health condition (Higher Education Statistics Agency, 2019) or who have left university early for mental health reasons (Marsh, 2017). Clearly, these are costs that are incurred by both young people themselves and society more broadly, both now and in the future. This places an imperative upon us all to consider how we can collectively meet this challenge. While recent proposals from the Department of Health and Department for Education[1] (ibid) are a welcome step forward in this respect, it has been argued that the UK government's proposed strategy needs to be more far-reaching and should include a greater emphasis on proactive and preventative approaches to supporting young people's mental health and well-being (Education and Health & Social Care Committees, 2018). The fact that 50 percent of all mental health issues are established before the age of 14 (DoH & DfE, ibid) further emphasizes the need for early intervention. It is in this context that we argue that the availability of personalised individual coaching could represent a valuable element of the support provided for children and young people in schools.

In recent years several publications have emerged which illustrate and inform the specific application of coaching with children and young people (e.g. Giant, 2014; Ratner & Yusuf, 2015; Abdulla, 2018), accompanied in parallel by a gradually developing evidence base regarding the impact of applications of coaching on young people's mental health and well-being. For example, Green, Grant and Rynsaardt (2007) found that female senior high school students' (mean age 16 years) participation in a 20-week programme of solution-focused/cognitive behavioural life coaching led to significant increases in levels of hardiness and hope, and significant decreases in levels of depression. More recently, two smaller-scale qualitative studies have offered an indication of the potential benefits of coaching with 'at-risk' young people, with some adolescent coachees who had participated in either individual or group coaching programmes reporting increased experience of positive emotions, enhanced self-belief/confidence, and a greater sense of choice and control over their thoughts, feelings and behaviour (Pritchard & van Nieuwerburgh, 2016; Robson-Kelly & van Nieuwerburgh, 2016).

In terms of *how* such gains are achieved, our contention is that coaching can positively impact on young people's mental health and well-being through two key mechanisms. In the first instance, coaching enables young people to constructively deal with day-to-day challenges, providing them with a confidential space in which (with support) they can plan strategies for tackling current situations and achieving greater well-being in their lives. However, as well as supporting young people to plan how to deal with their situations 'in the moment', coaching potentially has longer-term benefits in terms of its ability to enhance young people's broader problem-solving capabilities. By helping young people to become aware of the thinking *processes* they have used to problem-solve an issue (a process known as *metacognition* – Flavell, 1976), they can also learn transferable skills that they can draw upon to help themselves in times of difficulty in the future. We will now use a short case study to illustrate these two mechanisms in action.

Case study

Andre was a Year 11 pupil (in his final year of schooling) who was struggling to attend school due to anxiety. Andre's family and school staff wanted to explore how they could help him to manage his anxiety – including, importantly, attendance at examinations – while also helping him to learn skills that would enhance his ability to self-manage in the future as he faced the challenge of increased independence.

Several interventions were put in place around Andre, one of which was a series of five monthly coaching sessions. It is important to note that Andre was on the waiting list for CAMHS (Child and Adolescent Mental Health Services) involvement given the severity of his situation and the nature of his mental health/well-being needs. However, given that he was in his final year of schooling, there was a need for timely support to (ideally) help Andre to make the best use of his remaining months in Year 11. Coaching was an appropriate form of support in this instance, providing Andre with sessions that were future-oriented (focused on goals that Andre wanted to achieve), time-limited, and which explored everyday aspects of his life rather than past history or the origins of his difficulties (which could be more the domain of a therapist, subject to their particular orientation and approach). Indeed, Giant (2014) has noted that coaching "can be utilized to address specific goals for a client with deep-seated issues or [who may be] receiving more intensive therapy elsewhere" (p. 12). The sessions were heavily informed by the principles and practices of Solution-Focused Coaching (Iveson, George & Ratner, 2012; O'Connell, Palmer & Williams, 2012; Ratner & Yusuf, 2015), in that there was a clear focus on the future Andre wanted to achieve and the resources he had that would help him to move towards it.

At the beginning of the intervention, Andre was encouraged to describe his 'preferred future', an image of life as he wanted it to be (Iveson, George & Ratner, 2012). He described a future scenario in which he was studying a Computer Science course at a college, a goal for which Andre knew he needed to achieve "good grades in Maths, English and Computer Science". To help him achieve this, Andre said that he would like to learn how to manage his anxious feelings more effectively. This goal then became the focus of the sessions.

Over the course of the five coaching sessions, Andre and the coach used a 0–10 rating scale to:

- Evaluate the extent to which Andre perceived he was able to manage his anxious feelings ("On a scale from 0–10, where 10 is that you can always manage your anxious feelings, and zero is that you can never manage them, where are you now?").
- Identify examples of ways in which Andre was already experiencing success, even if only in part (e.g. "What is happening that means that you are at 5 out of 10 on the scale and not any lower?").
- Explore the resources and strategies Andre was using which seemed to help him (these were: walking half-way to a place and then pausing to re-group before continuing; distracting himself by talking with another person about something else; using a computer; and thinking about his dog).
- Develop Andre's conscious awareness of his effective strategies and prompt him to think about when and where the use of each strategy might be most helpful.
- Identify what a sign of a step forward on the scale would look like (e.g. attending more Maths and English lessons, attending a mock exam, completing some work in a 1:1 session).
- Review Andre's progress on the scale and clarify the actions, skills and thought processes that were helping him ("Where are you now on the scale? What has helped/been less helpful? What next?").

Across the coaching engagement some demonstrable gains were observed. Although Andre's attendance at lessons did not noticeably improve, he attended many (though not all) of his mock exams, stayed in those exams for longer than the minimum time, and became more conscious of strategies that he could use to help him to manage his anxiety. Towards the end of the coaching engagement, Andre went for an interview at a college and was offered a place on a college course.

Discussion

This case study has illustrated the applicability of coaching as an intervention to support a young person to achieve improved mental health and well-being. In this case, a solution-focused coaching approach was used to support a young person (Andre) who was struggling to attend school due to anxiety. The coaching relationship provided Andre with a safe-but-challenging non-judgemental space in which he could reflect on his goals and his progress towards them. Across the series of five sessions, this enabled Andre to begin making progress in terms of his ability to manage his anxious feelings and move towards his goal of accessing a college course. At the same time, Andre was also learning to use transferable thinking strategies that could be applied to other future situations. For example:

- Imagining a preferred future and using that as both motivation and as a reference point.
- Planning how to move towards his overall goal by: (i) considering his current position in relation to the goal; (ii) identifying existing successes and resources; (iii) setting small-step goals; and (iv) reviewing and evaluating progress, including the value of incremental change. In this particular example each of these was achieved through the use of a 'scaling' approach.
- Selecting the most appropriate strategy from the range of those available for a given task.

In this way, coaching can support young people not just to manage their immediate realities, but to also learn skills that can enhance their capacity to face future challenges. The benefit of this taking place in a coaching engagement is that it enables the young person to learn and apply specific strategies as they are relevant to the real-life situations they are facing. This approach is consistent with recent guidance on the use of metacognitive approaches with children and young people which states: "While concepts like 'plan, monitor, evaluate' can be introduced generically, the strategies are mostly applied in relation to specific content and tasks, and are therefore best taught this way" (Education Endowment Foundation, 2018, p. 14).

While a solution-focused coaching approach was used in this case-study, other engagements could be informed by a range of other psychology-informed approaches, for example:

- Using cognitive-behavioural approaches to enhance the young person's ability to recognise and transform self-limiting thoughts and behaviours.

(e.g. Stallard, 2019)

- Using Acceptance & Commitment Therapy-informed approaches to help the young person to clarify their values, set values-congruent goals, and learn new ways of relating to troublesome thoughts and feelings.

(Hayes, 2015)

Whichever method is used, young people could be supported to apply the approach to their present realities, while adding specific strategies to their repertoires for use in future situations. Such strategies could represent valuable protective factors to help safeguard against current and future issues with mental health and well-being.

It is important to note that Andre was actively involved as an equal collaborator in the process of change. He was not *done to* but was rather *worked with* to determine goals, develop strategies, and review progress. Indeed, research into the effectiveness of helping relationships consistently demonstrates that the client's experience of a positive *collaborative alliance* has a far greater influence on the outcome than the specific techniques that might be applied (Murphy & Duncan, 2007). In other words, people tend to do better in a helping relationship if they: (i) feel listened to, trusted and respected; (ii) are working towards goals that matter to them, and; (iii) feel they have a say in the tasks that are carried out both in and between sessions. Coaching enables young people to experience such a relationship, and to be active participants in determining both the outcomes that they want to work towards and the strategies for achieving this. In the process, our hope is that young people who experience such a relationship may also learn that talking to others about concerns at an early stage can be a positive and helpful step to take.

In this case, coaching was applied with a Year 11 (aged 16 years) young person; however, in our view it would be preferable to provide coaching for young people from an earlier age so that they have more opportunity to learn skills that will support them in dealing with the range of life's challenges. Although the prevalence of mental health issues in young people arguably points to the need for broader systemic changes in our society and education systems (Education and Health & Social Care Committees, 2018), in our view the provision and evaluation of effective support mechanisms for young people – including coaching – should be a component of any school's planning. As we have seen, coaching can be a helpful intervention for supporting young people (including those possibly experiencing mental health issues) to problem-solve daily aspects of living and move towards enhanced mental health and well-being.

It is important to acknowledge that coaching (in this context) focuses primarily on the individual, and the evidence suggests that schools need to also adopt a more systemic approach to improving well-being and mental health for young people. Weare (2015) outlines a framework to guide schools' planning in this respect, which locates individual interventions in a broader context. As well as individual-focused interventions, the framework also encompasses whole-school work to improve well-being (see Gillard, Flaxman & Hooper, 2018), supportive policies, staff development and ways to engage the broader community to this end. Children/young people do not exist in isolation of their contexts and, in our view, coaching should ideally complement a broader range of approaches at different levels of the organization.

Coaching can be effective even through a limited series of relatively short sessions and may well enhance young people's ability to cope both now and in the future. While we would argue that this is money well-spent, schools will have to consider questions of affordability and the availability of resources. One possible solution to achieve cost-effectiveness would be to train more adults in schools with these skills – for example, Learning Mentors, Learning Support Assistants, pastoral staff, and those with key responsibilities for mental health and well-being. In this way, the capacity of schools to proactively and preventatively enable young people to become better 'self-managers' would increase, potentially reducing the number of young people who may go on to develop mental health issues in the future.

2. Coaching for staff mental health and well-being

Working in education in the United Kingdom in the twenty-first century can be a fast-paced, high-pressure endeavour, with multiple demands (e.g. workload, pupil behaviour, school inspections, changes to national initiatives) exacting a toll on staff (Ofsted, 2018). Our education workforce therefore needs to be effectively supported if they are to be in the best place to give to the children under their care. Unfortunately, current evidence regarding the well-being of education staff suggests that we may be falling short in this challenge. For example, a recent survey of education professionals in the United Kingdom (Education Support Partnership, 2017) found that nearly a third of education staff overall (29 percent) and more than a third of senior leaders in education (37 percent) said that their job had made them feel stressed "most or all of the time in the past few weeks", a figure that is in contrast with 18 percent of UK employees overall (CIPD, 2017). In the same survey, 75 percent of respondents indicated that they had experienced either behavioural (e.g. irritability, mood swings), psychological (e.g. depression, anxiety, panic attacks) or physical symptoms (e.g. raised blood pressure, dizziness, headaches) due to work or where work was a contributing factor (ESP, ibid). These stark findings are perhaps reflected in: (i) the rising proportion of working-age teachers leaving the profession each year (from 9–11 percent for primary school teachers and from 11–13 percent for secondary school teachers – Worth & De Lazzari, 2017); and (ii) the numbers of teachers leaving the classroom within five years of qualifying (30 percent of the 21,400 teachers who began teaching in state schools in 2010 had left the classroom within five years – see Weale (2016)). Similarly, over half of the respondents in the 2017 ESP survey (53 percent) indicated that they had considered leaving the profession over the last two years as a result of health pressures.

If we do not look after the well-being of staff, how can we expect them to adequately attend to the well-being of others along with their many other priorities? As Weare (2015) notes:

> Wellbeing in schools starts with the staff: They are in the front line of this work, and it is hard for them to be genuinely motivated to promote emotional and social wellbeing in others if they feel uncared for and burnt out themselves.
>
> (p. 6)

Similarly, a recent survey of education practitioners indicated a consensus view that a focus on teacher well-being also promotes student well-being (Roffey, 2012). As one respondent noted:

> When teaching staff feel appreciated and empowered, they are much more likely to show patience and empathy for their students; to go the "extra mile" for the students in their care. They are also more likely to share and work with others in order to support their students and promote wellbeing.
>
> (Roffey, ibid, p. 15)

Certainly, we would argue that if people are to give effectively to others, we need to ensure they have the capacity to do so, with outlets for both communicating about and, where possible, problem-solving issues at an early stage. Unfortunately, the ESP report has indicated that there may be a tendency for education practitioners to suffer in silence, with almost two-thirds (64 percent) of those surveyed declaring that they would not feel confident in disclosing unmanageable stress or mental health problems to their employer (ESP, ibid.). This suggests the need for the provision of appropriate support structures for staff which normalise the process of checking-in and reviewing their capacity, health and well-being. To this end, Weare (ibid.) argues that schools should foster the development of a school climate and ethos which:

> routinely acknowledges the reality of staff stress and finds ways to make it safe for staff and leaders (as well as pupils) to acknowledge their human distress, weakness and difficulty and seek support for their mental health needs in non-stigmatising ways.
>
> (p. 7)

It is with this aim in mind that we propose that regular coaching for staff could be a valuable component of a school's strategy in this respect. Indeed, there is already some evidence to suggest that the provision of coaching for staff can have a positive impact on a range of outcomes, including staff well-being. For example, Grant, Green and Rynsaardt (2010) found that high school teachers' participation in a 20-week coaching programme was associated with increased goal attainment, reduced stress, enhanced workplace well-being and resilience, and improved leadership style. The authors concluded that coaching "has great potential to contribute to the development and wellbeing of society" (p. 151). The following case study shows how coaching has been used in a UK educational setting to support staff performance and well-being.

Case study

The authors were commissioned by a specialist primary school which provides for young people with social, emotional and mental health needs. Given the high level of need of the children, and the magnitude of the challenge this can present, staff at the school are arranged into classroom teams comprising one teacher and one or two additional Learning Support Assistants (LSAs). Following previous experience of the benefits of coaching in schools, the school's leadership decided that they wanted to provide the classroom teams with coaching to support their performance, development and well-being. The sessions would provide the staff with a confidential space in which they could offload their emotions, reflect on practice, problem-solve difficulties (if applicable), and plan how to move towards goals. It was agreed that sessions could be used to explore matters relating to personal and team well-being as well as day-to-day practice.

Rather than being provided on an ad-hoc or as-needed basis, sessions were timetabled to take place termly (six sessions over the year, approximately six weeks apart), with each session lasting for 45 minutes. Sessions were informed by core coaching skills and frameworks (e.g. the I-GROW model – Whitmore, 1992, 2002), supplemented by methods drawn from other psychology-informed coaching approaches (e.g. person-centred coaching, solution-focused coaching, cognitive-behavioural coaching – see Palmer & Whybrow, 2007, 2019; Adams, 2015). In each session the coaches would endeavour to draw the participants' attention to their strengths and successes while supporting them to reflect on their situations and plan how to move forward. Towards the end of each session the participants would review the possible actions considered and make their own decisions about what they would or would not pursue.

At the end of each academic year, the teams were interviewed and asked to: (i) rate the extent to which the coaching support had achieved the desired aims; and (ii) discuss what had been helpful about the sessions and how they might further be improved. This allowed the coaching relationship between coach and team to be reviewed and shaped over time. Table 12.1 shows the median rating provided by the teams over three academic years:

Table 12.1 Median rating provided by the teams over three academic years

Academic year	Number of teams	Median team rating (out of 10) for "the extent to which the coaching support achieved the stated aims (of enhancing performance, development & well-being)".
2014–2015	7	9
2015–2016	8	8
2016–2017	8	9

In their qualitative feedback, participants reported a range of outcomes that they experienced because of the coaching sessions. This encompassed positive changes in relation to well-being (e.g. "[It] takes stress levels down, gets stuff off our chests") and classroom practice (e.g. "The strategies help make life easier in the classroom"). Others reported further emotional benefits (e.g. "Increased confidence in what I am doing and my ability", "Helped our ability to remain resilient during challenging work") and noted that the very experience of "feeling listened to helps well-being." One participant observed, as discussed in the introduction to this chapter, a link between their own well-being and their ability to provide for the pupils, saying: "It gets everything out of my head – this helps my well-being which means I am better able to support the pupils with their well-being and needs. . . . Staff well-being is key so that we can support them."

In terms of what helped to achieve these gains, participants reported that it was important to experience the coaching sessions as a safe place to discuss issues – "[A] safe space to offload confidentially" where they could be "validated and not judged" and "talk through difficult situations with a fresh pair of eyes." A key element for achieving this sense of safety, in the view of the participants, was that the coach was independent to the organization ("A coach that is objective and confidential", "A supportive person who is not emotionally involved"). As one Learning Support Assistant summarized: "It's crucial to have a safe, confidential space with someone external to the organization. . . . Someone listening and shining a light on things." Another participant noted that the provision of time and space for coaching helped them to "feel valued" by their school. Similarly, humour was thought to be an important component of the sessions for helping the staff to "not feel like it is all doom and gloom".

A number of comments referred to the benefit of having space to discuss issues and plan constructive ways forward (e.g. "Talking properly about issues and coming to a forward plan", "Devising practical ideas", and "Thrashing out ideas so that we [can] improve situations"). One respondent noted that the sessions "Helped [us] prioritise what needs addressing and find ways to improve it".

Participants also commented on the role of the coaches in terms of being able to structure and guide conversations, observing that: "The coach helps us to move the conversation from negative discussions to positive ways forward. The coach judges [this] so we feel listened to but have more time to be positive." Similarly, another comment referred to "reflection with a structure that the coach builds into the session", while another noted that "the coach helps us stay on track". Other comments referred to the regularly timetabled coaching sessions as providing valuable reflection time, representing "[an] allotted space to reflect with guided communication by the coach." This was perceived as important in that "It gives us time to properly reflect, otherwise it's all ad-hoc", and provided staff with "a time with no other pressures to discuss a problem and decide on plans to implement to overcome it."

Finally, one participant reported that they had grown to value coaching despite harbouring initial reservations about the process, saying: "We very much value it, it's really important. I was sceptical at first but it's valuable in the environment we work in."

Discussion

In this case study, teams of education practitioners (teachers and LSAs) reported that they experienced termly coaching as supporting improvements in their performance, development and well-being, citing specific gains such as reduced stress, improved confidence, and enhanced capacity to provide for the pupils under their care.

Practitioners reported that they valued the sessions as providing them with a non-judgemental, safe, confidential outlet in which they could feel listened to and understood, and in turn felt valued by their organization as a result. Furthermore, the removal of the threat of judgement from the conversation enabled the participants to speak and behave openly and honestly, with the aim of increasing the likelihood that they would feel comfortable disclosing possible issues with well-being or performance at an early stage. Within this climate the participants self-selected themes for discussion, thereby respecting their autonomy and enabling them to choose topics and strategies that were most relevant to their individual situations. This also serves to engender the sense of agency and control that Weare (2015) advocates as being so crucial for the well-being of staff in the education sector. Thereafter, participants were afforded time and space to explore their experiences, thoughts and ideas for solutions, a privilege that can be all-too-rare in the maelstrom of twenty-first century education.

As the discussions unfolded the participants valued the coach providing structure or steer to the sessions to draw their attention to strengths and successes, keep the conversations on-track and guide the participants towards constructive solutions. This illustrates the need for the coach to be able to supplement a non-directive person-centred approach with other models or frameworks (e.g. I-GROW, solution-focused, cognitive-behavioural) as befits the needs of the coachee(s) and the situation. Moving forward, the approach described in this chapter could be further developed by incorporating a greater psycho-educational component – for example, explicitly teaching staff skills of stress-management, mindfulness, and ways to respond to negative self-talk (Weare, ibid; Palmer & Cooper, 2000).

The practitioners valued the coach being external to the organization, someone who was not emotionally involved in the day-to-day affairs of the setting and who could bring "fresh eyes" to situations. This, for the participants, was a key ingredient for achieving the desired sense of safety and objectivity. However, other research regarding the use of in-school peer coaches has shown that peer coaching can also have a positive impact on a range of variables including staff well-being, teachers' daily practice, and collaboration across the school (Lee, 2013, 2017). In some circumstances, therefore, peer coaching may represent a more cost-effective way of providing coaching support. Of course, this places an additional demand on schools in terms of providing training for those who will carry out the coaching and raises ethical questions regarding professional competence if matters of personal well-being are to be discussed (as opposed to purely practice-based discussions, say). Given this complexity, the respective pros and cons of the use of external or internal coaches will need to be carefully considered for any given context and purpose.

The sessions in this example were timetabled on a regular basis, providing practitioners with a recurring outlet in which they could access protected time where reflection on practice and well-being was accepted as part of the culture. Given the reported reluctance of education staff to discuss mental health or well-being issues with their line manager (ESP, 2017), this presents an alternative to deficit-driven support which first relies on the practitioner reporting an issue and seeking help. Regular termly sessions circumvent this problem and provide each practitioner with six opportunities over the year to disclose and problem-solve any possible issues in a safe environment. Repeated sessions also allow the coaching relationship to be shaped over time as coach and coachee(s) build trust and become more familiar with each other's styles, preferences and approaches. This enhances the development of the *collaborative alliance* (Bordin, 1979; Murphy & Duncan, 2007) which has been shown to be so crucial for achieving positive outcomes. Furthermore, repeated sessions allow change goals to be revisited and reviewed, underlining the message that change is an iterative process in which small-step improvements and 'relapses' are a common feature of the journey (DiClemente & Prochaska, 1998).

As previously mentioned, the provision of coaching support from external coaches has a clear resource implication for schools, in terms of both the fee for the coaching support and the additional cost of enabling staff to have time away from other commitments. The temptation to regard such support for staff as a luxury must be balanced against the available evidence regarding the extent of educational practitioners' well-being issues, and the possible costs of poor performance, sickness and recruitment resulting from a lack of suitable well-being support. Cost-effective ways of providing coaching for staff could include the use of peer coaching or staff being coached in small groups to reduce the number of sessions required.

It is important to clarify that we are not advocating the use of coaching as a sticking plaster while broader systemic issues are left unaddressed. In some contexts, a high number of significant well-being issues and frequent turnover of staff may indicate the need for broader systemic or contextual changes (e.g. measures to reduce workload, improve communication, and ensure that leadership are approachable – ESP, 2017), and we would not want the provision of coaching to detract attention away from these other actions. However, as we have seen in this section, the provision of regular psychology-informed coaching from external coaches may provide staff with a valuable outlet to proactively and preventatively explore and address issues with practice and well-being. As part of a broader strategy, this could help to achieve the aim advocated by Weare (2015) of schools developing a climate or ethos which finds ways to make it safe for staff to acknowledge their difficulties and seek timely support in non-stigmatising ways.

Conclusion

In this chapter we have illustrated how psychology-informed coaching could be a valuable approach for addressing current challenges regarding child and adult mental health and well-being in education. There is an emerging evidence base regarding the positive impact of coaching on mental health and well-being in both children and adults, although more research will be required to further explore this relationship. As we have illustrated, coaching provides coachees with a safe, confidential outlet in which they can explore their own specific aims and concerns while learning transferable skills (e.g. goal-setting, problem-solving, reviewing the application of helpful strategies) that they can then take forward into other situations. This enables strategies from evidence-informed psychological approaches (e.g. solution-focused coaching) to be incrementally applied to the coachees' day-to-day realities and added to their repertoire of strategies that they can call upon in future. As such, coaching engages the participants as active collaborators in reviewing their situations and problem-solving emerging issues, enhancing their sense of agency and autonomy in the face of external pressures or life challenges. The availability of timetabled coaching sessions can provide children and adults with regular 'check-in' opportunities, enabling possible issues with performance and well-being to be identified and addressed proactively and preventatively. In our view this helps to normalise the process of using support structures and enables people to access support from others in non-threatening and non-stigmatising ways.

Whether coaching is provided by external coaches or in-school peer coaches will be a matter for each individual setting to decide, taking into consideration factors such as e.g. the competence of staff to provide coaching, any training and supervision required, the extent to which staff/pupils experience the sessions as safe and confidential, the culture of the school, and available resources; however, whichever option is pursued, the key aim is for young people and adults to have regularly occurring outlets for exploring their situations, discussing challenges, and finding ways forward.

With this in mind, we would suggest that the following questions and conversations will be important for our society to consider:

- How can we continue to support the creation of cultures in which people can seek support and acknowledge their difficulties in non-stigmatising ways?
- What proactive support mechanisms (for young people and/or adults) do our schools have to act as a "buffer" to externally driven stresses? How can such support mechanisms, including coaching, be realistically provided? Is it acceptable for this to only take place where individual school budgets allow?
- What would be the 'return on investment' from investing in such support mechanisms?
- When might external coaches or in-school coaches be more appropriate?
- What training and supervision would education practitioners require in order to equip them to provide coaching support (either for children/young people or each other)?

Of course, coaching is not a panacea, and other interventions or changes in the individual's context may also need to be considered. However, we would argue that coaching could well be an important component of a broader strategy for supporting pupil and adult mental health and well-being in our education settings. In this way, coaching has the potential to make a significant contribution to both current and future generations, and towards the further development of supportive cultures in schools.

Note

1 As set out in *Transforming Children & Young People's Mental Health Provision: A Green Paper,* the government proposes: (i) To introduce Designated Senior Leads for Mental Health in schools; (ii) to establish new Mental Health Support Teams, and; (iii) to reduce waiting times for young people's access to child and adolescent mental health services.

References

Abdulla, A. (2018). *Coaching Students in Secondary Schools: Closing the Gap Between Performance and Potential*. Abingdon: Routledge.

Adams, M. (2015). *Coaching Psychology in Schools: Enhancing Performance, Development and Wellbeing*. Abingdon: Routledge.

Bordin, E. S. (1979). The generalizability of the psychoanalytic concept of the working alliance. *Psychotherapy: Theory, Research & Practice, 16*(3), pp. 252–260.

Campbell, J. (2016). Coaching in schools. In C. van Nieuwerburgh (Ed.), *Coaching in Professional Contexts* (pp. 131–144). London: Sage.

CIPD (2017). *Employee Outlook Spring 2017*. Cited in Education Support Partnership (2017), p. 8.

Department of Health & Department for Education (2017). *Transforming Children and Young People's Mental Health: A Green Paper*. London: DoH & DfE.

DiClemente, C. C. & Prochaska, J. O. (1998). Toward a comprehensive, transtheoretical model of change: Stages of change and addictive behaviors. In W. R. Miller & N. Heather (Eds.), *Applied Clinical Psychology. Treating Addictive Behaviors* (pp. 3–24). New York: Plenum Press.

Education Endowment Foundation. (2018). *Metacognition and Self-Regulated Learning: Guidance Report*. Retrieved 15 January 2018 from https://educationendowmentfoundation.org.uk/public/files/Publications/Metacognition/EEF_Metacognition_and_self-regulated_learning.pdf.

Education and Health and Social Care Committees. (2018). *The Government's Green Paper on Mental Health: Failing a Generation. First Joint Report of the Education and Health and Social Care Committees of Session 2017–19*. London: House of Commons.

Education Support Partnership. (2017). *Health Survey 2017: The Mental Health and Wellbeing of Education Professionals in the UK*. London: YouGov/Education Support Partnership.

Flavell, J. H. (1976). Metacognitive aspects of problem solving. In L. B. Resnick (Ed.), *The Nature of Intelligence* (pp. 231–235). Hillsdale, NJ: Lawrence Erlbaum Associates.

Giant, N. (2014). *Life Coaching for Kids: A Practical Manual to Coach Children and Young People to Success, Wellbeing and Fulfilment*. London: Jessica Kingsley Publishers.

Gillard, D., Flaxman, P. & Hooper, N. (2018). Acceptance and commitment therapy: Applications for educational psychologists working with schools. *Educational Psychology in Practice, 34*(3), pp. 272–281.

Grant, A. M., Green, L. S. & Rynsaardt, J. (2010). Developmental coaching for high school teachers: Executive coaching goes to school. *Consulting Psychology Journal: Practice and Research, 62*(3), pp. 151–168.

Green, L. S., Grant, A. M. & Rynsaardt, J. (2007). Evidence-based life coaching for senior high school students: Building hardiness and hope. *International Coaching Psychology Review, 2*(1), pp. 24–32.

Harris, R. (2009). *ACT Made Simple: An Easy-to-Read Primer on Acceptance and Commitment Therapy*. Oakland, CA: New Harbinger Publications.

Hayes, L. (2015). *The Thriving Adolescent. Using Acceptance and Commitment Therapy and Positive Psychology to Help Teens Manage Emotions, Achieve Goals, and Build Connection*. Oakland, CA: New Harbinger Publications.

Higher Education Statistics Agency. (2019). *Table 15 – UK Domiciled Student Enrolments by Disability and Sex 2014/15 to 2017/18*. Retrieved 25 October 2019 from www.hesa.ac.uk/data-and-analysis/students/table-15.

Iveson, C., George, E. & Ratner, H. (2012). *Brief Coaching: A Solution-Focused Approach*. Hove: Routledge.

Lee, J. (2013). *Coaching in Secondary Schools: An Exploration of the Benefits for Individuals and School Improvement Through Professional Learning Communities*. Unpublished doctoral thesis. University of Bristol.

Lee, J. (2017). 'We can't do it just to make them feel good!'– An exploration into the benefits of coaching in secondary schools. *International Coaching Psychology Review, 12*(2), pp. 42–56.

Marsh, S. (2017). Number of university dropouts due to mental health problems trebles. *The Guardian*, Tuesday 23 May 2017. Retrieved 15 January 2018 from www.theguardian.com/society/2017/may/23/number-university-dropouts-due-to-mental-health-problems-trebles.

Miller, W. & Rollnick, S. (2002). *Motivational Interviewing: Preparing People for Change.* New York: The Guilford Press.

Miller, W. & Rollnick, S. (2013). *Motivational Interviewing: Helping People Change.* New York: The Guilford Press.

Murphy, J. J. & Duncan, B. L. (2007). *Brief Intervention for School Problems: Outcome-Informed Strategies.* New York: The Guilford Press.

Neenan, M. & Palmer, S. (Eds). (2012). *Cognitive Behavioural Coaching in Practice: An Evidence Based Approach.* Hove: Routledge.

O'Connell, B., Palmer, S. & Williams, H. (2012). *Solution-Focused Coaching in Practice.* Hove: Routledge.

Office for Standards in Education, Children's Services and Skills. (2018). *Teacher Well-being and Workload Survey: Interim Findings.* Retrieved 25 October 2019 from https://educationinspection.blog.gov.uk/2018/11/30/teacher-well-being-and-workload-survey-interim-findings/.

Palmer, S. & Cooper, C. (2000). *How to Deal with Stress.* London: Kogan Page.

Palmer, S. & Whybrow, A. (Eds). (2007). *Handbook of Coaching Psychology: A Guide for Practitioners.* Hove: Routledge.

Palmer, S. & Whybrow, A. (Eds). (2019). *Handbook of Coaching Psychology: A Guide for Practitioners* (Second Edition). Hove: Routledge.

Pritchard, M. & van Nieuwerburgh, C. (2016). The perceptual changes in life experience of at-risk young girls subsequent to an appreciative coaching and positive psychology interventions group programme: An interpretative phenomenological analysis. *International Coaching Psychology Review, 11*(1), pp. 57–74.

Ratner, H. & Yusuf, D. (2015). *Brief Coaching with Children and Young People: A Solution-Focused Approach.* Hove: Routledge.

Robson-Kelly, E. & van Nieuwerburgh, C. (2016). What does coaching have to offer young people at risk of developing mental health problems? A grounded theory study. *International Coaching Psychology Review, 11*(1), pp. 75–92.

Roffey, S. (2012). Pupil wellbeing – Teacher wellbeing: Two sides of the same coin? *Educational & Child Psychology, 29*(4), pp. 8–17.

Rogers, C. (1951, 2003). *Client-Centred Therapy: Its Current Practice, Implications and Theory.* London: Constable & Robinson Ltd.

Rogers, C. (1961). *On Becoming a Person: A Therapist's View of Psychotherapy.* London: Constable & Robinson Ltd.

Ryan, R. M. & Deci, E. L. (2000). Self-determination theory and the facilitation of intrinsic motivation, social development, and well-being. *American Psychologist, 55*, pp. 68–78.

Seligman, M. & Csikszentmihalyi, M. (2000). Positive psychology: An introduction. *American Psychologist, 16*, pp. 126–127.

Snyder, C. & Lopez, S. (Eds). (2005). *Handbook of Positive Psychology.* New York: Oxford University Press.

Stallard, P. (2019). *Think Good-Feel Good: A Cognitive-Behavioural Therapy Workbook for Children and Young People.* Chichester: John Wiley & Sons.

van Nieuwerburgh, C. (2012). *Coaching in Education: Getting Better Results for Students, Educators and Parents.* London: Karnac.

Weale, S. (2016). Almost a third of teachers quit state sector within five years of qualifying. *The Guardian,* Monday 24 October 2016. Retrieved 15 January 2018 from www.theguardian.com/education/2016/oct/24/almost-third-of-teachers-quit-within-five-years-of-qualifying-figures.

Weare, K. (2015). *What Works in Promoting Social and Emotional Well-being and Responding to Mental Health Problems in Schools?* Advice for Schools and Framework Document. London: National Children's Bureau.

Whitmore, J. (1992, 2002). *Coaching for Performance: GROWing People, Performance and Purpose.* London: Nicholas Brealey Publishing.

Worth, J. & De Lazzari, G. (2017). *Teacher Retention and Turnover Research. Research Update 1: Teacher Retention by Subject.* Slough: NFER.

Chapter 13

Coaching is growing up

How a pluralistic perspective might help

Tim Walker

This chapter acknowledges the diverse body of theory, experience and practice that can be collectively considered coaching (and those who might consider themselves coaches, in whatever capacity). While celebrating the strength of this 'broad church', it identifies some of the key challenges this diversity presents to coaches, would-be coaches, coaching supervisors and, not least, the market for coaching, our clients! Finally, I want to suggest how a pluralistic approach might offer an organising framework in which to conceptualise and deliver coaching practice.

Another way of thinking about this is to consider the times that you might have felt 'stuck' in your coaching practice, as I certainly have as a coach and therapist! This might be due to a whole raft of different challenges. A few that spring to mind for me are:

- Struggling to find a 'point of contact' or common ground with my client – a sense that we are not aligned in the coaching process
- A feeling that the model I am working with is not appropriate
- Finding it difficult to be understood by my client
- Frustration expressed by my client in the process
- Managing my own frustration
- Lacking faith in my ability to help my client

Pluralism isn't a 'holy grail' here but invites us to think more broadly about ourselves, our clients and the way in which we work, and might offer a way to become 'unstuck' in our coaching process.

Pluralism, as a concept and philosophy, has a long history, which involves embracing diversity, tolerance of different ideas and perspectives alongside a deep sense of 'valuing the other' in relationships. It asserts that multiple competing perspectives can all be valuable in addressing the same objective, and that no single 'truth' is likely to exist.

As I'll explore further in this chapter, a pluralistic perspective might also helpfully be applied to many issues we face in our modern world, notably in addressing the increasing polarity in political debate but also in considering increasing diversity in social and consumer identities. But, how specifically can pluralism be helpful to coaching practice?

As coaches, we are constantly grappling with the questions and challenges our client work, not to mention our own professional and personal worlds, bring us. Endless efforts searching for the 'right answer' may, in many situations, not be the most helpful approach to our work, especially if we might not even be looking in the right place for that answer!

I recall one of my psychology lecturers in research methods recounting an anecdote about someone walking down a street at night and encountering a person on their hands and knees on the pavement under a streetlight. When asked 'what are you doing?' the other person replied, 'searching for my keys'. 'Ah' said the first person, 'is this where you saw them last?'. 'No', came the reply, 'I last saw them over there', pointing to the other side of the street. 'Then, why are you searching here?' The answer: 'because the light is better here!' My take on this is that it is human nature to look for answers in places we are familiar with or are easier to access. It's efficient to adopt an approach and, through experience, become increasingly adept at applying it. Is that *always* the most effective way of helping clients, especially those who don't seem to be 'getting it'? This is something to consider as I make my case for pluralism.

A pluralistic approach to coaching offers a framework which opens up possibilities, as well as encouraging genuinely collaborative work. It helps to 'shine a light' on other options and ways of engaging with our coaching clients.

Mick Cooper and John McLeod (2011, p. 6.) succinctly state that pluralistic practice should be based on two key principles:

1   That lots of different things can be helpful to clients.
2   If we want to know what is most likely to help clients, we should talk to them about it.

It would, of course, be important to consider more fully the nature of this 'conversation'. A pluralistic approach would place increased emphasis on the importance of the coachee's views and perspective, both in terms of *what* they want to achieve from the coaching process but also *how* they would want to work. This is unlikely to be a one-off decision made at the start of the coaching engagement but would form part of an iterative process drawing from both coach *and* coachee feedback.

Challenge to expertise?

There is also something inherent in this pluralistic way of thinking that poses a significant challenge to the idea of 'expertise' in coaching and where such expertise sits in the process. For many of us, being an 'expert' is something that we have aspired to, bolstered by notions of excellence, nowhere better exemplified than by 1982's *In Search of Excellence* by Tom Peters and Robert Waterman, a staple for many MBA students of the 1980s and 1990s, of which I was one. Given the broad nature of our clients' backgrounds, experiences and challenges, however, how helpful is it to aspire to be, let alone present ourselves as, an 'expert' who has access to 'the answers'? Although the idea of challenging our own expertise might seem threatening to our sense of professional identity I would argue that doing so helps open up the options to us as coaches, especially where 'stuckness' is the issue.

Carl Rogers (e.g., 1961) challenged the notion of expertise in *psychotherapy* (I'll use this term to refer to all forms of 'talking therapy'), cautioning therapists to hold their expertise 'lightly' when working with clients. Failure to do this would inhibit the client's potential for growth, and therefore his or her ability to achieve 'self-actualisation' in humanistic/person-centred therapy terms. In more recent years we have experienced more emphasis on the active role of clients in therapy, with the emergence of terms such as 'experts by experience'.

To illustrate how it can be helpful to challenge our own sense of expertise, and be willing to engage in pluralistic thinking and practice, I was personally involved in an innovative research study in the NHS in 2016 where the concept of 'making sense of voices' was adopted to work with clients who had experienced (in many case) years and even decades of active psychosis which had not responded to medication or 'conventional therapy'. The approach had been pioneered by Dr. Marius Romme, a Dutch psychiatrist, who had appeared on Dutch television in 1987 with a patient of his, Patsy Hague. The purpose of this appearance was to reach out to 'voice-hearers' (i.e., those experiencing active psychosis) that were not engaged with mental health services in order to understand how they had coped with their experience. Dr. Romme was very open in admitting how little mainstream psychiatry understood about psychosis, and therefore how best to support patients. The psychiatric profession, in other words, was stuck on this issue.

The training that I (alongside a small group of fellow NHS psychologists) received was led by two professionals alongside voice hearers who had made sense of their experience, and who were able to discuss the process that had helped them do so. At the beginning of the training there was considerable scepticism expressed by the trainers about whether or not our 'psychology mindset' would prevent us from engaging with clients' subjective experiences.

Along with my colleagues I felt a sense of huge discomfort (and some indignation!) at the outset but, as the process evolved, came to realise that this process or 'model of therapy' could never have been generated from within the psychiatry/psychology 'establishment' in which we had trained. I would suggest that pluralistic thinking had led to this innovative approach, allowing clients (*and* many mental health professionals) to become 'unstuck' from an idea that their voice hearing was due to a biological problem with their brains or some form of 'madness'. For those wishing to read further, a good start would be Romme's book *Making Sense of Voices*, published in 2004, but in essence the approach requires helpers (who might be mental health professionals but could equally be peer support workers) to work in a more 'journalistic' way with clients, building up a detailed contextual history of the client's life and in particular the context in which they first began to experience 'voices'. The underlying premise behind this being that voice-hearing (psychosis) is an understandable response to life events rather than a biological problem with the brain. If the voice-hearer can make sense of their experience they can develop a different relationship with their voices (typically, voice-hearers will experience 5–7 different voices, each with a different meaning or message).

I hope you will agree that this is somewhat fascinating in itself, but I include it to prompt the question 'who might the equivalent of voice-hearers in your client group be?' Which individuals or groups of individuals don't seem to respond to your typical approach, and with whom the coaching process might benefit from a more open conversation?

Another example of trying to understand what clients find important in therapy is a study carried out by Bedi and Duff (2014) which found that the two most important factors were *feeling that their therapist validated their experience* and *being asked about their life beyond their presenting issues*. The implications of this seem to be that 'problem solving' may not be central to many clients' needs in therapy, and similar research is important in coaching to explore what factors our clients consider most important. I include some nascent examples of this later in the chapter.

Cooper and Norcross (2016) have taken this idea further forward in developing an 18-item measure to use with (psychotherapy) clients to help 'operationalise' their preferences. The measure is based on four key scales:

- Therapist directiveness vs. client directiveness
- Emotional intensity vs. emotional reserve
- Past orientation vs. present orientation
- Warm support vs. focused challenge

It doesn't seem too much of a stretch to imagine this research being adapted to identify relevant scales in the coaching process.

Why does contemporary coaching invite pluralism?

Any definition of coaching should allow for a diverse range of coaching practitioners, models of coaching and coaching clients, in itself suggesting that the activity invites a pluralistic approach

Practitioners

Coaches enter the coaching profession from a multitude of backgrounds and training routes. There is little overall consensus in what makes an 'accredited coach' (Bachkirova et al., 2017b) and a huge range of coaching training/qualification routes exist, from relatively short, skills-focused programmes through to more comprehensive programmes which perhaps focus more on research and critical thinking.

As the coaching world grows and matures, greater emphasis is perhaps required on thinking about an organising and/or over-arching framework to conceptualise how any coach interacts with any 'coachee' (coaching client). This can help inform all coaches, from those who are well-established to those just beginning their coaching practice. Bono et al. (2009) reported that the average age of coaches was a little over 48 years, and with an average of almost 10 years of coaching experience. Bachkirova and colleagues (2017a) acknowledge the benefits that this maturity can bring but also raise some concerns that this demographic profile may also tend to be more entrenched in its views on human behaviour in the world (and, by implication, the workplace).

Models

It seems three 'streams' of models have emerged with, and catalysed the growth of, coaching.

One stream is that developed from the application of theories from the world of education, notably those related to reflective and experiential learning. Whereas reflective dialogue might be considered a coaching tool or technique, Colin Beard and John Wilson, writing in 'Experiential Learning: A Handbook for Education, Training and Coaching', position experiential learning as an "underpinning philosophy that acts as a thread joining many of the learning theories together in a more unified whole" (2013, p. 17). 'Learning by experience' is perhaps one of the most enduring and accessible forms of personal and professional development any of us can engage in.

Beard and Wilson also make some interesting connections between experiential learning and the notion of 'the experience economy'. The idea is that, as our basic commodity needs continue to be more than met (in most modern economies at least) we, as consumers, increasingly seek out and place value on experiences rather than 'material things.' Two examples that I worked with in my own business career are music and video, which can now of course be streamed 24/7 from a multitude of devices with no physical carrier. This has not only transformed the traditional supply chain/value chain but has also required 'providers' to re-imagine how consumers interact with their 'product'. Those who have failed to grasp this imperative have fallen by the wayside. Another fascinating example in this context is the current enormous popularity in the UK of the 'Secret Cinema' concept (www.secretcinema.org), in which the 'cinema-goer' becomes immersed in the experience and, having been allocated a character to play, comes dressed for the part. The boundary between performers and audience members is deliberately blurred to allow for a more rewarding experience and a real sense of 'co-creation'.

The relevance of all this to coaching might be in striving to adopt a much broader perspective of our *coachee's experience*, which itself is a pluralistic idea.

As coaches we may be very focused on our experience, qualifications and the models that we work with, but what else constitutes our coachee's experience? That might begin when they engage with our marketing material (website, brochure etc), or perhaps from the first email or telephone exchange we have with them. What physical (or virtual) coaching environment do we offer? Is coaching something we 'do to them' or are they immersed in the experience through preparatory exercises or giving us regular feedback, for example?

A second stream of coaching models seems to be clearly identifiable as 'coaching models inspired by/derived from traditional models of psychotherapy'. Examples include coaching from psychodynamic, cognitive-behavioural, solution-focused, person-centred, existential and Gestalt perspectives. Additionally, I have been very interested and active in the increasing application of ACT (Acceptance and Commitment Therapy) to coaching over the past few years (increasingly referred to as ACC or Acceptance and Commitment Coaching). ACT is an excellent example of applied pluralistic thinking; it builds on concepts derived from behaviourism and the broader behavioural sciences, a theory of language development as an alternative to cognitive therapy, Buddhist practices, and also draws from existential philosophy in its emphasis on identifying 'personal values' as a way of guiding behaviour and providing motivation to do the 'difficult things' that are important in living a meaningful life. It's beyond the scope of this chapter to describe ACT in detail, but for those wishing to read further, I'd suggest Acceptance and Commitment Therapy (2nd ed.) by Hayes et al. (2012) as a starting point.

The third stream of models in coaching I'd like to discuss are those which are 'acronym/mnemonic' based such as GROW (as developed by Sir John Whitmore and colleagues in the late 1980s). Other models using this style of approach include (but are not limited to); PRACTICE (e.g., Palmer, 2008), SPACE (Edgerton & Palmer, 2005), ENABLE (Adams, 2015), CLEAR (Hawkins & Smith, 2013), LEAD, LEARN & GROW (Watts & Corrie, 2013) and LEARN (Watts, 2017). This third stream of approaches attempts to provide coaches with a simplified structure in which to develop their practice: a sequence of 'steps' to follow and apply, often sequentially, in order to 'know what to do' with clients from session to session. Although the benefits seem clear, the seemingly inevitable downside to this array of acronym-based approaches is that it makes coaching 'seem simple' to some of those wishing to coach or be coached. In the same way, many self-help books tell us to follow these 'n' steps, or to develop these 'n' habits, promising that some form of success will surely follow. There is a danger that the process of coaching will be reduced to simply 'doing' the four steps of GROW, for example. If we see coaching as 'goal setting', 'reality checking', 'option generating' and 'will-finding/motivating' then is there a danger that we reduce it to something akin to a 'brainstorm' session, or simply 'problem-solving' in a narrow sense. Also, much as the mantra of SMART goal-setting (specific, measurable, achievable, realistic, time-bound) has been successfully applied to projects (whether in business or personal contexts), are these simplified ways of approaching problems appropriate to the increasingly complex, diverse world we find ourselves inhabiting? Does *GROW* in itself lead to sustainable *growth*, or is it a somewhat reductive notion?

Daniel Kahneman (2015) highlighted the tendency for humans to use heuristics ('cognitive short cuts') in order to effectively 'automate' our thinking processes when we are faced with 'similar problems'. This efficiency is often helpful (for example when we are driving – not needing to analyse every action; or perhaps when avoiding the proverbial 'dark alley' late at night, not needing to spend ten minutes analysing risk versus taking a longer route home). It can also, of course, lead to unpleasant biases and prejudices, of which I'm sure you can easily think of without examples. More pertinently perhaps, in a coaching context, might this 'efficiency process' result in us working in the same tried and trusted way without stopping to reflect on the uniqueness of each encounter, and how we might vary our approach accordingly.

The process of wanting/being inclined to think fast was also harnessed by Steve Peters in his excellent book The Chimp Paradox (2013), where the 'computer in our head' represents the fact that many of our thought processes are automatic (though based on algorithms that can be programmed by high-speed, emotionally driven 'chimp thinking' or more measured, rational 'human thinking').

The coaching environment

Having considered some of the options in terms of how to 'supply' coaching, I'd now like to consider some of the key changes in the 'demand side' or the environment in which coaching is now being delivered, and how a pluralistic perspective might help us adapt to this and thrive as coaches. It is unarguable that business and society have changed rapidly in recent years. One of the key drivers for this change has been the emergence of the internet, and digital technology more generally. While much of this has been highly enabling, and has delivered many efficiencies and positive change, it can also be argued that these rapid changes have also brought with them much uncertainty to our ways of doing business and of life in general. It has also informed a theoretical underpinning for a new relationship between consumers and suppliers of services and products, one which I was able to explore through my own career in music and media retail and also as a visiting lecturer in digital marketing and strategy throughout a key transformational phase in digital media technology from the late 1990s until the end of the following decade.

In this account digital technology could effectively reduce consumerism to the 'market of one'. Each consumer would no longer be defined by a large corporation's idea of the 'market segment' they represented. Perfect information would mean that consumers would simply 'consume what they wanted/liked'. Emphasis needed to shift towards a more meaningful relationship with each consumer, not based on the old ways of 'push marketing' but to enable consumers to access the products and services they wanted, in the way they wanted. This would mean a different way of engaging consumers – a 'new dialogue'. Of course, social media and internet-based marketing would help, but only if the consumer felt 'heard' and the relationship seemed authentic and genuine

This also led into an important discussion about the blurring of traditional boundaries between producer and consumer. If consumers had increasing input into products (via more direct feedback or the ability to 'customise' their product or experience) were they therefore becoming part of the production process itself ('prosumers' – an inelegant word but you get the drift)? Are our coaching clients, with increasing access to information alongside changes in business practice such as 360-degree feedback processes, becoming our 'prosumers'?

Societal changes also affect wider aspects of our lives: how we work and communicate; valuing diversity; how we express identity. Much is made of generational trends in society, with so-called millennials now reaching ages where they will be occupying increasingly senior positions in business, and therefore increasingly likely to seek coaching input. There is also a huge increase in the awareness of mental health issues. Whilst I am unequivocally in support of this trend, it does bring with it a sense for many that there is 'something wrong' with them, which may not always be helpful.

For the coach, it is important to have an understanding of how the environment for coaching is changing, and how to position our coaching offer to best cater for this new (and evolving) environment.

In my practice, I work with a significant number of clients who engage me for 'coaching' rather than 'therapy.' Many of these do so because I have a background which spans both the business/organisational world and the 'mental health' world. Of course, I realise that some of these clients suspect that they have broader mental health challenges but feel more comfortable engaging with a therapist/coach who has experience of 'both worlds. I think this group of clients would be unlikely to engage with a 'pure mental health specialist' because of the implications (for them) of doing so – why would any 'sane person' see a shrink?! As a consequence much of my client work involves blending coaching and more therapeutic work, and I firmly believe my pluralistic approach enables me to work effectively with each client. This involves careful listening and sensitive questioning at the assessment/planning stage of our work to ensure that I understand my client's needs and objectives clearly.

One 'crossover' that I do see with increasing regularity is the (often highly) successful professional who really struggles with both personal and professional relationships. Their professional expertise has invariably helped them to achieve success at work, but they are now experiencing some form of discomfort. This might be some kind of 'exit' from their employment, or perhaps an appraisal process which has identified a problem with interpersonal skills that is a barrier to future development. I will always seek to understand how this 'plays out' for my client in their personal lives, and often the pattern will be repeated there, though manifesting in a different way. This might lead me, for example, to focus on the relationship between my client and I and how that plays out in the 'here and now' of our interactions.

Something else I experience on a regular basis is the client struggling with 'workplace burnout' of some description. Sometimes these clients find me directly but often they are referred by their employer or outsourced occupational health provider. Pluralistic thinking helps me move beyond typical 'stress management' techniques with clients experiencing this kind of problem. Many of these individuals are highly conscientious and find it difficult to manage work-life balance. Working with 'values' is one way that I have found highly beneficial in helping these individuals 'unhook' from the rules that they perhaps may have learned in not thinking about their own needs, or understanding the long-term impact of neglecting their personal lives and health. I also find working with professional values helpful in identifying changes that clients want to make at work, even if that might ultimately mean a change of employer or work environment.

Towards a pluralistic framework

It seems clear that coaches have an increasingly broad range of models and approaches to select from, both when choosing a training route and when practicing as a coach. This would seem to make sense in an increasingly complex coaching environment. However, just as our clients might be looking for a way to simplify their objectives and deal with issues that might get in the way, so it might be appealing to a coach to decide on an approach which might either reflect their own experience/training or one they have become aligned with for other reasons.

Psychotherapy: how its approach might illuminate coaching

The field of psychotherapy provides warnings for the dangers of adopting a singular approach and the benefits of pluralism in coaching. It was estimated in 2005 (Norcross & Goldfried, 2005) that over 400 different approaches existed. Despite this, less than 25 percent of therapists registered with the BACP (British Association of Counselling & Psychotherapy) report having been trained in 'integrative approaches': working with a single model in a focused way still seems to prevail. This, of course, has advantages. Therapists can become extremely proficient in an approach; they can perhaps feel comfortable in assessing the progress made by their client in therapy, and there is an ability to conduct research in a consistent way. The IAPT service in the UK's National Health Service, for example, has been grounded in carefully developed, structured, targeted, manualised therapies.

However, there are also potential pitfalls to 'single-model' approaches, which the coaching profession might be wise to heed. Cooper and McLeod (2011) use the phrase 'schoolism' to describe the tribalism and binary thinking that leads to much energy being spent on championing and/or defending one's favoured model: if one is right, then the other must be wrong! This might all too easily create a barrier for coaches which prevents them from learning from and about other approaches, as well as a focus on building ever greater *efficiency* in *our approach* over perhaps the *effectiveness* of a broader perspective. Equally, it can create a 'blinkered' approach to coaching which renders it inflexible to our clients' needs and perspectives. As Abraham Maslow wrote when outlining his 'law of the instrument', 'I suppose it is tempting, if the only tool you have is a hammer, to treat everything as if it were a nail' (1966, p. 15).

Research such as that by Asay and Lambert (1999) indicates that models and techniques only contributed 15 percent of improvement in therapy clients. Client variables and extra-therapeutic events (40 percent), the therapeutic relationship (30 percent) and expectancy/placebo effect (15 percent) complete the picture they paint of key factors.

In psychotherapy this debate has been pitched as 'specific' versus 'common' factors: whether a specific model of psychotherapy is 'king', or to focus on the 85 percent of change (in the Asay and Lambert study) that is the result of non-specific (or common) factors.

If we are edging towards an argument that there is no one right way to 'do therapy' it seems logical to apply this argument to coaching, which bears many similarities. Common factors research has indeed been applied to coaching. An exploratory study by Erik de Hann and colleagues (2012), identified the following factors as being highly significant to positive coaching outcomes:

- the coaching relationship ('working alliance') between coach and client, as defined by *the client*
- client 'self-efficacy' (i.e., the client's belief in their own ability)
- perceived range of 'coach techniques'

As coaching outcome research is also beginning to indicate that specific models may not be the most important determinant of outcome, can we therefore apply a framework which has been helpful to many working in psychotherapy/counselling settings, that of pluralism? Mick Cooper and John McLeod (mentioned in my introduction) have developed a framework for pluralistic psychotherapy and counselling (2011) and discuss with colleagues (Zsofia Anna Utry and Stephen Palmer) in a 2015 paper published in The Coaching Psychologist how this might be applied to coaching. The paper references Diana L. Eck, head of The Pluralism Project at Harvard University, selecting the following pertinent terms describing pluralism:

- . . . the energetic engagement with diversity . . .
- . . . the active seeking of understanding across lines of difference . . .
- . . . encounter of commitments . . .
- . . . based on dialogue . . .

Pluralistic practice can therefore draw on a broad array of approaches, but places 'constructive dialogue' at the heart of the process, rather than a practitioner's specific range of skills and experience, or any integrative or eclectic approach they might work with. This does not mean that the 'customer is always right' either; the process of dialogue should be two-way in arriving at the most helpful approach. The 2015 paper goes on to introduce the concept of 'metatherapeutic communication', in other words a dialogue about the process of therapy as it progresses. This not only serves the function of feedback and collaboration, but also assists the client to develop skills in becoming more reflective and 'active' in therapy. If you will allow me to re-visit ACT (in a pluralistic way) this also speaks to the idea of 'perspective taking' and contacting the 'observing self' (an idea itself borrowed from Buddhist practice). Awareness, in this context, is the vital precursor to choices of either change or acceptance.

It then seems to be a short hop to think in terms of what 'metacoaching communication' might mean. The paper cites research (Ely et al., 2010) which found that executive coaches typically ask for feedback in an ad hoc manner rather than as part of a 'built-in' process. How might you, as coach, build in regular feedback to your practice?

Pluralistic coaching practice

Again, the 2015 paper seeks to apply the core 'steps' of pluralistic psychotherapy to coaching.

These steps are to think firstly about the client's *goals* for coaching (of course, mirroring to some extent the 'G' of GROW). Secondly, the *tasks* that need to be undertaken (these are conceptualised as the macro-level areas of change to focus on), and thirdly the *methods* that will deliver this change (referring to the micro-level activities that will deliver on the tasks identified. This is demonstrated in Figure 13.1.

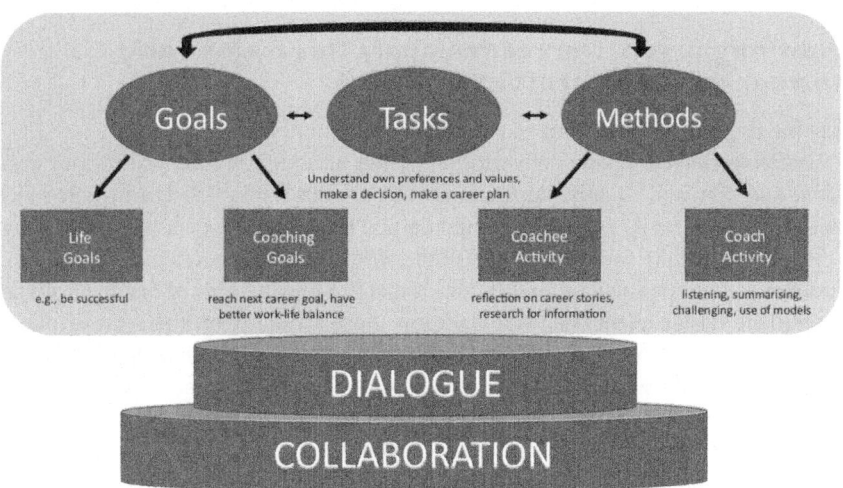

Figure 13.1 Application of core 'steps' of pluralistic psychotherapy to coaching
Source: Utry et al. 2015

Research into pluralistic coaching

I am only aware of one research study looking at a pluralistic approach in coaching, that conducted by Andy Pendle, and published in the International Journal of Evidence Based Coaching and Mentoring (2015). This was a qualitative study involving semi-structured qualitative interviews with five practicing coaches, exploring their attitudes towards a pluralistic framework for coaching. The broad findings were that the participants seemed comfortable with incorporating different approaches into their coaching practice and were strongly in favour of a collaborative approach. There seems to have been some issues in how they were able to make sense of the philosophical position of pluralism, and also in effecting close collaboration and dialogue about the coaching process throughout their client work.

In general terms, and learning again perhaps from the psychotherapy world, research is a significant issue in terms of how pluralism can and should be understood. Cooper and McLeod (2011) discuss the increasing trend towards both an 'evidence-based' research culture, and specifically the prioritising of 'empirically supported' therapies. They argue that that UK's National Institute for Health and Clinical Excellence (NICE) draws almost exclusively from empirical research in making recommendations for practice. There are clearly strong efficiency and limited-resource arguments for why this should be the case, but the counter-argument is that the outcome of such research is gauged on a narrow range of 'measures' and research methods. Such methods rarely, argue the authors, include factors such as the client's preferences, the role of supervision, and the therapist's own reflections and personal experiences. The reader is pointed to research that reviews how these and other more 'pluralistic characteristics' of psychotherapy are associated with beneficial outcomes.

How might you, the reader, apply this framework to your coaching practice?

Let me use my own coaching experience to try and illustrate.

I often arrange a phone conversation before arranging a first face-to-face session, and this will usually set the tone for ongoing work. There are sometimes specific references to issues that might call on the clinical aspects of my training (e.g., 'I would like to understand if I am on the autistic spectrum, or bipolar'), but more often the focus is on difficulties that are playing out for the client in the workplace. These clients will want to know more about my business background, and how I draw from that experience to relate to workplace challenges. Beyond that, there is often a sense of the potential coachee wanting some reassurance that I will be able to deal with more personal and sensitive issues should they arise as part of our work – a 'safe pair of hands' if you like.

It's quite common for these clients to have already experienced coaching provided by their current or previous employers, and many will be familiar with their Myers-Briggs typology (or comparable psychometric profile). One of the most common things I hear about prior coaching is that it was very focused on workplace problem solving but, for the coachee, had failed to draw from or explore their wider experiences in life and, as such, the coachee didn't believe that they had learned broader life-skills that could be applied not just to the workplace but to all the 'other stuff' in their life. Many tell me that as soon as they attempted to move a coaching conversation beyond a very specific workplace problem they felt closed down.

The topic of coaching: mental health boundaries is discussed elsewhere in this book, but I believe it's important to understand that moving beyond a strict workplace agenda does not necessarily mean venturing into specialised mental health work; it might simply mean making more links between what is happening for the coachee in the workplace and what is happening (or has happened) elsewhere in their life. The 'entry point' may often be workplace-focused but as some of the examples I discuss in the following demonstrate, the coaching conversation can often involve much broader considerations.

Typical issues for me in my coaching role have included:

- Dilemma over a job offer (and needing to work through the implications of accepting or declining)
- Loss of motivation at work
- Feeling bullied or excluded at work (often linked to a 'problematic' boss)
- Being identified *as* a 'problematic' boss
- Difficult relationships at work more generally
- Successful entrepreneurs struggling to adapt to being 'people managers'
- Equally, successful entrepreneurs who have exited/cashed out and are now struggling with 'what next'
- Clients struggling to manage stress at work (including a number who are referred to me by occupational health professionals who specify 'coaching' rather than 'therapy' as a brief)

Let's take a couple of these and consider how I might apply a pluralistic framework:

Table 13.1 Problematic relationships at work

Goal	Tasks	Methods
Improve relationships at work	Identify the key problems client is experiencing	Non-directive discussion
		Review any appraisal or feedback from colleagues
		Cognitive-behavioural formulation to identify any unhelpful patterns of thinking or behaving which may be maintaining problem
	Develop strategies to address these	Assertiveness skills training
		Role-play examples of difficult situations the client has experienced
		Behavioural experiments to challenge current unhelpful thinking by client
	Evaluate progress	Client to keep weekly diary
		Client seeks feedback at work
		Plan review session

Table 13.2 Loss of motivation at work

Goal	Tasks	Methods
Re-discover motivation for work	Understand how loss of motivation relates to client, job role, organisation	Non-directive discussion to understand client's career background to date
		Socratic questioning to identify key factors resulting in current problem
		Motivational interviewing (MI) to agree rationale for change-focused work
	Identify key changes that need to be made	(could include)
		Values work to identify what makes work meaningful to client
	Implement changes	Set values-based goals and identify likely problems
		Problem-solving/Skills training as appropriate
	Evaluate progress	Regular reviews to reinforce progress and learn from setbacks

I have, of course, kept these examples relatively uncomplicated, to demonstrate the framework. The reality is that significant issues/challenges might emerge at any point in the coaching encounter, as they do in therapy. The clients I am working with are all individuals and bring with them a vast range of backgrounds and experiences, which will inform their personal struggles and goals for coaching.

Any one of these 'straightforward' problems are likely to bring with them a huge range of underlying challenges, including those related to mental health, neurodiversity, personal relationships, addiction in its many forms, health/disability, 'existential crises' of various kinds, loss/bereavement, sexuality/gender identity, culture or ethnicity. In my experience, clients increasingly want to debate political and societal issues – are these 'outside our agenda' or a vital part of how our clients are trying to understand their identity and values, and how they make sense of their own experiences.

For anyone engaging in the 'professionalised conversation', it seems hugely important that we consider all the possibilities that might present themselves as part of this endeavour. Pluralism is not a technique, or even a set of techniques. It is a position that we take with regard to our clients. It is not the same as being pragmatic, or expedient. Equally it doesn't require that we are trained in every possible approach. Whatever our core training it's likely and highly sensible that we will use that as at least a building block, as well as a key reference point in engaging with our clients. I am happy to acknowledge that I still view behavioural psychology as an 'approach' which is most likely to inform the way I conceptualise (or 'formulate) my work with clients. However, I remain open to dialogue with them throughout the process of coaching or therapy about the directions we take. This may involve incorporating elements of other recognised therapies or perhaps working with clients to help them make sense of religious or spiritual beliefs in the context of their challenges. These are often outside my range of training or direct experience but by engaging in active discussion we are usually able to identify a way of integrating these critical elements into our overall work.

Clients communicate in many different ways, and non-verbal communication can often be a window into their inner worlds. One client I recall very vividly, asked at our first session if he could read aloud a poem he had written about his life and struggles. Even though I felt very unsure and somewhat uncomfortable I said yes. The poem took maybe ten minutes to read but was more powerful and informative than many longer assessment sessions I have had (not to mention more moving). Yes, it was verbal, but very different from a 'usual' conversation. I have also had clients share art and music with me on numerous occasions, and there has always been meaning beyond the art itself in terms of what the client is communicating.

Cooper and McLeod (2011) make the distinction between a *pluralistic perspective* and *pluralistic practice*. Even those practitioners working with a single approach can endeavour to make this more flexible to individual needs, to engage in regular dialogue about the process of, and the client's experience of, coaching. Recognising, perhaps, when they are not best placed to help a particular client and making appropriate onwards referrals, or perhaps seeking external input to the coaching process from other professionals (of course, in agreement with the client and discussed in supervision).

This raises questions for those considering beginning a coaching career, or those seeking to develop their own expertise through training/CPD. It also raises questions about supervision – would it be helpful to consider supervision from an alternative or multi-disciplinary perspective, rather than maybe from a supervisor more skilled and experienced in our own approach(es)?

Returning one more time to my experience of working with change in the digital music and media sector, the phrase 'co-opetition' also comes to mind. In that context it meant forming alliances and partnerships with those who might otherwise be considered competitors – a recognition that 'smaller players' with limited resources might be better off pooling some of these to offer a better overall service to their customers.

How might this idea apply to your coaching practice? Could you re-visit your sense of who you might view typically as competitors and consider how some form of collaboration might be helpful, to you and your clients?

As our clients' lives, workplaces and world views change and become more diverse and (perhaps) complex, shouldn't we as coaches be developing a broader view of how we can best support them? Pluralism doesn't offer a neatly packaged set of tools to draw from, but is a personal stance that we can adopt in order to embrace and work with difference and uncertainty. That, inevitably, will require a willingness to challenge ourselves in many aspects of our practice. Are you ready to accept that challenge?

References

Adams, M. (2015). *Coaching Psychology: Coaching Psychology in Schools*. Abingdon: Taylor and Francis.

Asay, T. P., & Lambert, M. J. (1999). The empirical case for the common factors in therapy: Quantitative findings. In M. A. Hubble, B. L. Duncan & S. D. Miller (Eds.), *The Heart and Soul of Change: What Works in Therapy* (pp. 23–55). Washington, DC: APA.

Bachkirova, T., Jackson, P., Gannon, J., Iordanou, I., & Myers, A. (2017a). Re-conceptualising coach education from the perspectives of pragmatism and constructivism. *Philosophy of Coaching: An International Journal*, 2(2), 29–50.

Bachkirova, T., Spence, G., & Drake, D. (2017b). *The Sage handbook of coaching*. Los Angles: SAGE Publications.

Beard, C., & Wilson, J. (2013). *Experiential Learning: A Handbook for Education, Training and Coaching*. London: Kogan Page Publishers.

Bedi, R. P., & Duff, C. T. (2014). Client as expert: A Delphi poll of clients' subjective experience of therapeutic alliance formation variables. *Counselling Psychology Quarterly*, 27(1), 1–18.

Bono, J. E., Purvanova, R. K., Towler, A. J., & Peterson, D. B. (2009). A survey of executive coaching practices. *Personnel Psychology*, 62(2), 361–404.

Cooper, C., & Norcross, J. C. (2016). A brief, multidimensional measure of clients' therapy preferences: The Cooper-Norcross Inventory of Preferences (C-NIP). *International Journal of Clinical and Health Psychology*, 1, 87.

Cooper, M., & McLeod, J. (2011). *Pluralistic Counselling and Psychotherapy*. London: SAGE.

Edgerton, N., & Palmer, S. (2005). SPACE: A psychological model for use within cognitive behavioural coaching, therapy and stress management. *The Coaching Psychologist*, 2(2), 25–31.

Ely, K., Boyce, L. A., Nelson, J. K., Zaccaro, S. J., Hernez-Broome, G., & Whyman, W. (2010). Evaluating leadership coaching: A review and integrated framework. *The Leadership Quarterly*, 21, 585–599.

Haan, E. de., & Sills, C. (2012). *Coaching Relationships: The Relational Coaching Field Book*. Oxfordshire: Libri Pub.

Hawkins, P., & Smith, N. (2013). *Coaching, Mentoring and Organizational Consultancy: Supervision, Skills and Development*. Maidenhead: Open University Press.

Hayes, S., Strosahl, K., & Wilson, K. (2012). *Acceptance and Commitment Therapy* (2nd ed.). New York: The Guilford Press.

Kahneman, D. (2015). *Thinking, Fast and Slow*. New York: Farrar, Straus and Giroux.

Maslow, A. H. (1966). *The Psychology of Science: A Reconnaissance*. New York: Harper & Row.

Norcross, J. C., & Goldfried, M. R. (2005). *Handbook of Psychotherapy Integration* (2nd ed.). Oxford: Oxford University Press.

Palmer, S. (2008). The PRACTICE model of coaching: Towards a solution-focused approach. *Coaching Psychology International*, 1(1), 4–8.

Pendle, A. (2015). Pluralistic coaching? An exploration of the potential for a pluralistic approach to coaching. *International Journal of Evidence Based Coaching and Mentoring*, Special Issue No. 9.

Peters, S. (2013). *The Chimp Paradox: The Mind Management Program to Help You Achieve Success, Confidence, and Happiness*. New York: Penguin Group.

Peters, T. J., & Waterman, R. H. (2015). *In Search of Excellence*. London: Profile Books.

Rogers, C. R. (1961). *On Becoming a Person: A Therapist's View of Psychotherapy*. Boston: Houghton Mifflin.

Romme, M., & Escher, S. (2004). *Making Sense of Voices: The Mental Health Professionals Guide to Working with Voice-hearers*. London: Mind.

Utry, Z. A., Palmer, S., McLeod, J., & Cooper, M. (2015). A pluralistic approach to coaching. *The Coaching Psychologist*, 11, 1.

Watts, M. H. (2017). The reflective practitioner: Some personal reflections. In R. Bor & M. H. Watts (Eds.), *The Trainee Handbook: A Guide for Counselling and Psychotherapy Trainees*. London: SAGE.

Watts, M. H., & Corrie, S. (2013). Growing the 'I' and the 'We' in transformational leadership: The lead, learn & grow model. *The Coaching Psychologist*, 9, 2.

Chapter 14

Welcome to our new economy cabin[1]

What new technology and a changing market for coaching will mean for the ethics of the profession

Andreas Kleinschmidt with Mary Watts

What is good coaching? What is ethical coaching? Is unethical coaching good coaching, when it is effective?

These questions will have to be asked and answered by every generation of coaches, and by every coach, again and again, as he or she grows. Some of the answers have found their way into ethics codes, of which there are many and more to be written. Their main points tend to overlap, in practice they often only offer limits and some guidance, but they can never replace a set of personal values.

This chapter will take a look at some of the thorniest ethical issues and dilemmas emerging for coaches today. It will take a look at the answers given by practitioners and coaching organizations. And it will look into the future: trying to predict which ethical questions will start to cause us headaches in the years to come. If you are looking for simple answers to ethical problems in coaching, presto, here are three dos and three don'ts, based on highly unrepresentative interviews with practitioners:

> *Respect your client.*
> *Help your client.*
> *Keep your client's secrets*
> *Don't harm your client.*
> *Don't lie to your client.*
> *Don't sleep with your client (even if both of you*
>   *were to consider it a gesture of respect).*

If you are ok with easy answers, you can stop reading now and use the time for some coaching or to find new clients. If you are keen to explore your own answers to current and future issues and dilemmas around ethics in coaching – as we would hope – the rest of this chapter is for you.

What will be the big topics tomorrow?

There are three megatrends in the coaching industry, which will change its shape and size in the next five years and which will throw new, painful ethical questions at us. The trends are: Digitalization. Democratization. Professionalization.

Digitalization: Machine Learning (often called Artificial Intelligence, or AI) is beginning to support coaches, and it will take over some aspects of coaching completely, especially in the area of skills coaching. Already, at the time of writing, you could use an app that helps you speak a bit more like Obama, for instance. This will mean better, measurable objectives for some coaching assignments. And it will bring cheaper coaching to more people. But it raises big questions in terms of accountability. If your coaching app were to lead you to bad business decisions, who is to blame? The self-learning algorithm? How will the algorithm deal with conflicts of interest? How comfortable will we be with its coaching if it were a black box, like many Machine Learning Applications are? Are human coaches not black boxes?

Democratization: Coaching has been a wildly successful industry over the last ten years, with lucrative growth rates. While growth *rates* will shrink gradually, growth as such is here to stay for years to come. We can expect coaching to become more widely accepted – and available to individuals lower down the corporate food chains. This is helped by three trends: the first we already know, cheaper, scalable, coaching through use of digital tools, partly drawing on Machine Learning. Second, the transformation of management styles toward flatter hierarchies and networks of teams. Third, the growing number of coaches on the market: "it is estimated by the International Coaching Federation that there were 71,000 coach practitioners, worldwide, in 2019, up from 47.500 part time and full time coaches in 2011." (LaRosa https://blog.marketresearch.com/us-personal-coaching-industry-tops-1-billion-and-growing; https://coachingfederation.org/app/uploads/2020/09/FINAL_ICF_GCS2020_ExecutiveSummary.pdf, pg 8; 20 February 2019).

Extrapolating current market trends, more work for coaches will also mean more coaches entering the market. If we assume the quality of coaches, whichever way we want to measure their quality, is a normal distribution, then more coaches in absolute numbers means, in absolute numbers, more underwhelming, worse than average coaches on the market. By which standards will we measure the quality of a larger coaching industry in the future? Who will have the power to define the standards? And how will we hold accountable those who train coaches for this growing market?

Industrialization of coaching: the ugly twin of democratization. Today, coaching lives a profitable existence in the cracks between professions: psychotherapy to the left, counselling to the right, consulting not far away, training a friendly neighbour, sharing the front lawn. And since we are talking about changing behaviour and mindset we cannot ignore the potential overlap with education, religion, cults, and sects for example. As the industry grows it will have to answer calls for it to define itself more clearly: Which distinct skills does a coach need? Which type of training and education is necessary? How will the profession police itself? What empirical proof is there for its claims to being effective (Iordanou et al. 2016; Athanasopoulou & Dopson 2015)[2]? Answers to these questions will likely raise barriers to entry. We will see the rise of larger players which are able to invest into technology, including supporting Machine Learning applications.

Coaching may turn from being dominated by freelancers into an industry of fewer, bigger players. Once we see a McKinsey – or maybe a Deloitte – of coaching, we will also see sales pressure, margin pressure and standardization of product. While this is partly great news, as it could bring coaching to more people, it might erode some hard to measure qualities of the better coaching we see today. What will happen to the human touch? To bespoke solutions? The spirit of true care? Will the employed coach of the future – enhanced by AI, incentivized through sales and volume targets – be able to create the safe space in which he or she can care and focus on the individual in the same way as today's great coaches claim to do?

Let's use an analogy from air travel to sum up these three trends. Executive coaching in the for-profit sector up until now is business and first-class travel. Expensive. Elite. For the few. Bespoke and exclusive. Sometimes a trophy item, to carefully boast about. Industry growth as well as lower cost and lower price through application of technology will add new segments: economy and premium economy cabins. (A lot of great coaching is already happening, by the way, at lower average hourly rates, in the public sector and charity contexts.)

This will be both helpful and challenging in terms of ethics. Coaches with less experience, less live weight, quickly trained in standard programs, maybe in undergraduate university courses, supported and guided by technology including AI, will service this cabin. Depending on the quality of the algorithms they are given as support, they might potentially offer more effective coaching in some areas than the most experienced coaches of the year 2019, who largely work without technology support.

But are they going to ooze out the seniority and confidence many clients seek and pay top dollar for? And given their relative lack of life experience, will they be able to coach in a way that reflects more than the very (sometimes narrow) objectives presented by their clients? Will they be willing and able to explore further? Will they negotiate their ethical perspective with both their client's and with ethical norms prevalent in the society they live in? If they are willing and capable to do so: Will their sales and margin targets allow them to do so? Or, on the flip side, will they potentially be so effective and cost-efficient in some areas, that they collectively undermine the business model of the seasoned, senior freelance coach of today? (If results are great, who should care about the seniority a coach oozes out?)

Before we explore the future, let's take a look at the most challenging ethical aspects of coaching here and now.

Ethics today

What are the big ethical questions that bite us today, in the pre-industrialized, pre-digitalized, pre-democratized world of coaching?

Let's look at the numerous codes of ethics, published by the equally numerous coaching organizations. Then let's put ourselves into the shoes of clients. And finally, let us listen to some practitioners and their experiences, which they shared with me, frankly and anonymously.

Diane Brennan and Leni Wildflower (2018) compared numerous codes of ethics published by coaching organizations. They have identified common themes:

1   Do no harm: do not cause needless injury to your client or others
2   Duty of care: act in ways that promote the welfare of other people
3   Know your limits: practice within your scope of competence
4   Respect the interests of the client
5   Respect the law

As it turns out, our tongue-in-cheek dos and don'ts are not too far off the mark. The issue with these codes is: some are very long and granular, apparently trying to regulate every conceivable case. Others are very high level. Both approaches are limited in their usefulness.

On top of it: There is not one organization that can claim to represent the industry on the whole. Even worse: the rules from numerous overlapping codes can't be enforced effectively. A coach may be excluded by a coaching association they are a member of. But they cannot be banned from coaching altogether (as can a surgeon who regularly forgets scissors in patients!). On top of it, many coaches are not members of any coaching organization at all.

Identify your favourite code, ideally the most demanding one, use it to give yourself a crash barrier in terms of ethics. Of course, you may be tempted to pick and choose and make your own code. Please do – it will make for great reflection. But also, please, don't use it in practice. Codes by professional bodies are updated regularly and you will benefit in the long run from the efforts other people put into keeping your code of choice in tune with the times.

The client perspective

Before we look at the experience of practitioners, let's put on the shoes of clients. What would they NOT want from their coach? Some lowlights:

A coach who makes them dependent, milking them through a never-ending series of sessions.
A coach who manipulates their thinking and their actions in ways that are not beneficial to them.
A coach who abuses them to feel good himself (the "narcissistic guru coach syndrome").
A coach who blackmails them with secrets shared in confidentiality.
A coach who tries to sell them a share in a holiday park after an uplifting, inspiring session.

A coach who, over drinks, boasts about the work done with the client or the high profile of the client – or even her identity.

A coach who uses information from coaching for insider trading.

A coach who insists on giving a relaxing oil massage at the beginning of a session. (Which might potentially work for some sports coaching.)

What else? Think of three more outrageous things you would not want as a coaching client:

(Of course, some of these points describe behaviour which is not just undesirable, unpleasant and unethical, but straightforward illegal, e.g. insider trading.)

Curiously, many clients assume impeccable ethical behaviour from their coaches from the beginning. One reason why so few questions are usually being asked around boundaries of the relationship may be the feeling of urgency on the client side. (When we urgently need a locksmith, it is understandable why one might rush the vetting phase.)

Experience of practitioners

So, what does the experience of practitioners tell us about ethical challenges and their ways of dealing with them?

There are seven big areas into which we can group ethical problems (Iordanou et al. 2016, p. 67). Let's take a look at each in turn and then see what coaching practice teaches us about their relevance and ways to mitigate conflict.

1 *Proposition*: Which skills and what level of experience does the coach advertise and what type of outcome from a coaching relationship is being suggested?
2 *Competence*: What credentials, experience and capability does the coach truly possess?
3 *Product quality*: What kind of service is actually delivered and at what level of sophistication?
4 *Contracting*: What exactly are the objectives, scope, mutual rights and obligations?
5 *Confidentiality*: Which pieces of information may (or must) the coach use outside the coaching arrangement, and how?
6 *Bias*: How aware is the coach of his or her biases and how well will these be managed before and during the coaching relationship?
7 *Role shift*: Do client and coach maintain a transactional relationship as equals, or does the coach, knowingly or not, willingly or not, foster dependency? Does a personal relationship grow out of coaching?

Let's take a look at these one by one.

Proposition: Which skills and what level of experience does the coach advertise and what type of outcome from a coaching relationship is being suggested?

Coaches who want to eat need to sell, (unless they rely on a generous partner or a trust fund, or eat very little). They happen to sell themselves rather than cars, zebras or luxury holidays. While for many excellent coaches this is the most difficult and unpleasant part, some thrive more on the sales side, than in terms of delivery of their service. A tad of overselling in terms of qualities or qualifications appears almost unavoidable: people do it on dating apps (add a centimetre or two?); investment banks do it when they boast with carefully calibrated league tables in which they miraculously come on top almost everywhere; and many coaches do it, when they suggest they work almost exclusively at C-level or that they were Senior VP of a multinational corporation (their wife's advertising firm with a total of three employees and an office at the holiday home in Greece). What about proposed outcomes: Are you proposing to make your client CEO? Are you proposing to help your client overcome depression? Does your website suggest this is what happens to your clients?

Where do we draw the line?

There are legal boundaries to misrepresentation and there are ethical boundaries. Where should your boundaries be? Here are two litmus tests. One is the *Financial Times* (FT) or *Wall Street Journal* test. The other is the Mom test.

Perform the FT test by asking yourself, what an investigative journalist would write after testing all the explicit and implicit claims made on your website and in communication with your clients leading up to a mandate. If after consulting with the legal team of the newspaper, the reporter could write about several misrepresentations, chances are that at some point, some client or competitor will make this point. The FT test is the legal test.

Now ask, what Mom would say to your marketing claims, (or anyone in your life who tried to make sure, you don't come out as a nasty piece of work). If either or both tests produce red flags, and you still keep making the exaggerated, incorrect or inappropriate claims, you fail.

Competence: What experience and capability is the coach able to apply to the coaching?

You may have accurately listed on your website your impressive Ivy League Education, your flawless career in investment banking, the numerous board memberships at profit and not for profit organizations and all the expensive coaching qualifications you have rightfully acquired. But you might still be a lousy coach. Bad product is usually weeded out in efficient markets, however, coaching is far from an efficient market. It lacks oversight and transparency; it consists of tiny submarkets with niches in niches (e.g. public speaking at financial institutions in the UK); coaches and clients find one another through word of mouth. Bad coaches exist and they can move to new niches after burning too much terrain in one, damaging the brand of coaching on the whole.

What makes things harder: competence (and outcomes of coaching) can currently hardly be measured. This makes it theoretically impossible to defraud coaching clients. How come? Fraud requires – from a legal point of view – intent. A bad coach may well live in the delusion of being a great coach, while delivering bad and expensive coaching. This would be a bad deal for the client, but from a legal point of view no fraud.

Know and communicate your boundaries: Don't do psychotherapy when you are not qualified. (And, by the way, numerous coaches are qualified to do so.) You would not try to fix a broken bone, either, would you?

Product quality: What kind of service is actually delivered and at what level of sophistication?

You have bought a package of coaching sessions. Your coach keeps you talking. You feel good about yourself. No one ever, anywhere, listens to you like your coach. Fair enough, not much has changed in your work life over the course of the six sessions – but you feel so good after each and every single session. Why not book six more? Also, your employer pays for it.

There is nothing wrong with paying people to make you feel better. Geishas get paid. Sex workers get paid. Violinists get paid. It becomes problematic when the label for it is "coaching", rather than entertainment. (Would the product be bought, if the label weren't coaching?)

Even when the client has specifically requested coaching, and hired you based on your stellar competence and based on an appropriate proposition on your end, delivering great coaching might still be the wrong thing to do. It happens frequently that executives are being offered coaching when really they would rather need training. Or – worst case – they may be on a performance plan and the idea truly is to get them out of the door. The coaching (which in this case is *meant to be unsuccessful*) is just a box to tick on the road towards an orderly, early exit. In the first case the sponsor for coaching is deluded. In the second case the client is deceiving both the employee and the coach. Clients can behave unethically, too.

Contracting: Defining objectives, scope, mutual rights and obligations

Many coaches insist contracting is the most crucial moment in the coaching relationship. It is not only about how often and how much. It is where the proposition (including any potential misrepresentation) gets baked into both a legal and an ethical commitment. And it is the moment where experienced coaches check who *really* is the client: often organizations get coaching for an employee and pay for it. Whom is the coach supposed to serve? Can the coach with good conscience coach a high-flyer out of her current role, leaving the contracting organization burnt? Would this be ethical? Should the coach avoid this potential outcome from coaching? Would it be ethical to exclude this avenue and opportunity?

Many coaches make a distinction between the sponsor (the party paying for the coaching) and the client (the individual receiving coaching). It may be agreed that the coach (or preferably the client) check in with the sponsor regularly to report on progress, which raises issues around confidentiality. The distinction between sponsor and client, however, only cosmetically addresses the problem, by naming it. Transparency goes a long way, by setting clear boundaries at the beginning.

Alas, some boundaries could mean lost business, if the sponsor does not play. Ethical behaviour sometimes has a price.

Confidentiality: Which pieces of information may the coach use outside the coaching arrangements, and how?

"Whatever is said between these four walls, remains between these four walls." This paradigm is powerful and necessary in privileged relationships: between priest and believer, between doctor and patient, between a lawyer and his client. And between coach and client. But is it realistic? In many countries, priests are obliged to report crimes against minors, even when they learnt about them during confession. Similar rules are in place in some jurisdictions for lawyers. By taking out health insurance, we usually sign away large parts of the confidentiality regarding our health. So, what about coaching?

Not all cases will be this severe, but what if a client talks about committing fraud? What do we do if a client talks about having forced someone into unconsensual sex? What if we pick up sexist bias that is likely to harm the culture of the sponsoring firm? Should whatever is said between these four walls, remain between these four walls under all circumstances? When it comes to psychotherapy, the UK Council for Psychotherapy's *Code of Ethics and Professional Practice* (2019) says no: and that while the psychotherapist commits to:

> *"Respect, protect and preserve clients' confidentiality"* they must also *"Notify clients when appropriate or on request, that there are legal and ethical limits to confidentiality, and circumstances under which confidential information might be disclosed to a third party".*
>
> (UKCP 2019, p. 3)

Coaches are encouraged to discuss their sessions with a supervisor who also adheres to a strict code of professional conduct. It may be tempting to do so informally with other coaches, to share success, to seek consolation about failure, and sometimes to boast a bit. However, even anonymous accounts can far too easily be traced to individual clients.

It gets even more difficult, when coaches serve in a dual role, for example a line manager who coaches an employee. Or when coaches work with several clients who work with one another; these may be competing companies or several individuals at the same organisation. The promise of confidentiality can lead to conflicts of interest.

Conflict of interest

Imagine a fantastic coach who is also a yoga enthusiast. Why not offer a couple of yoga sessions to a stressed-out client? It may do her good? Why not do them in your own new studio? Conflict of interest or enhanced product offering?

Many coaches are not only coaches: They have grown out of flourishing careers, they have a wide network of friends and business partners, they have lots of interests, personal and commercial. It is in part the richness of their lives and experiences which makes them attractive as coaches. It can make them crossroads of opportunities and therefore crossroads for conflicts of interest.

These conflicts can take mild forms – our yoga example. They can take severe forms: buy some stock after becoming aware of preparations for a merger? Propose client A for a promotion, since you also coach his boss, or hint at reasons that should forbid such a promotion? Managing such boundaries gets easier after good contracting but often remains a case by case task in complex settings.

Bias: How aware is the coach of his or her biases and how well will these be managed before and during the coaching relationship?

Coaching is not a science. It is not clean, it is hardly empirical. And we are humans. The human element in coaching is one of the elements which makes it powerful (a notion to be revisited once we see results from "Robo-Coaching", coaching empowered by Machine Learning). The way we think and feel – and coach – is underpinned by our experiences, our cultural context, by the way we see ourselves and the world. The way we think and feel influences how we see clients, the options and opportunities we accredit to them. Without bias, we would not function efficiently, including as coaches. (Ever tried to discover the world every single day anew, like a newborn baby?)

What research tells us about our biases – regarding gender, age, race, sexual orientation and so much more – is that most of them are unconscious. And that even when we make them conscious, we still have a hard time overcoming them. One avenue taken by large companies is to create systems that counterbalance unavoidable bias: for instance creating more checks and balances when it comes to new hires and promotions, like involving diverse teams in making such decisions. In coaching we usually don't have these resources. Digital tools might be helpful in the future, by matching coaches and clients in a way that mitigates biases, by providing second opinions in real time, by adjusting for a sticky bias of a coach. In the meantime supervision is the best tool coaches can use to challenge their own biases.

Role shift: Do client and coach maintain a transactional relationship as equals, or does the coach, knowingly or not, willingly or not, foster dependency? Does a personal relationship grow out of coaching?

You really like your client. Your client really likes you. How about a coaching session over dinner? With a glass of wine? Or a bottle? Let's do a city trip together to see a few Rembrandts at the Alte Pinakothek in Munich? Wouldn't that be a great setting for some good coaching? This is the beautiful side of role shift. Friendship. Most coaches will in such a case draw a line at some point and suggest to end the professional relationship. How could they objectively coach when they have become part of the system that potentially feeds the challenges a client brings to coaching?

Few would argue that lovers should or could effectively coach one another for money. Codes of ethics for psychotherapy and counselling – as well as coaching – explicitly forbid practitioners to engage romantically with their clients. Coming back to our last Don't from the introduction: don't sleep with your client. Even if you personally find it ethically acceptable, the quality of your (coaching) service is likely to suffer.[3]

The practitioner's view

Now we know what can go wrong. How relevant are these aspects in practice, though, according to seasoned coaches? What are the biggest ethics topics in today's coaching landscape? Unstructured interviews with our unrepresentative sample of coaches from different countries and with different specializations make three big ones stand out:

- Incompetence
- Conflict of interest
- Abuse

These three cut across the seven fields we have identified. And in practice they arguably carry the greatest potential for harm of clients and the reputation of the coaching profession.

Incompetence

Coaching is an unregulated profession with lots of good and lots of bad coaches. You want to be a coach: get a business card, with the title "coach" printed next to your name. (To be fair: highly regulated professions like psychotherapy also have better and worse practitioners.) As coaching grows, more individuals are attracted to this field. Expensive and cheap training programs woo entrants into the profession. The main gauge of quality appears to be whether a coach gets booked and at what rate.

There are currently no effective filters that keep the greedy and the seedy out of the industry. Buyer beware. Still today, coaching clients often have no previous experience with coaching and will not be in a good position to judge the qualification of their coach, nor the quality of the product. The presumed gate-keepers – coaching associations – are numerous and largely represent coaches and their interests, they are also financed by coaches. A bad doctor usually gets into trouble, after a while. A bad coach can currently fish elsewhere, in a large and growing pond.

Conflict of interest

A lot of coaching happens in companies, predominantly larger organizations which have the resources to pay for it. It is not uncommon for coaches to work with several individuals in the same organization. How can a coach keep confidential information confidential – but fully serve the organization? How about a client with a drinking problem which has not yet been noticed higher up in the hierarchy? What if the coach were to work with the employee afflicted by addiction and her boss, at the same time? Should the coach, in another scenario, avoid any allusion to the fact that the promotion her client is preparing for eagerly, has long been earmarked for someone else (as the CEO had revealed in confidentiality in yesterday's session)?

Abuse

Abuse takes many forms. (Practicing in spite of incompetence can be interpreted as one.) A particularly common and damaging form is baked into the prevalent business model of coaching and requires a lot of discipline on the side of coach and client to steer around: raking up hours.

Most coaches currently work based on billable hours.

Packages are booked, for example for six sessions. Retainers exist, much rarer is coaching based on measurable outcomes. Some coaches go as far as requesting a share of additional profits or even equity in a company. But the hourly model prevails, partly because it is easy to understand and measure. Other providers of professional services go with the same model. (It is interesting to note that this model is also a favourite with many of the coaching professional bodies where the level of accreditation and, implicit in this, the assumed level of coaching competence, are linked directly to the number of coaching hours completed).

However, it creates a vicious incentive structure for coaches. More hours mean more income. It sweetens the deal for coaches when their clients develop a dependency – for example consulting always with their coach before important decisions. It can motivate coaches to create pleasant sessions, which invite repetition of the experience, while an unpleasant session can at times be more impactful for the client. Sometimes "a kick in the behind" is a great move that speeds things up. Coaches who prepare solidly before sessions and reflect and document after sessions, are indirectly punished; it is hard for them to bill time and work which is not witnessed by the client.

Law firms have traditionally worked on the basis of billable hours, however, clients today are pushing for new models, which are more clearly aligned with outcomes. A tough call for coaching. An ethical challenge for coaches, to push for results more quickly, when it means they may get less from an individual assignment.

Ethics tomorrow

The topics described in the previous sections will not go away as coaching evolves as a profession. But technological change, and the changing shape and size of the coaching industry will throw up new issues. So how will the three megatrends of digitalization, democratization and industrialization affect the ethics of coaching?

First of all: the three trends will bring good things. Coaches and their clients will get great digital tools to make their work both more efficient and more effective. Digital tools will also enable better measurement, which might open the door for better billing models, especially outcome-based fees. More automation – in line with democratization and industrialization – will also mean more coaching for more people. This in turn means more data points from digitally enhanced coaching, which will increase the effectiveness of coaching even further, as supporting algorithms will learn and improve.

On top of it, more automation in coaching needn't mean we move to "one size fits all". Algorithms will start to cater to individual needs, and pick up nuances in interactions which even the most seasoned human coaches would not pick up without help. The bigger risk is bias, which to date has been found in Machine Learning solutions, e.g. for credit scores. First steps are being taken to both make bias in AI solutions transparent and to remove it (or at least mitigate its consequences). This mindset and practice needs to inspire all AI ventures in the space of coaching going forward.

Assume bias can be mitigated and the digital coaching assistants – or automated coaches – deliver great outcomes for clients. Will we know what they are actually doing? Complex systems which rely on deep learning usually cannot explain why they are doing what they are doing. In critical applications, like self-driving cars or autonomous weapons systems, that is already an obvious problem. Should we take billions of leaps of faith and blindly trust an algorithm that had taught itself through billions of data points over time? Or should we insist on understanding every decision it takes – meaning we may end up underusing this resource where it can't explain itself to mortals? What does this mean for coaching? Usually, no one dies during coaching. And, assuming satisfactory outcomes from their work, would algorithms really have to be able to explain what they are doing and how and why? Nevertheless, be prepared to see lawsuits from disgruntled clients of robo-coaching.

Digitally enhanced coaching will produce data on human behaviour and cognition. What should happen with it? Who will own it? And who will be allowed to draw valuable conclusions from it and monetize these? The question mirrors the current debate around collection and use of online data which is monetized through advertising. Will there be one dominant player reaping outsized benefits from a quasi-monopoly on coaching data, with the outsized scaling and network effects it may bring? Or should future coaching clients co-own the data and the observations coaching-machines produce? And how will we as a society negotiate this decision?

Even if regulation were to forbid the emergence of one dominant player, consolidation in the coaching industry is likely to take place; more likely than in therapy, in any case, as coaching will for the foreseeable future evolve outside the realms of regulation from bodies of the public health system. The required investment for technology will drive consolidation further.

What will this mean for standards of best practice, training, measurement, supervision and – of course – ethics? Here is the sober view: as other consolidated professions show, the winners, the dominant players of the market, tend to define the market standards over time: by offering only what allows for high margins and thereby "educating" the market; through their ability to advertise and market; by means of lobbying; and by forming and dominating industry associations which codify standards, including ethical standards. They build de facto standards, which over time become codified standards.

Here is the idealistic perspective: whoever dislikes this scenario has two choices. Start building a big player in the future coaching industry and use your market power to try and establish standards you deem ethical. Or attempt the grassroots approach, herd the cats and try creating binding standards for coaching through international consultation and consensus (also, good luck).

While consolidation might be bad news for mediocre freelance coaches whose market will be served by others and better, it may very well be great news for coaching clients: they will have the choice between more automated, affordable coaching, and what we had called business and first-class cabins. (These premium cabins, by the way, will in their own right become better, as they will also be able draw on new technology, including AI, while delivery will remain high touch.) At the same time the future mass market will allow more people to benefit from coaching.

But let's brace ourselves for a few bumps on the road. Yes, there will be growth, yes, coaching will be more of a formal profession, yes, standards will start to converge. But we are not there, yet. Currently, coaching relies on self-regulation, which is a privilege. As the industry grows, incidents of malpractice will become more numerous in total numbers and thereby more visible. Coaching might be up for a cathartic moment in the next few years, a moment of judgment by public opinion – modulated and amplified by media and social media – if and when self-regulation fails, as, unfortunately, it so often does.

If coaching were to be struck by a moral crisis, let's not waste that crisis, and use it to build a better industry. Also, we can start today: by reflecting on our own practice, the ethics of our practice, and how we can improve both.

Conclusion

What we learn from the experience of coaches: small infractions, ethical missteps may be overlooked by both coach and client. They can cause – invisibly at first – great damage. At the same time, masterful coaching can draw on elements that might appear ethically borderline, but which turn out to be spectacularly successful. In the space of psychotherapy, for instance, "provocative therapy" comes to mind (Farrelly & Brandsma 1989).

So, what is ethical coaching? Is unethical coaching good coaching, when it is effective? It is time for you to give a first version of your own answers. And feel free to revisit them as often as you like, ideally before and after every session. As coaching evolves and grows as a profession, we will see a convergence of rules and norms, in the same way as this happened with other professions, like psychotherapy. However, ethical behaviour will always be enmeshed with the ideologies prevalent in the societies and the segments of society that we coach in (Watts et al., 2020).

To make an extreme example: had coaching techniques been popular in Nazi Germany, the rulebook around the ethics of using them would surely have looked very different from today's codes. Because ethics is also a function of social context, previous experience, and numerous individual factors; because ethics differ between societies; because ethics are always evolving; because of this, ethical behaviour in coaching is more about thinking for yourself and challenging yourself, rather than simply following rules.

Questions for reflection

What are the underlying values that inspire your own ethics around coaching?

If you had to sum up your ethical principles in three bullet points: What would they be?

What was the trickiest ethical challenge you faced in your own coaching practice?

Go through your own marketing materials and do the Financial Times and the Mom test.

When coaching was effective in the eyes of client and coach, but breached ethics codes, is it still good coaching, according to you?

If you didn't bill by the hour, which other billing methods would you consider? For each method you come up with, think through how the changed incentive structure might change your approach, methods or delivery.

Can you think of a situation where you did breach client confidentiality? What have you learned from this?

Notes

1 Thanks to: Prof. Mary Watts (for challenging expertly at every stage), Emilio Galli-Zugaro, Jonathan Hartley, Dr. Guljit Kohli, Anne Scoular, Katarina Skoberne, Dick Tyler and many more.
2 While numerous studies tried to measure the return on investment (ROI) of coaching interventions, the results of these studies differ wildly, albeit most suggest a staggeringly high positive return, often several 100 percent.
3 The acutely in-love coach or coachee might want to make the case that a patient undergoing therapy is vulnerable, whereas a coaching client on the other hand is by definition in an equal position to the coach and should be able to give consent to move to a more romantic place.

References

Athanasopoulou, Dopson (2015) *Developing Leaders by Executive Coaching*, Oxford: Oxford University Press.

Brennan, D. & Wildflower, L. (2018) Ethics and Coaching. In E. Cox, T. Bachkirova & D. Clutterbuck (eds) *The Complete Handbook of Coaching*, ch 32 ps 500–517, London: SAGE Publications.

Farrelly, F. & Brandsma, J. M. (1989) *Provocative Therapy*, London: AbeBooks.
LaRosa, J. *U.S. Personal Coaching Industry Tops $1 Billion, and Growing*. https://blog.marketresearch.com/us-personal-coaching-industry-tops-1-billion-and-growing; 20 February 2019.
Iordanou, C., Hawley, R. & Iordanou, I. (2016) *Values and Ethics in Coaching*, London: SAGE Publications.
UK Council for Psychotherapy (2019) *UKCP Code of Ethics and Professional Practice*, UKCP, London.
Watts, M., Kleinschmidt, A. & French, D. (2020) Ethics Challenges – Challenging Ethics: Keeping an Open Mind on Ethics and Professionalism. In M. Watts, R. Bor & I. Florance (eds) *The Trainee Coach Handbook*, London: SAGE Publications.

Chapter 15

Conclusion

Ian Florance and Mary Watts

Our introduction to this book suggested three overall sources for emerging conversations around coaching: within the discipline itself; within a range of health-related disciplines such as psychology; and within wider society. In turn, these categories raise wider aspects of coaching which need discussion, for instance:

- how coaching is done: the chapters in this book on pluralism, reflective learning, ethics and supervision provide examples.
- areas where coaching might become increasingly relevant: mental health and trauma are considered in Chapters 6 and 7.
- new coaching populations, or changes of emphasis in existing populations: chapters within Emerging Conversations address education, leadership and increasingly diverse general populations.
- the sorts of specialist areas coaches might need to know about: trauma, neuroscience and assessment all present challenges to generalist coaches.

We knew from when we started planning this book that it couldn't even cover all of the issues that had emerged in the recent past. The areas we have outlined have evolved while the book was being written and produced. In addition, new forces for change and development have appeared.

So, what other factors might affect coaching's evolving future?

Other developing issues in coaching

Given contemporary priorities, it is perhaps no surprise that some issues stem from environmental and ecological concerns and a consequent desire, among an increasing number of people, for an increasingly close relationship with, and care for, the natural world.

Environmental issues

One example of this might be fairly traditional coaching which focuses on an issue of growing importance: environmentalists', policy makers' and activists' environmental goals and how they can be achieved urgently.

Another might address the sorts of fears about future environmental effects that young people and their parents in particular are reporting. These fears have already been given the title Eco-Anxiety: a fear of environmental doom. While this is not yet a defined syndrome in the Diagnostic and Statistical Manual of Mental Disorders (American Psychiatric Association, 2013), a cursory web search will find references to it in any number of web sites (see Fawbert, 2019 and Smith and Hughes, 2013 as just two examples). Eco-Anxiety could become as ubiquitous a reason for being coached as over work, stress, depression and performance anxiety are now.

As well as influencing *what* issues coaching will need to address, environmental/ecological issues may pose questions for the existing models of *how* some coaching is done. Face-to-face leadership coaching, for instance, often involves long-haul air travel for relatively brief meetings. Coachees often have to travel reasonably long distances by car to a coach's office or consulting room. How far will the adoption of the sorts of technologies Carol Braddick outlines in her chapter be driven by a desire for coaching to become greener? Indeed, how could certain coaching applications and arrangements become greener unless they take digital technologies more seriously?

The use of animals

Compared with the large-scale, socially driven issues already outlined, this is a much smaller and more focused example of developments sourced in the natural world. Our increased interest in animal behaviour has led to the use of cats or dogs plus horses as aids to coaching with people who are happy to have animals present. This has resulted in a research effort to understand the efficacy of a range of approaches to the use of animals in coaching, as well as counselling (see, for instance, Grajfoner, 2012).

If the presence of an element someone likes, or reacts well to, improves coaching outcomes, then the use of art, music, poetry and other phenomena may become more important as part of the generalist coach's skill set. The use of art and music in other therapeutic relationships is long-established.

Quite apart from environmental/ecological issues, other developments in society at large will increasingly affect what coaching addresses and how it's carried out.

Emerging identities

Claudia Filsinger's chapter on diversity and coaching addresses questions raised by the recognised growing diversity of many national populations. Identity politics grew as a movement in the late 20th century and its influence is pervasive. It is therefore likely that more and more identities will need to be considered with reference to Claudia's ideas and arguments, in any future discussion of widening diversity among coaches and coachees.

Mass migration and refugees

Driven by both internal and external conflict and the effects of global warming, migration is one of the key problems facing human beings in the future. Coaching has a huge role to play, among other interventions, in helping refugees address their experiences. The topics range from the traumas they undergo to navigating new cultures and finding jobs that fit their talents and interests (see Tribe, 2019 and Tribe and Patel, 2007 for introductions to this area).

Career coaching

Although this might seem an established application, careers coaching is going to become far more widely needed in the future because of changes in life expectancy, career shapes, ways of working and future economic developments (see Gratton and Scott, 2016 for a succinct and entertaining review of the issues). Career coaching will require an increasing ability to cope with different situations: not just career reorientation of already successful executives within their fields, but the frequent changes of direction, job requirements and personal aspirations among workers of all ages (Rogers, 2019 is a very good book-length study of careers coaching which recognises its growing importance).

Spirituality (including formalised religions)

This is a rich area for discussion and one which has practical implications.

Many coaching techniques were originally used in religious practice: the use of silence, visualisation, confession, meditation, breathing, repetition of phrases as cues and Q&As are cases in point. The huge popularity of mindfulness which sources in the practice of Zen, *Vipassanā*, and Tibetan meditation techniques shows that this is not just an historical process but a contemporary one. The same is true of the increasing popularity of retreats involving silence or quasi-coaching techniques, particularly in both life and business coaching (for examples, see Retreats Association, 2020)

A number of books and groups have started to address this issue (van Niewerburgh and Allaho, 2018; Hyson, 2013 are initial ways into this area).

Groups

Sasha Webster argues in her chapter that certain sorts of coaching need to be more widely available. Refugee/immigration coaching, outlined earlier, presupposes a great increase in coaching capacity. If these insights are correct and Tor Levin Hofgaard's keynote address at the 2019 European Congress of Psychology in Moscow (which we referenced in our Introduction) can be applied to coaching, there are simply not enough coaches to go around (and some of those are untrained or only loosely familiar with coaching's techniques). It is unlikely that training courses can increase the number of trained coaches by the required amount in a short time. We will therefore need more models for coaching groups of people together. Some exist but how we do this becomes an urgent issue.

Cybernetic coaching

Carol Braddick's chapter on technology gives an overview of how technological developments might change how coaching is done. But there is another sense in which coaching might be affected by technological advances. It is predicted that the singularity – the point at which intelligent machines become self-conscious – is a matter of decades away (see, for instance, Kurzweil, 2006). Even if this is boosterism, human beings are going to have to cope with increasingly competent and intelligent machines which make certain skills and attributes, previously seen as uniquely human, relatively common and, in some cases, redundant. What will this do to human beings' confidence, self-image, employability, creativity – in fact our whole view of ourselves?

The on-line description of the British Psychological Society's Cyberpsychology Section reads:

> Cyberpsychology is a scientific inter-disciplinary domain that focuses on the psychological phenomena which emerge as a result of the human interaction with digital technology, particularly the Internet.
>
> (British Psychological Society, 2019)

It is, we believe, realistic to imagine not only that machines will help in the process of coaching people as Carol Braddick's chapter shows, but that, in the foreseeable future, an intelligent, self-aware machine may present itself as a coachee to a human or machine coach. Even if this sort of prediction is wide of the mark it can be used as a thought experiment to raise important issues for the discipline.

Coaching and politics

Another area which seems ripe for development and expansion is the application of coaching to politics in the widest sense, and most particularly political leadership and representation. Political turmoil has been strongly influenced by global and transnational issues. This has called into question such issues as the motivations and personalities of people who stand for political office; mental illness among politicians; selecting applicants who will make good candidates and representatives; and the attitudes that inform people's voting preferences. One of the editor's interviews with Ashley Weinberg provides a good starting point for this topic (Weinberg, February 2018). The time is ripe for coaching research to address this issue and feed its findings into practice.

These are not entirely new issues and some progress has been made in many of them but they will help to steer coaching's future. No doubt readers will be able to add further influences to this initial list.

What is coaching? The key questions and oppositions this book raises

Coupled with these potential growth areas, the discussions in this book's chapters stimulate a number of overarching, linked issues which could profoundly affect future coaching practice.

Is coaching an applied science or a humanist / natural activity or an art?

This opposition was referred to in this book's chapter on psychometric assessment. Of course, there's no reason coaching can't be all of these things. But again, to look at psychology as a model for coaching, the art vs science debate has been a consistent element in psychology's reflective practice. The different views of coaching's development outlined in the Introduction highlight these alternatives. Of course, this opposition is too stark.

'An evidence-based activity which utilises creative, human-centred techniques to maximise individual and group potential' might be the best way to describe what coaching often is at the moment. Thus, for instance, Mary Watts' chapter on reflection, Sasha Webster's on a more human-centred approach to leadership and Tim Walker's on pluralism emphasise a less 'hard scientific' approach to coaching; while Ian Florance on testing, Sarah Corrie on research and others might seem to emphasise the need for coaching to become more scientific in its approach – at the very least that it draws on more formal evidence than the justification of using what seems to work in practice.

The quotation used in our Introduction from Jenny Rogers, typifying coaching as 'a pragmatic trade drawing on borrowed theory' (Rogers, 2016, 6) is moot here. In addition to research on its effectiveness, there are important conversations to be had about coaching's theoretical basis: in what sense it adds anything to what other disciplines do; where does theory inform practice and where are coaches working on 'rule of thumb' and 'common sense'? One could state this baldly and give it more focus as follows . . .

Is coaching psychology-lite?

It has sometimes been thought of in this way. Coaching psychology (as opposed to coaching) has had some difficulty defining itself. A good place to start looking at this is a presentation made at the Australian Psychology Society Interest Group in Coaching Psychology Conference 2008 (Whybrow, 2008). It quotes some useful definitions of coaching psychology which could equally be applied to coaching.

Implicit in the presentation, and in this question, is the difficulty psychologists' institutions (such as the British Psychological Society) experience in differentiating coaching psychology from coaching (if, indeed this can or should be done); and in categorising coaching psychology alongside the other main applications of the discipline. Hence, in the British Psychological Society there are clinical, occupational and other divisions but coaching psychology is served by an interest group. Their Register of Coaching Psychologists is open to all chartered psychologists who can demonstrate the necessary level of knowledge skills and experience in coaching. This has the advantage of creating a very diverse mix of psychologists with specialisms in mental health, business, education and neuropsychology for example. However, coaches who are not psychologists can only become associate members without voting rights. This is an interesting, slightly clumsy arrangement, which the Society is examining, and reflects the, at times, uneasy relationship between coaching and coaching psychology.

Coaches use many theories and techniques developed within more mainstream psychology but most coaches would deny the idea that coaches want the kudos of practising elements of psychology without going through the long and expensive training it takes to become a registered or chartered psychologist (of which more later). They would claim that coaching is not contained within psychology but overlaps with it.

Sarah Corrie and Andrew A. Parsons refer to 'wicked problems' in their chapter on mental health coaching: these are problems that 'require transdisciplinary innovations in thinking and practice'. Perhaps coaching as a whole is a 'wicked discipline' and the chapters in this book on diversity and pluralism hold the key to its future. The word 'wicked' may carry too many negative implications which could be avoided by calling coaching a cross-border discipline. But if that is true, it makes the issue of ethics, addressed in Chapter 14, a thornier problem. It also links to . . .

Training: generalist or specialist or both?

Chapters in this book imply that there is specialist knowledge from other domains that coaches may need (Table 15.1).

This raises a huge number of questions. Is the role of the generalist coach still feasible or is it exactly the generalist skills of the coach which fill the gap left by specialisms? Should basic coach training cover specialist areas or should they form part of CPD or very focussed applied qualifications? If the latter, is some sort of official recognition of coaches' status the only way to make sure further training takes place after initial courses?

Many coaches would claim, and many experts argue, that the key to successful coaching is relationship building (see Schnell, Searle, and Stoneman, 2020) with coaching's specific techniques and knowledge being of secondary importance. These chapters at the very least raise questions about this assumption. Is coaching knowledge based or relationship based? Which links to the question . . .

Table 15.1 Possible domains of specialist knowledge needed by coaches

Chapter Subject	Areas where more detailed knowledge may be needed
Psychometrics	Testing, statistics, personality psychology
Research	Research methodology
Mental Health	Clinical psychology, various therapies
Trauma	Psychology
Diversity	Different cultures
Neuro-coaching	Neuroscience
Technology	AI, big data, statistics, specific packages
Executive coaching	Business issues

Can anyone coach?

Can you train someone to coach? For that matter, can you coach someone to succeed in a goal of becoming a coach? Is this possible for people who have few skills in relationship building and little knowledge of coaching (let alone the other areas we've outlined)?

Is coaching for the few or for the many?

Sasha Webster's chapter, in particular, challenges certain ways of offering work-placed coaching: in particular that it serves a largely leadership-based audience. Andreas Kleinschmidt's and Mary Watts' chapter on ethics raises issues across a wider domain of coaching. Is coaching only for the few, defined by income, access to resources, job title or, for that matter, type of distress? Or, do we believe coaching offers a solution to a growing range of specialist and general, scarce and ubiquitous problems? In either case – to move back up this list of questions – who can offer this service; how can they be trained; what sorts of training should be offered, how; and how far should these coaches be expert in specialist areas they might encounter?

As one ponders the challenges posed by the emerging conversations in this book and also those highlighted in this conclusion as ripe for further and deeper conversation, one can't help but notice the complexity of the issues associated with them. This complexity raises questions around boundaries and professional relationships; for example, between coaches and psychologists, trainers and educators, researchers and practitioners. It also flags up fundamental issues around training – for example do we train generalists or specialists? Should one come before the other? And at what level should training be? But in addition, it raises questions around some of the pre-suppositions upon which much coach training is based. For example, are the competency models we currently use in coach training and accreditation fit for purpose and sophisticated enough for the complex global issues that our emerging conversations have highlighted?

Surfacing emerging questions will help to guide coaching's future but this will only happen in the context of initiating new emerging questions and conversations and continuing to challenge our thinking in relation to these. We hope that the chapters in this book are just the beginning of an ongoing journey of emerging conversations

Bibliography

American Psychiatric Association. (2013). *Diagnostic and Statistical Manual of Mental Disorders -5*. 5th ed. Washington, DC: American Psychiatric Publishing.

British Psychological Society. (2019). Accessed December 2019 www.bps.org.uk/member-microsites/cyberpsychology-section

Brock, Vikki G. (2014). *Sourcebook of Coaching History*. 2nd ed. Ventura, CA: CreateSpace Independent Publishing.

Fawbert, Dave. (2019). 'Eco-anxiety': How to spot it and what to do about it' 27 March 2019, Accessed 20 January 2020 www.bbc.co.uk/bbcthree/article/

Grajfoner, Dasha. (2012). 'The introduction of animal assisted coaching psychology: Definition and challenges' *Coaching Psychology International*. 5, 1, 22–25.

Gratton, Lynda and Andrew Scott. (2016). *The Hundred Year Life*. London: Bloomsbury.

Hyson, Peter. (2013). *Coaching with Meaning and Spirituality*. London: Routledge.

'Identity Politics'; Stanford Encyclopedia of Philosophy, Winter 2012 Edition Accessed 30 January 2020 https://plato.stanford.edu/entries/identity-politics/

Kurzweil, Raymond. (2006). *The Singularity Is Near*. London: Duckworth.

Retreats Association. (2020). *Retreats 2020*. Princes Risborough: Retreats Association.

Rogers, Jenny. (2016). *Coaching Skills: The Definitive Guide to Being A Coach*. 4th ed. Maidenhead: McGraw Hill Education.

Rogers, Jenny. (2019). *Coaching for Careers: A Practical Guide for Coaches*. Maidenhead: McGraw Hill Education, p. 6.

Schnell, Sabine, Searle, Jonny, and Stoneman, Richard. (2020). 'The coaching relationship' in *The Trainee Coach Handbook*, edited by Mary Watts, Robert Bor and Ian Florance. London: Sage, pp. 27–46.

Scoular, Anne. (2011). *Business Coaching*. Harlow: Prentice Hall Financial Times.

Smith, Andrew and Hughes, William. (2013). *Ecogothic*. Manchester, UK: Manchester University Press, p. 148.

Tribe, Rachel. (2019). *Refugees and Psychology – The Accelerating Change*. Presentation. Conference of the European Test Publishers Group. Ljubljana, June 7th. Unpublished.

Tribe, Rachel and Nimisha Patel, eds. (March 2007). 'Refugees and asylum seekers'; Special Issue. *The Psychologist*. 20, 149–151.

van Niewerburgh, Christian and Raja'a Allaho. (2018). *Coaching in Islamic Culture: The Principles and Practice of Ershad*. London: Routledge.

Weinberg, Ashley. (February 2018). 'I'm happy to be a psychologist committed to positive change' *The Psychologist*. 31, 42–43.

Whybrow, Alison. (2008). 'Coaching psychology-coming of age' *Australian Psychological Society*, 22 August. Accessed 15 December 2019 https://groups.psychology.org.au/Assets/Files/Whybrow-A.pdf

Wildflower, Leni. (2013). *The Hidden History of Coaching*. Maidenhead: Open University Press/McGraw Hill.

Afterword

Coaching in a time of crisis

Mary Watts

March 27, 2020

Yesterday was something of a defining day for me and I knew this morning that this book couldn't go to print without acknowledging the enormity of what is happening globally right at this moment.

I'm sitting at my computer looking out of the window. Rays of sun are shining through some huge protected pines, leaving a dappled effect on the old roof opposite and on the spring shrubs and flowers that are growing particularly well this year. Their colours are even brighter and crisper than usual. We've had the most perfect weather in the suburbs of London for some days – the sort of weather that I recall when I think of my childhood wearing what I imagine are very rose-tinted glasses. I wonder what glasses I shall be wearing when I look back at this period, if indeed I'm lucky enough to have the opportunity to do so. It's March 2020 and in the last few days we have learned from the UK government that we are all to be confined to our homes apart from essential trips out for food, medicine and one exercise event – a 'social distance' of two metres being kept from others at all times except with family members with whom you're living. Only essential workers are allowed to work away from home, and the only schools left open are those designated for their children so that they can continue in their front-line roles of protecting the rest of us against the deadly Covid-19 virus. The first UK doctor has just died from the disease and the UK Prime Minister and Prince Charles have tested positive. It is a disease that has respect for no one. In its sights we are all equal!

For the last few weeks Ian Florance and I have been striving to get this manuscript ready to send to Routledge, fearful that we will be the only people with access to it. A shared drive now including just the latest version of chapters gives access to others, in case something should happen to us. Perhaps it's something that we should have done right from the start and the fact that we didn't maybe reflects something of our complacency about life, its stability and its ongoing nature.

Had I been writing this only six months ago what I'm describing would have been thought the stuff of fiction. Had any of the authors of this book created a potential scenario similar to the one that each of us, together and separately, is now living, in order to demonstrate a particular coaching theme, they would not have been taken seriously. In this book of Emerging Conversations in Coaching and Coaching Psychology, change is a recurring theme but I'm absolutely sure that none of us, as we wrote, could have imagined the tsunami of change that would so rapidly envelope the whole world in little more than a matter of weeks.

For a few days my mind has been in turmoil at a personal and professional level. Today the mist is clearing. At one level nothing has changed but some events of yesterday helped me to focus more clearly on one area at least, which relates closely to the contents of this book. Each of the chapters has been written by authors who each in their own way are committed to making the world a better place through the ethical empowerment of individuals, organisations and whole societies. Never has that been more needed than now and as the weeks and month pass by this imperative will become even greater.

An experience yesterday brought to life for me, in a very unsure Covid-19 world, many of the themes and issues addressed in this book. I took part in a live online introduction to mental health first aid (MHFA). It lasted half a day and would normally have been offered as a face-to-face course. Each of the 15 attendees were there as we had a real interest in the topic and had agreed to be 'guinea pigs' for the trialling of the online version. Being something of a technophobe and incompetent, it also gave me the opportunity to 'face my fears' as my grandson puts it, and to deal with a new reality. I'm proud to say that I feel I coped well with break-out rooms for small group discussion, using thumbs up and clapping symbols in the multiple choice quiz to indicate a yes or no response, contributing to some of the written chats and spoken discussions that took place, and mastering turning my video and speaker on and off at various times to cope with dog barking at my end and short breaks when we left for a coffee so that I wasn't seen or heard after leaving the meeting. In a small but important way I was able to take control of an area of my life, tackle a fear and learn a lot in the process.

So, what did I learn that went beyond the technology? It was commented on that the course was designed in 'peace time' as one might say. A pre-Covid-19 world when we all went about our daily business in what now seems a pretty routine sort of way. Its focus was not on creating mental health counsellors or psychologists but alerting us to the basic skills that can better enable us to help others as well as ourselves by applying them in a range of situations in which mental health first aid could make a real difference to someone's well-being. The real-life examples shared by participants were easy to relate to.

As we know from physical health first aid, early action can, at the extreme, save lives, and in less dramatic contexts make a vast difference to someone's pain and recovery from injury or ill health. As I listened to the teaching and discussions, and later read the manuals (MHFA 2018), it became clear that all of it applied equally, and maybe even more so, to our current very troubled times. Many of the key skills highlighted overlapped closely with many core coaching skills, for example: engaging in deep, non-judgmental listening; knowing how to engage with someone in distress rather than avoid them as so often can happen;

showing empathy; being alert to vulnerability, both our own and that of others; and being knowledgeable about, and open to, referring people to a range of alternative resources that may be of help to them.

Interestingly many of the core triggers for needing mental health first aid are those that we see as triggers for distress in our coachees, such as rapid change and the uncertainty that may go with this; personal and interpersonal conflict; health and well-being issues; feeling powerless to bring about even the smallest of changes to enhance the quality of life; existential crisis and related questions such as what is my life for and about? And perhaps above all, experiencing loss in a variety of ways, for example, of our freedom, income, and, sadly, even of loved ones. All or any of these may be experienced at any time – even, for example, when we've just achieved a much-wanted promotion, a pay rise, or our new business is thriving.

As I reflect on yesterday's course I'm thinking of how we might read and reflect on the contents of this book in ways that will enable us to be most effective as coaches in a dramatically new era – one that, at this stage, we have no idea what it will look like. A review of the chapters this morning has reinforced for me that each is hugely relevant right now and will continue to be as we move forward. But each chapter is no more than an emerging conversation, and changing life circumstances and our lived experience of these will feed into the direction that these conversations will now take.

A second event yesterday has also impacted on my today and what I'm now writing about. My husband has been using his time at home to do some sorting out. He's in what has been designated as the particularly vulnerable group in terms of Covid-19 as he is over 70 and has Parkinson's disease. He came across a couple of old videos filmed many years ago when I was working at a London University, teaching trainee counselling psychologists. In the first video an extremely distressed lady was talking to the therapist about her obsessive-compulsive problems, which were totally wrecking any possibility of 'normal' and fulfilling living. She had acute fears of contamination, and hand washing, and avoidance behaviours had taken over her everyday living. In the second, an equally distressed lady was talking about her anxiety and extreme panic attacks which had led to recent agoraphobia. So changed was my self-presentation that my husband was some way into the first film before he realized that the client was me. I had lived and worked with the pain and anxieties of such clients for many years and as a colleague therapist interviewed me, watched by a large group of students, it was easy to be a real, feeling person. I wasn't an actor – I just was . . .

At that time, I could go home, leave distress behind me and re-enter my personal and 'normal' world. This was vital to the maintenance of my own health and well-being, which, in turn, was needed to support me in the challenging yet rewarding work that I was doing. Today I suspect there are very few who can honestly say that they experience nothing of what I was demonstrating in those old videos. We have essential workers putting themselves at considerable risk on a daily basis; expectant mothers who are anxious that they will be giving birth without their birthing partner; people whose businesses are rapidly failing and others who have been laid off from work; many people who, whatever their age, are fearful of stepping outside to buy food or other essentials; and perhaps most tragically we have people suffering alone, maybe with a loved one in hospital and dying alone. We have always known that medical interventions can have significant side effects, but the side effects of what we are now living are almost impossible to contemplate and will be with us for many years.

Why, I wonder, is there so little discussion on how we can best support each other from a mental health perspective? Why is little being said openly about the mental health side effects of the bitter pill that we are all swallowing? Is this a stark reflection of the way that for so many years we have stigmatized those who have spoken out about their own mental health issues and difficulties?

There is huge scope for mental health first aiders and coaches to learn from and collaborate with each other and for this shared learning to include, amongst others, counsellors, psychologists and other health professionals, educators, social care professionals, those from business and industry, and politicians. All of us will have experienced the fallout from Covid-19 and maybe will have to face similar events in the future. This work will be challenging and personal well-being will be core to it.

Over the last few days communications with health-related colleagues in various parts of the world have reinforced for me the enormity of the challenges that together we face. I share in what follows a few anonymised snippets of these. They have come from people in various parts of Europe, the UK, Asia and the USA.

> *We are in the midst of gearing up and radically changing our work and life.*
> *I'm working full time at a primary care clinic. It has been stressful these past few weeks. We too are lacking the valuable PPE (personal protective equipment) that we need. . . . Our patients are flipping out with anxiety and feelings of panic . . . and we have no training in mental health. . . .*
> *Things are not easy at the moment but they are going to get worse in the next few days. . . . All physicians at the hospital have been asked to help as volunteers. . . . I really, really appreciate your offering*
> *Our work is changing rapidly, we are preparing for the Covid-19 emergency. This is a highly crucial phase for us because if this spreads badly in my country, we don't have the resources that the western world does to handle the situation.*
> *I really appreciate your sorrow. . . . . We are at the calm before the storm . . . when things have run in (I don't expect it to calm down anytime in the near future) I would really like to reflect on this with you.*
> *Thank you for the time you spent listening to my fears and problems. It makes me really happy to share my thoughts with someone not involved in my daily practice and to get inputs from outside my usual environment.*
> *Having the opportunity to talk makes a real difference*

As I re-read these communications I found questions formulating in my mind.

Will the events of today help to reduce and hopefully eliminate the stigma so often associated with admitting to mental distress?

Can any of us, whether in our personal or professional life, ignore the fact that we are all vulnerable and that it is a sign of strength rather than weakness to be aware of this?

Can we ever only work with a part of a person, or do we delude ourselves when we believe we're doing this?

How might we in our everyday lives and as coaches engage constructively with these issues, the conversations that emerge from them and with the people who are affected by them?

How can we all, whether coach or not, further develop our skills in ways likely to be of help to people in distress, for example in times of rapid change, in situations where they are fearful and feel powerless, times when they want a solution but there doesn't appear to be one, and at times when they are alone and their pain goes unheard and unnoticed?

And turning this around into a more hopeful scenario, how can we best support people as they seek solutions and ways to turn them into action?

From these snippets we are reminded of the power of having the opportunity to *talk*, of sorrows being shared, and of being really *listened* to.

As you read the chapters in this book some will have very obvious and direct relevance to these questions, for example the chapters on the contribution of coaching in mental health care, trauma coaching and education. However, each chapter in its own way has huge relevance to these questions and the broader issues raised in this Afterword. One health care colleague says how, when things are calmer, he will want to reflect on events with his coach, which raises questions about what reflection is and can be, and how it might best be used to support clients – all issues addressed in the reflections chapter. The psychometrics, research, and neuro coaching chapters each introduce us to new perspectives relevant to gaining insights into the whole person. These insights are exemplified and added to when we move to a whole-person approach to leadership coaching. When we open our eyes to the whole person it's impossible to ignore the issues raised in the chapters on diversity and pluralism in terms of our understandings, insights and practices in coaching. The chapter on technology-mediated coaching is hugely relevant to all of us right now: not only to professional coaching activity but to an even greater extent to the daily living of the majority of us as we strive to stay connected with family and friends, and as businesses rapidly seek new ways to survive.

Coaching is enormously rewarding, yet can be challenging, stressful for the coach as well as the client, and there is always something new to learn, new insights to be had. This is likely to increasingly be the case as the role and boundaries of coaching expand. The chapter on coaching supervision initiates new conversations to complement and support these changes.

Finally, the ethical challenges for coaching are magnified hugely by Covid-19 and are relevant for us as individual coaches and for the profession as a whole. For example, can we as a profession continue to remain largely voiceless politically or are there ways in which we can and should make a difference to the lives of many through various forms of coordinated political representation? If so, can we achieve our political goals when we have no overarching professional organisation to represent coaching at national and international levels?

It's time to draw a close to this Afterword before yet more questions and conversations emerge – yet as I do so I'm reminded of the power of hope, of positive thinking, and the resilience of the human spirit that clients and others have so often shown me. In working together, we can harness these as we focus on enhancing and advancing coaching knowledge and practice in ethical and humane ways, for the benefit of all not just the few.

Ian and I hope that you will enjoy exploring and reflecting upon the emerging conversations presented by chapter authors and that you allow your thinking and learning to be open ended. We also encourage you to actively engage in initiating, sharing and extending your own emerging conversations in coaching. We also very sincerely hope that over the coming months and years that you find ways to preserve and enhance your own health and well-being as you continue to support others in doing the same.

Reference

MHFA England (2018) *Adult Mental Health Aware Half Day Course Manual & Adult Mental Health Aware Half Day Workbook.* MHFA England. For more information on MHFA England go to www.mhfaengland.org & info@mhfaengland.org

Index

Note: Page numbers in *italic* indicate a figure and page numbers in **bold** indicate a table on the corresponding page.